Criminology
Goes to the Movies

Criminology
Goes to the Movies

Crime Theory and Popular Culture

Nicole Rafter and Michelle Brown

NEW YORK UNIVERSITY PRESS
New York and London

NEW YORK UNIVERSITY PRESS
New York and London
www.nyupress.org

References to Internet websites (URLs) were accurate at the time of writing.
Neither the author nor New York University Press is responsible for URLs
that may have expired or changed since the manuscript was prepared.

Library of Congress Cataloging-in-Publication Data

Rafter, Nicole Hahn, 1939–
Criminology goes to the movies : crime theory and popular culture /
Nicole Rafter and Michelle Brown.
p. cm.
Includes bibliographical references and index.
ISBN 978–0–8147–7651–3 (cl : alk. paper) — ISBN 978–0–8147–7652–0
(pb : alk. paper) — ISBN 978–0–8147–7741–1 (e-book)
1. Crime in popular culture. 2. Criminology.
I. Brown, Michelle, 1971–
II. Title.
HV6030.R34   2011
364—dc22   2011012522

New York University Press books are printed on acid-free paper,
and their binding materials are chosen for strength and durability.
We strive to use environmentally responsible suppliers and materials
to the greatest extent possible in publishing our books.

Manufactured in the United States of America

c   10 9 8 7 6 5 4 3 2 1
p   10 9 8 7 6 5 4 3 2 1

Nicole Rafter dedicates this book to her daughter,
Sarah Rachel Hahn.

Michelle Brown dedicates this book to her daughter,
Sabine Wren Brown-Hoffman.

Contents

Preface

    This book grew out of conversations about two problems we repeatedly encountered in our scholarship and in our teaching. As specialists in the area of crime and the media, we long ago realized that criminology is produced by not only scholars but all participants in popular culture, including everyone who rents or downloads a crime film or buys a ticket to a movie theater. In the past, we have written about the relationships between popular and academic criminology, demonstrating their overlaps and arguing that crime, while it is indeed negative phenomenon, is also a cultural resource, one into which everyone dips for ideas about crime and justice. Discussing these matters in our writing and teaching, we often use movies as examples. This created the first problem. Not every reader of our books or student in our courses had seen the films we mentioned as illustrations. In the lead-up to this book, we tried to find a way to get our audiences on the same page— or, rather, the same screen—so they would all understand our examples.

    The second and much more general problem that this book addresses is pedagogical. All students majoring in criminal justice and criminology are required to take a course in criminological theory, but as any instructor can attest, about four weeks after the course has ended, if you ask a former student something about, say, strain theory, you get an anxious look and a bit of head-scratching. Even top-notch graduate students, when asked after a lapse of several months to relate a new idea to social disorganization theory or differential association theory, will respond uncomfortably, "Which one was that again?" We concluded that students have few ways to connect the criminological theories they study with actual criminal behavior; they simply cannot visualize the theories in action. Another aspect of this problem, unfortunately, is the deadly dullness of most criminology textbooks—huge costly tomes that mainly inspire a hope for the course's speedy conclusion.

    When we asked students if keying each theory to a specific movie would help, they responded with something close to joy. Narratives that exemplify the theories, they told us, would help them remember theoretical abstractions. Characters and their stories would give them examples of what the theories were all about. Movies could bring the theories to life. When we discussed our idea with other instructors and researchers, they too were excited about rethinking theory in terms of popular culture. In this book we take an entirely new approach to criminological theory, encouraging students, scholars, and general readers to gain a deeper appreciation of the ways in which theory is at work in our lives and in cultural imagination.

Criminology Goes to the Movies aims at advancing understandings of the sources and nature of criminological theory. In this respect, it proposes theory of its own. It also aims at making criminological theory comprehensible, engaging, and memorable. We want to make criminology pleasurable and at the same time to show students and other readers that key explanations of crime lie buried in films, just below the surface. Our job is to show how they can be excavated. We hope that in the process of that excavation, we all will learn more about the role of theory in culture and culture in theory.

We are grateful to many people who helped with this book, most especially Robert Hahn, Majid Yar, and Per Ystehede. Friends and colleagues whose efforts in many spheres of life provided time and support to see this volume through include Leon Anderson, Ekaterina Botchkovar, Steven Chermak, Joseph De Angelis, Ellen Dwyer, John Gilliom, Carol Greenhouse, Eric Lockmer, Abigail McDonald, and Martin Schwartz. Ilene Kalish, our editor for earlier books we wrote separately, has been a delight to work with, a steady source of wit, inspired ideas, and encouragement—and patience! Family members, including Dennis and Cindy Pope, Rick and Peggy Butler, Mandy and Patrick Gould, and grandparents Ruth and Lowell Hoffman, provided child care in every sense of the word; without it, this volume would not have materialized. Finally, Michelle Brown dedicates this volume to her beautiful new daughter. Sabine, here is your first "picture" book—welcome to the wonderful world of theory and images.

Note on Use of Dates

We give the date of release whenever a movie is first mentioned in a chapter. The appendix lists all crime films referenced in the text and their release dates, so readers who want to look up a date in midchapter can find it there.

Introduction

Taking Criminology to the Movies

What is the relationship between criminology and crime films? What kinds of intellectual enterprises occur at the intersection of criminological theory and cinema? What sorts of encounters might occur were criminology to go to the movies? These questions lie at the heart of this volume.

Theory—whether it be theory of crime or of the image—has a bad reputation. Students often find theory dry and abstruse, and they discover that it is difficult to relate theory to practice. Scholars are in part responsible for theory's bad reputation, for too often they take a narrow and rigid view of theory, positioning themselves in relation to a particular set of propositions that they then spend their lives elaborating. But theory, as we understand it, is exciting terrain—dynamic, fluid, plural, accessible, and part of the lives of ordinary people. In other words, theory is not confined to academic criminology. Criminological theory is at work all around us—in daily conversation, news media, prime-time television, music, cyberspace, mystery novels, and film.

In this volume, we begin with the assumption that criminology is hard at work in culture and that culture is hard at work in criminology. To illustrate this process, we focus on the cultural site that exemplifies this engagement perhaps better than any other—Hollywood cinema. We hope to show how ideas about crime develop in the cultural imagination and, in turn, shape and are shaped by theory as well. We argue that criminological theory is produced not only in the academic world, through scholarly research, but also in popular culture, through such vehicles as film. Our goal is to reconceptualize criminological theory in relation to culture—and, in particular, cinema.

This book builds upon an article in which criminologist Nicole Rafter asserted that crime films play an important role in relation to criminology, constituting a "popular criminology, a discourse parallel to academic criminology and of equal social significance."[1] Here we set out to examine the space where popular culture and academic criminology meet (see Figure 1.1). We are

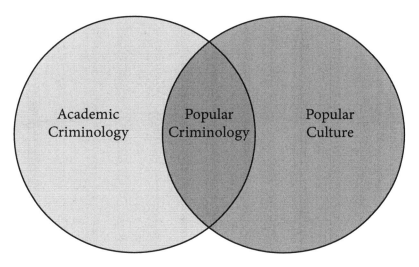

Figure 1.1. Popular Criminology: Where Academic Criminology Meets Popular Culture

not merely interested in showing how crime theories constitute a subtext in many films. We are much more interested in demonstrating that popular culture can expand formal theory—and that the encounter of theory with cinema is an engagement that leaves both fundamentally transformed. Using crime films to investigate the overlaps of criminology and popular culture, we analyze how these domains interpenetrate and cross-fertilize one another.

In what follows we first discuss how academic criminology can benefit from closer connections to popular culture. Next we address the compelling role that crime plays in the popular imagination and ordinary life. The third of the following sections is devoted to a discussion of popular criminology, the innovative discourse that emerges from the intersection of academic criminology and popular culture. This chapter concludes with an overview of the volume and a note on the topsy-turvy manner in which the book can be read.

Academic Criminology

"Academic criminology can no longer aspire to monopolize 'criminological' discourse," write two of the field's most sophisticated observers, "or hope to claim exclusive rights over the representation and disposition of crime."[2] Yet most academics who write and teach about causes of crime ignore popular culture, perhaps because they do not know how to conceptualize their relationship to it. Others use film snippets in classes or write about cases famous in popular culture—but without theorizing the inter-relationships between the examples and scholarly work. At the same time, specialists in popular culture, while increasingly engrossed by criminologi-cal matters, lack a conceptual scaffolding for bridging the two fields. This volume shows how to deal with such problems through a move beyond descriptive efforts toward a rigorous theoretical interpretation of popular culture. The first question in such a pursuit is one for academic criminol-ogy, and it is a question of the image's significance: Why take seriously "criminology in the image"?[3]

The first and foremost answer to this question is found in the overwhelm-ing presence of crime in popular culture. To ignore cultural representations of crime is to ignore the largest public domain in which thought about crime occurs. (In fact, if our diagram were drawn to show the relative importance of the two domains, the circle on the left, representing academic criminol-ogy, would be the size of a pinhead, while the circle on the right, representing popular culture and its ideas about crime, would fill the page.) But academic criminology has been slow to focus on popular culture, and it has tended to push such inquiries to the margins of the field.

To be sure, some criminologists have engaged with aspects of popular culture.[4] For example, some have conducted psychological studies of media effects, examining the impact of violence in representations on violence in real life.[5] Others have studied the role of media-amplified moral panics, epi-sodes in which the media suddenly define a group previously regarded as harmless as a social threat.[6] A far more profound and theoretically fertile engagement with popular culture appears in the recent work of cultural crim-inologists, who examine the intricate media environment of a globalized, late modern world.[7] Given the unprecedented and all-encompassing role of media in contemporary life, cultural criminologists are critical of an older idea that "pictures" show "reality," which in turn affects social action and crime policy through direct lines of causality. Older "gap" studies focused on discrepancies between images and what they purported to represent—as, for example, when scholars examined ways in which films inaccurately depicted police corruption or women lawyers. In the view of cultural criminologists, in contrast, "the media is no longer something separable from society. Social reality is experienced through language, communication and imagery. Social meanings and social differences are inextricably tied up with representa-tion."[8] But even within cultural criminology, film analysis has lagged behind studies focusing on television, print news, and mystery stories.

In bringing film analyses forward in criminology, we hope to expand criminology's boundaries, laying the groundwork for engagements that extend beyond past and present theoretical understandings. For example, many criminologists reject psychological explanations because they focus on individual, rather than social, factors in offending. However, psychological explanations circulate widely in crime films, serving as a cultural resource for viewers working through issues like the responsibility of the mentally ill offender, the role of science in court, and the advisability of behavioral modification as a tool for social control. As we show, films like Alfred Hitchcock's *Psycho* (1960), Fritz Lang's *M* (1931), *The Boston Strangler* (1968), and Stanley Kubrick's *Clockwork Orange* (1971) illustrate problems in not only psychology but also psychoanalysis and psychiatry. Many films depict the interplay of multiple and sometimes contradictory psychological impulses. While a psychological study must examine mental abnormalities and discuss variables in a scientific register that often obscures this complexity, film allows a broad public to explore and develop positions on the value of psychological perspectives on crime. Recognizing how cinema extends criminology into the realm of the psychological moves us well beyond debates about, for instance, the effects of media violence. These discussions also alert us to the reality that psychological theories of crime circulate broadly and deeply in the cultural imagination, regardless of criminology's distance from these perspectives.

Cinema also serves as a popular source for articulating, modeling, and critiquing theories in ways that academic criminology often cannot. Attention to these possibilities initiates interdisciplinary alliances and promises a more democratic, less exclusionary view than that of academia of what it means to do criminology and be a criminologist. Taking criminology to the movies fosters theoretical development. If criminology accepts the validity and necessity of the kinds of analysis we propose here, the stage will be set for new questions about crime and its explanations to emerge.

Popular Culture

Clearly, it has become increasingly difficult for academic criminology to maintain boundaries between itself and popular culture—to ignore the explanations of criminal behavior generated so powerfully and prodigiously by movies, novels, television, and other cultural discourses. Most impressive is the fact that criminology has managed such a feat as long as it has, given crime's ubiquity in popular culture.

Academic criminology can do many things that popular culture cannot, such as discovering the prevalence of specific crimes, the effects of drugs and alcohol, and why people may be reluctant to report offenses to police. On the other hand, popular culture brings to discourses about crime some attributes that scientific criminology cannot claim. One of these is an ability to speak to diffuse cultural anxieties. There is a quality—or texture—to crime and victimization in everyday life that formal criminology and other social scientific studies miss. As numerous "culture of fear" studies point out, popular fascination often revolves around the anecdotal, the violent, the sex scandal, the serial killer, the child abduction and murder.[9] From novelist Truman Capote to television crime journalist Nancy Grace to the television show *Law and Order*, graphic and detailed accounts of crime pervade everyday life. Dismissing these accounts as voyeurism or schlock limits our understanding of their social functions. Instead of ignoring or correcting these spectacles, we ask how such cultural focal points are relevant to criminology.

Even more pertinent is the fact that one cannot really pull apart image and meaning. We are not claiming merely that movies create cultural focal points and reproduce the emotional textures of crime in ways that formal criminology cannot. Rather, we are claiming that images organize our worlds and that representations are central to our lives. Representations shape how we think about crime and formulate public policy. Our beliefs about serial killers and child molesters are closely bound to the images with which popular culture bombards us.

One characteristic of popular discourses about crime that is usually absent from academic criminology is its strong emphasis on emotive elements in crime—its adrenaline rush, pleasure, desperation, anger, rage, and humiliation.[10] Film, unlike academic criminology, provides a broad window into the ways in which criminal behavior is shaped by values and emotional contexts. The same is true of film's ability to make us aware of the emotions of victimization and even the experience of people who work in criminal justice professions. For instance, *The Silence of the Lambs* (1991) shows us the vulnerability, terror, and determination of FBI cadet Clarice Starling (Jody Foster) as she confronts first the masculine world of law enforcement and then the obsessions of two very different serial killers. Similarly, *Thelma & Louise* (1991) portrays the profound anger that fuels a crime spree after one of the women is almost raped. Films can vividly depict how people caught within worlds of crime and victimization cope and ultimately survive, for better or worse.

One of the most intriguing and troublesome developments in recent popular culture is the appearance of major films that blatantly defy criminological explanation. They have no heroes, and the crimes of their leading characters are either random or inexplicable. In films like *Taxi Driver* (1976), *Mystic River* (2003), *The Departed* (2006), *Before the Devil Knows You're Dead* (2007), *No Country for Old Men* (2007), and *There Will Be Blood* (2007), crime and extreme brutality are ultimately incomprehensible. These films show bleak, violent worlds where the villains often go unpunished and the innocent unsaved. A sense of desolation and loneliness drives protagonists toward transgressive and sometimes pathological behavior. Viewers are often left, as in *No Country for Old Men*, with no clear way of making sense of the criminal; such films challenge the very idea of criminological explanation. In other films, social order is cautiously reasserted but not without a sense of irony and despair, as with the ignominious death of contract killer Vincent (Tom Cruise) in *Collateral* (2004) or the sudden and strange celebrity of Travis Bickle (Robert De Niro) after his murderous rampage to save a child prostitute in *Taxi Driver*.

This trend is associated with postmodernism, the late twentieth-century aesthetic development characterized by irony, fragmentation, instability, and playfulness about violence. It is also a trait of late modernity—the period in which we live—which is defined by a rapid global tempo that is often atomizing and isolating in its effects upon the individual. In this context, capitalism reigns supreme, inequalities flourish, and faith in progress has vanished. Future horizons are overshadowed by new and unprecedented forms of mass violence, war, and disaster, all capable of ending human life in apocalyptic annihilation.

Another by-product of late modernity is films with byzantine narratives and numerous major characters who intersect across a background of globalization. *Traffic* (2000), *Syriana* (2005), *Crash* (2004), and *Babel* (2006) depict disconnected lives of multiple characters, crisscrossing globally, their fates interwoven by invisible narrative connections. In this kind of film, characters' lives are often marked by a sense of futility, moral ambiguity, and doubts about the possibility of justice.

Another way to think of these cinematic developments in popular culture is as part of an alternative tradition in Hollywood production, out of which emerges a new category of critical crime films.[11] In contrast to conventional narratives characterized by easy resolutions, where heroes win out and villains are punished, critical films are dominated by open endings and characters who are neither good nor bad but inscrutable. In these contexts, the world, the self, and truth are volatile, unpredictable, and never fully knowable. Such tendencies in popular culture raise questions about the very possibility of theory.

Popular Criminology: Criminology Goes to the Movies

Popular criminology begins from the standpoint that crime films are integral to crime, criminology, and culture itself, comprising a popular discourse that must be understood if thinking about the nature of crime is to be fully understood.[12] "Given the ascendant position of the image/visual in contemporary culture," writes cultural criminologist Keith Hayward, "it is increasingly important that all criminologists are familiar with the various ways in which crime and 'the story of crime' is imaged, constructed, and 'framed' within modern society."[13] A popular or cultural criminology, by broadening the parameters of knowledge about crime and criminality, provides a point from which to develop a more contemporary set of questions foundational to the field. It promises simultaneously a more expansive and better unified body of knowledge about crime. What is most noteworthy about the comments of Hayward and other recent writers on representations in criminology is the manner in which they call for reinvention, for research on crime that can bring together theory and image. They all assume that in order to do criminology, we must pay close attention to the act of representation.

Popular criminology, as criminologist Eamonn Carrabine points out, is in the air, with growing attention from scholars working independently of one another.[14] Rafter's article provides a useful starting point, defining *popular criminology* as

> a category composed of discourses about crime found not only in film but also on the Internet, on television and in newspapers, novels and rap music and myth. Popular criminology differs from academic criminology in that it does not pretend to empirical accuracy or theoretical validity. But in scope, it covers as much territory—possibly more—if we consider the kinds of ethical and philosophical issues raised even by this small sample of movies. Popular criminology's audience is bigger (even a cinematic flop will reach a larger audience than this article). And its social significance is greater, for academic criminology cannot offer so wide a range of criminological wares.[15]

But, as Carrabine points out, "the two are not equally valued."[16] Academic criminology still has a long way to go to make good use of popular culture as a resource. Carrabine adds—contradicting the conventional view—that "the media do not just provide us with endless, worrying accounts of social problems or distract us with unchallenging diversions, but are fundamentally involved in how existence is organized in the contemporary world."[17]

While it is true that many crime films have no criminological implications whatsoever, others are so well developed theoretically as to perfectly illustrate specific criminological perspectives. In these cases, popular culture and academic criminology not only overlap; they almost coincide. All of the films we discuss at length in this book echo one or more criminological theories. For instance, the first film we analyze, *Double Indemnity* (1944), exemplifies the criminological theory termed *rational choice*, while the second, *Frankenstein* (1931), illustrates an early biological theory of crime. This does not mean that filmmakers consciously set out to embody rational choice or biological theory in their movies; rather, it suggests that the general ideas of criminological theories circulate freely in popular culture, with filmmakers drawing on them as appropriate. Moreover, certain film genres readily suggest certain explanations of crime. Film noir, the genre of black-and-white films popular in the 1940s and 1950s, often featured a male hero making rational but doomed choices. Thus it is not surprising to find *Double Indemnity*, a classic film noir, telling the tale of an insurance salesman getting involved in crime through poor but rational choices. Similarly, the horror genre lends itself to depictions of menacing freaks of nature. When James Whale, the director of *Frankenstein*, set out to make a motion picture of the novel of that name, he naturally used the conventions of horror to depict his biologically freakish killer.

But films can fill several theoretical molds at once. As open texts, they have the ability to engage with multiple perspectives simultaneously. In fact, most of the films we examine are open to a range of theoretical interpretations. *Frankenstein*, a film that draws on biological theory of crime, also uses sociological factors to explain the monster's criminality: from the moment he is "born," his creator neglects, rejects, and abuses him.

In some ways, films are even better equipped than the analytical language of formal criminology to voice an explanation of crime. In *City of God* (2002), for example, handheld cameras, zooms, split screens, rapid editing, visual fragmentation, and a nonlinear narrative capture the frenetic violence and chaos of one of Rio de Janeiro's infamous favelas, a neighborhood isolated from other parts of the city by what criminologists would describe as its subculture of violence. Another example can be found in *Capturing the Friedmans* (2003), in which director Andrew Jarecki stitches together documentary footage, interviews, and courtroom and media footage to raise profound questions about the process of criminalization and, inter alia, illustrate what criminologists call *labeling theory*. Film's endlessly flexible, intricate rhetoric enables it to present explanations of crime that are in some ways more persuasive than those of expository criminological discourse. In fact, sometimes crime theories receive more multifaceted treatment in film than in scientific discourse. This complexity takes a variety of forms. *Double Indemnity*, for instance, is not simply a pure application of rational choice theory but also a contradiction of it, for the film's narrative strategies suggest a fatalism that negates the very idea of free will. Other films, like *Capturing the Friedmans*, end without closure or resolution. Such narratives imply a rejection of theory, a denial that criminal behavior can be explained. In each chapter we ask how explanations of crime generated by popular culture coincide with those of formal criminology: Do they confirm them, contradict them, or both?

In our discussions of film, we have tried to respond to criminologist Alison Young's call for "an approach to film analysis, both in cultural criminology and in law-and-film studies, that does not simply relate depicted events to questions of the social . . . but which also engages with the *cinematic nature of the medium of film*."[18] Young calls in particular for an engagement "with cinema's unique harnessing of image, sound, affect, memory, plot, episode, character, story and event" that will restore "the overlooked cinematic dimension to scholarship on crime and justice in film."[19] By *cinematic* she means the rhetoric through which films draw us into their stories, including the processes through which they construct their images. For Young, these are the very ways in which films make meaning and cause us to attach ourselves emotionally to their narratives. Thus in our analysis of *Taxi Driver*, for instance, we discuss how director Martin Scorsese uses voice-over narration, camera points of view, and carefully planned settings to create an intense character study of alienated war veteran Travis Bickle, who travels the redlight districts of New York City at night in his cab, observing the sleaze with ethnographic (albeit obsessive) detail. (We argue that Travis's tours of the city and keen eye for the textures of deviance in some ways reproduce the methodology of social disorganization theory.) Similarly, in our discussion of *Traffic*, we show how intersecting narratives of the drug trade invoke aspects of what criminologists call *strain theories*. *Traffic*'s strategies illuminate strain theory in a manner that is original in terms of visual qualities as well as character and narrative development.

Finally, for us, the experience of working in unfamiliar and challenging terrain, exploring theories in a manner that is atypical of the field, and building methodological approaches and insights that cross disciplinary boundaries, has led to thinking about our subject and ourselves as researchers in ways that we ordinarily would not have done. Film captures aspects of the experience of crime that are rarely mentioned in academic scholarship—need, loss, violation, desire, even mourning. From the sexually abused serial killer Aileen Wuornos (*Monster* [2003]; *Aileen Wuornos: The Selling of a Serial Killer* [1992]) to the suicide of Arnold Friedman (*Capturing the Friedmans*); from the spiraling pain of a violence-ridden community in *Mystic River* to the tragic fate of the *Frankenstein* monster, films depict the experiences that drive criminality.

Overview of Volume

The arrangement of this book's chapters reflects the sequence in which the theories themselves emerged. Each chapter concentrates on a single theory and a key illustrative film. In each chapter readers will find a summary of the theory, a description of the social context in which it was first formulated, and an analysis of its development over time. The film section of the chapter allows for greater elaboration of the theoretical perspective, examples of related films, and special attention to ways in which film may modify the theory or push it in new directions. Each chapter concludes with a "Further Viewing" list of films related to the theory but not discussed in the chapter.

Chapter 2 focuses on the theoretical perspective that is the oldest and today still one of the most popular explanations of criminal behavior, rational choice theory, which it examines through the lens of what many consider to be the definitive film noir, Billy Wilder's *Double Indemnity*. We show how the conventions of film noir (its fatalistic worldview, moral ambiguity, pessimism, and sense of alienation) intersect with rational choice theory, complicating the idea of the rational actor. Chapters 3 and 4, respectively, cover biological and psychological theories of crime. James Whale's *Frankenstein* incorporates (while it gently parodies) one of the earliest and most famous of all biological theories, Cesare Lombroso's notion of the born criminal, a brute incapable of obeying laws. The cinematic centerpiece of our discussion of psychological perspectives (chapter 4) is Alfred Hitchcock's *Psycho*, whose obsessive killer, Norman Bates, is perhaps the most riveting psychopath in movie history.

Whereas chapters 3 and 4 deal with theories that explain criminality in terms of individual failings, the next set of chapters focuses on theories that explain crime in terms of social factors. Chapter 5, on social disorganization theory, uses Martin Scorsese's classic *Taxi Driver*, with its vivid depictions of transitional zones in New York City and the city's nightlife, to illustrate not only the types of settings that social disorganization theorists had in mind but also one of their research methods—that of having an observer traverse the city and soak up its character, just as Travis Bickle does as he noses his cab through the nighttime metropolis. Chapter 6, on strain theories, draws on several films to illustrate the various types of strain theory but concentrates on Steven Soderbergh's *Traffic* and the variant called *institutional strain theory*. Chapter 7 turns to social learning theories, including subcultural theories of crime and the work of Edwin Sutherland, the dominant figure in late twentieth-century criminology. To illustrate subcultural theories, it uses *Mystic River*, Clint Eastwood's dark tale of a tightly knit, culturally isolated community in which a subculture of pedophile priests sets the plot in motion while the values of another criminal subculture dictate a kind of fratricidal murder.

The next set of chapters is devoted to critical perspectives in criminology. The labeling approach to crime, discussed in chapter 8, takes as its starting point the notion that crime is a socially constructed event. Andrew Jarecki's *Capturing the Friedmans* offers a disturbing look at how the definitional and constructivist processes identified by labeling theories work. Because this documentary gives no clear answers to the question of whether the Friedmans actually molested children, it forces viewers to live with the ambiguous results of the processes through which the Friedmans were rendered deviant and criminal. For conflict theorists, the topic of chapter 9, crime is fundamentally about power: those without it are far more likely defined as criminals and processed as such. With its Marxist overtones and emphasis on social structure, conflict criminology insists on taking relationships between social actors and social institutions into account, including the race, class, and gender divisions that emerge out of political, economic, and historical contexts. Spike Lee's *Do the Right Thing* (1989) illustrates how structural inequalities can lead to violence in everyday life. Chapter 10 deals with feminist perspectives that have transformed the work of at least some criminologists through their attention to gender, patriarchy, and both crime and victimization. *Thelma & Louise* takes up several of the most intriguing assertions of feminist criminology, including the claim that women's pathways into criminality often include prior victimization and the idea that criminality itself is a gendered performance.

Chapter 11 examines a theoretical perspective that has recently achieved a good deal of popularity among criminologists: life-course theory, which tracks trajectories of criminal behavior across the life span, paying special attention to turning points that may encourage desistance from offending or, alternatively, keep one locked into a life of crime. Our example here, *City of God*, Fernando Meirelles and Katia Lund's bravura foray into the slums of Rio de Janeiro, shows how one gang member takes the usual route into drug dealing (there is nothing to encourage desistance here, in this world of impoverished hyperviolence) while another escapes through small turning points that enable him to become a photographer. In the final chapter, we summarize the volume's main arguments, emphasizing the theoretical richness that emerges when academic criminology engages with crime films. Taking criminology to the movies can transform traditional criminology, demonstrating the folly of its attempt to lock itself into an academic bastion, and stimulating the creation of a new discourse: popular criminology.

A Note on Film Selection and Chapter Flipping

We established several criteria to guide us in selecting films to illustrate criminological theories. First we looked for movies that illustrated the theories well. Second, we looked for movies that were either classics or the subjects of recent critical acclaim; this criterion guaranteed that the examples would be not only good films but also easily accessible to those who wished to watch them in conjunction with the chapters. Third, we picked films that collectively covered the history of moviemaking from the earliest talkies into the present, to give a sense of how closely film, since its inception, has been engaged with criminology. Finally, we looked for morally ambiguous films that avoid analyzing crime in simplistic terms. The films that we finally selected portray perpetrators and victims in ways that complicate easy categorizations of good and evil. The cinematic worlds we examine are gray and morally murky, and their plots often lack clear resolutions.

As a group the films enable us to raise important issues in relation to popular criminology: What is the role of such sociological stalwarts as race, class, gender, and age in the depiction of crime? How do rationality, power, and institutions as well as biological and psychological factors figure in cinematic accounts of crime? What role do cities, neighborhoods, and subcultures play in the popular imaginary of crime? What additional factors do movies use to explain crime? How do those explanations invoke, subvert, or move beyond criminological theory? In short, we chose films that would bring breadth, depth, and innovation to our theoretical discussions.

Although we present the criminological theories chronologically, in the order in which they were formulated, we have written the book so that the chapters can be read in any order. Because no chapter depends on earlier material, readers can flip among them, fast-forwarding and rewinding at will.

"For Money and a Woman"

Rational Choice Theories and Double Indemnity

Billy Wilder's *Double Indemnity* (1944) begins with the film's protagonist, Walter Neff, mortally wounded and confessing to murder. "Yes, I killed him," declares Neff. "I killed him for money and a woman. And I didn't get the money and I didn't get the woman. Pretty, isn't it?" Here the conventions of film noir, Hollywood's most original and distinctive mode of crime drama, and rational choice theory, the oldest criminological perspective, converge in a narrative that depicts crime as the calculated choice of individuals who weigh crime's benefits against its costs in the headlong pursuit of their own self-interests. Hollywood cinema has long relied on the image of the rational actor to explain crime. Heist films, thrillers, and noirs, in their many classic and contemporary incarnations—including such titles as *The Asphalt Jungle* (1950), *Oceans 11* (1960; 2001), *Reservoir Dogs* (1992), *Bottle Rocket* (1996), *The Departed* (2006), and *Before the Devil Knows You're Dead* (2007)—portray individuals' choices to pursue crime and the consequences that follow. However, as a genre, film noir may best illustrate the key points of rational choice theory due to its characteristically flawed heroes, calculating dames, voice-over narration, dark visual style, and pessimistic worldview. [1] In this chapter, we examine the main principles of rational choice theories, including their perspectives on human nature, criminal behavior, and punishment, through the lens of what many consider to be the definitive film noir, *Double Indemnity*—a movie nominated for seven Academy Awards and routinely listed in the top 100 films of all time. [2]

Rational Choice Theories

The origins of the idea of crime as a rational act lie in the late eighteenth-century Enlightenment, a historical moment that privileged reason and freedom over superstition and religious oppression. Out of this historical shift emerged what became known as the Classical school of criminological thought, a set of perspectives shaped most prominently by the philosophers and utilitarian social reformers Cesare Beccaria and Jeremy Bentham.

In 1764, at the youthful age of twenty-six, Beccaria, the son of an Italian aristocrat, published a brief treatise, *Dei delitti e delle pene* (*On Crimes and Punishments*), a work that had incalculable impact on the future of criminal justice reforms and criminology. Beccaria began by assuming that in their natural state, humans are ferociously selfish, waging constant "war" against everyone else. To reduce this endless strife, individuals must concede a small portion of their own freedom by entering into a social contract, a kind of peace agreement, with others. In doing this, they create a social order that is no longer based on the power of the strongest or the dictates of religion but instead on a liberalism authored by and representative of the people. Social stability can then be measured by its usefulness in achieving "the greatest happiness shared among the greater number."[3]

At the time Beccaria wrote, criminal behavior was most often equated with sin and frequently involved cruel, excessive punishments, including torture, for all aside from powerful aristocrats. But the new ideas based upon humanist, scientific, and democratic ideals percolating through societies, including the American colonies as well as Beccaria's Italy, challenged the stranglehold of Catholic noblemen on the criminal justice apparatus. In this period, the simple accusation of having committed a crime was enough to merit interrogation, torture, and, in some cases, a painful, public death. Beccaria advocated a new model of governance in which the fear of others would be replaced by a fear of law, and in which punishment would be calibrated to fit the crime. To develop law as a rationalizing force, he insisted that laws need to be clear and that punishment, as a mechanism for law's enforcement, "should not be an act of violence perpetrated by one or many upon a private citizen" but rather "public, speedy, necessary, the minimum possible in the given circumstances, proportionate to the crime, and determined by the law."[4]

The state's right to punish, a principle central to Beccaria's sociolegal ideas, reflects his understanding of the criminal as a rational actor. He and many of his followers, in conceptualizing the democratic citizen as a rational actor who weighs the costs and benefits of crime, constructed a subject who must be deterred from committing such acts through the very idea and promise of punishment. For Beccaria, deterrence is a formula in which "our own good [self-interest] can be controlled only by equal and opposite obstacles [consequences]."[5] However, within this framework, he argued that punishment should be used minimally, with its severity carefully limited. Prevention is better than punishment, he taught, and it is—or should be—the overriding aim of criminal justice. Ultimately, for Beccaria, it is the act of crime and its effects, best conceived as harm done to society, that should guide the proportionality of punishment and serve as the main measure of the law.

Beccaria and related thinkers pictured the ideal citizen as someone who engages in a cost-benefit calculation before deciding to engage in or avoid criminal behavior, a person capable of reasoned judgment, deliberation, and a clear understanding of the law. Their theory, with its view of a symbiotic relationship between crime and punishment, seeks to channel human behavior through a series of rational decision-making processes carefully moderated by the criminal code. Today, rational choice theorists continue to assume that human behavior, including criminal activity, can be controlled through attention to the principle of obstacles or consequences. Beccaria's project, ultimately reformist in orientation, provided scholars and jurists with a formula that would use rationality to harness crime.

Judges and juries found it impossible to follow Beccaria's injunction to ignore the attributes of individual offenders in deciding punishments. Children seemed to merit special consideration and protections, as did mentally ill defendants. Thus, more reforms were added to legal and penal codes. More recent critics have argued that Classical theory overlooks the role of social forces in the construction of crime. In particular, they argue that because of the way in which social class shapes the law, Classical theory ignores the manner in which the law itself may reproduce the status quo, exacerbating inequality and protecting the interests of the powerful. In stratified society (these critics continue), inequality is imprinted on the law, and the social contract, if it exists at all, favors the interests of the powerful over others. These criticisms notwithstanding, Classical theory at its origins transformed ideas about crime and punishment through its stress on rationality. Its principles eventually developed into a coherent body of criminology and left a substantial imprint upon Western legal codes, justice systems, and popular perceptions of crime and punishment.[6]

Classical theory, by the criminal as a rational actor who weighs the pain of punishment against the profit (or pleasure) of offending, emphasized the agency and responsibility of the individual. Centuries after Beccaria wrote his treatise, this individualistic focus forms the foundation for today's rational choice theories, explanations that emphasize responsibility, routine activity, and situational crime prevention.[7] Rational choice theories experienced a revival in the 1970s, in a era characterized by the emergence of a punitive public attitude toward crime. Advocates of greater punitiveness insisted that the source of crime was not to be found in social structure but rather in the individual; their arguments shifted attitudes toward punishment away from rehabilitation toward deterrence.[8] Criminologist James Q. Wilson, in his influential volume *Thinking about Crime*, argued that we need to rethink our ideas about crime causation, dropping the environmental explanations of the past hundred years and replacing them with something like Beccaria's pessimistic view of the nature of man:

> As much as anything, our futile efforts to curb or even understand the dramatic and continuing rise in crime have been frustrated by our optimistic and unrealistic assumptions about human nature. . . . I argue for a sober view of man and his institutions that would permit reasonable things to be accomplished, foolish things abandoned, and utopian things forgotten.[9]

Such arguments carried great weight politically, bound up as they were with the general public's revulsion toward the "moral decadence" and "hedonism" of 1960s hippies and its growing anger toward the welfare state, countercultures, and the civil rights movement. (These changes in attitude were caught perfectly in the 1971 film *Dirty Harry*.)

In response to their sense of social disorder and misdirection in the criminal justice system, social conservatives like Wilson reframed discussions of crime in terms of "choice" and personal responsibility. They channeled Beccaria's arguments, designed to limit the harshness of punishment, into a mood of deep punitiveness that gave birth to a so-called law-and-order society in the United States.[10] Late twentieth-century forms of rational choice theory again assumed that crime "pays" and that its benefits outweigh its costs, but they emerged against the background of mass incarceration and renewed support for capital punishment. Today's rational choice perspectives continue to assume that imprisonment reduces crime, but this assumption has not been proved—indeed, the majority of people released from prison on parole soon recidivate. Moreover, by interpreting crime solely as the result of individual choice, these theories deny the role in crime causation of poverty, race, class, and gender.

Environmental or opportunity theory, one of today's most prominent rational choice theories,[11] argues that the key to crime prevention lies not in deterrence (Beccaria's position) but in the architecture and ordinary patterns of lived experience. For example, a playground with bright lights is less likely to be vandalized, and new communities can be designed so that the houses are close together and look out onto common recreational spaces. Opportunity theory focuses on "situational crime prevention"—physically removing opportunities to commit crime from the spaces of everyday life. "In general," criminologist Marcus Felson writes, "crime can be viewed as a routine activity that feeds on routine legal activities as people proceed to gain their daily bread."[12] Making crime difficult to pursue, in Felson's view, makes it less likely to occur.

> Settings change choices by providing temptations and control. These are mediated by various tangible cues that tell people what they might get away with. People make decisions accordingly. They are somewhat constrained, but not necessarily all day or all week. The constraints shift from one setting to another. By making our insights about crime control more tangible, we are better able to examine whether and when people will make illegal choices.[13]

For opportunity theorists, the criminal act is the outcome not simply of decisions but of contexts and opportunities that converge in time and space with offenders' decisions. Offenders must be motivated, there must be suitable crime targets (potential victims) and, in addition, capable guardians who might prevent the crime from occurring. For instance, a pickpocket at a rock concert packed with a drinking audience might have a heyday, but a ban on alcohol and the presence of security officers might deter the pickpocket from even buying a ticket.

To summarize: Rational choice theories are based on the Classical school's pessimistic vision of human nature, which views individuals as inherently selfish and hedonistic. They picture the criminal as a rational actor who weighs costs and benefits and must be deterred through the promise of punishment, physical reduction of opportunities for crime commission, or deployment of guardians whose watchfulness will deflect criminals to other venues. These theories fundamentally favor individual responsibility in their account of crime, discounting the contribution of social conditions. As we shall see, *Double Indemnity* relies heavily upon elements of rational choice theories, even while it simultaneously contests some of their basic assumptions.

Double Indemnity: *Rational Choice Meets Film Noir*

You want to know who killed Dietrichson? Hold tight to that cheap cigar of yours, Keyes. I killed Dietrichson. Me, Walter Neff. Insurance salesman. Thirty-five years old, unmarried, no visible scars . . . 'til a while ago, that is.

Double Indemnity follows Walter Neff's murder confession through flashbacks as he records it by dictating machine in the office of his colleague and friend, Barton Keyes. This setup produces a step-by-step narrative of the decisions Neff makes in his descent into crime—a plan that, despite its careful organization, ultimately unravels. A key convention of film noir, the voice-over narration of events by the film's protagonist, gives viewers access to the character's thoughts and decision-making processes.[14] The crime originates when Neff (Fred MacMurray), an insurance salesman, in the course of attending to business in a Los Angeles residential neighborhood, remembers a set of auto renewals at a nearby address. Arriving at the home of his client, a wealthy oilman, Neff locks eyes with his client's wife, Phyllis Dietrichson (Barbara Stanwyck), standing at the top of a staircase clothed only in a towel. "To tell you the truth, Keyes," Neff explains in his recorded confession, right then "I wasn't a whole lot interested in . . . auto renewals or in Mr. Dietrichson and his daughter, Lola. I was thinking about that dame upstairs and the way she had looked at me and I wanted to see her again up close without that silly staircase between us."

Another major convention of film noir is the "femme fatale," a seductive woman who captivates the male lead, leading him into dangerous, illicit, and frequently deadly situations. From a rational choice perspective, clearly "the woman" is part of Neff's incentive for engaging in crime. Barbara Stanwyck as Phyllis Dietrichson is an archetypal femme fatale as she seduces Neff and then persuades him to kill her husband. Their flirty discussion of insurance quickly reveals to Neff that Phyllis is a bored, discontented housewife, seeking to purchase accident insurance on her husband without his knowledge— an illegal act. Although she justifies this pursuit in terms of the hazards of his work in the oil fields, Neff quickly rejects her proposal and accuses her of duplicity, indignantly asking, "Who'd you think I was anyway? The guy that walks into a good-looking dame's front parlor and says, 'Good afternoon, I sell accident insurance on husbands. . . . You got one that's been around too long? One you'd like to turn into a little hard cash?'"

Nonetheless, Neff finds himself distracted the rest of the afternoon and into the evening. "I was all twisted up inside and I was still holding on to that red-hot poker. Right then it came over me that I hadn't walked out on anything at all, that the hook was too strong, that this wasn't the end between her and me. It was only the beginning." In the midst of his musings, Phyllis arrives at Neff's apartment, this time making clear her romantic attentions and characterizing her husband as controlling, abusive, and alcoholic. In the end, Neff commits to following through with the murder, taking over much of the planning, periodically pointing out the risk of both prison (he refers to "Tehachapi," a famous California women's prison) and death in the gas chamber, providing viewers with a rational choice exemplar of a potential offender weighing the pleasures of crime against its potential costs. Neff insists there must be no slipups—the crime has to be "perfect, . . . straight down the line." Significantly, Neff reveals that his decision is not as sudden as it seems but rather is "all tied up with something I'd been thinking about for years, since long before I ran into Phyllis Dietrichson. Because you know how it is, Keyes, in this business you can't sleep for trying to figure out all the tricks they can pull on you." Neff's expertise in the insurance business serves as what today's opportunity theorists call a *structure* of opportunity. He knows all he needs to know to commit massive fraud. In fact, he pushes fraud to a new level in his planning with Phyllis Dietrichson, pointing out that certain kinds of death—those that are least likely—are subject to a double indemnity clause that doubles the accident insurance from $50,000 to $100,000. With their decisions made, Neff alludes forebodingly to the now predetermined quality of their plan: "The machinery had started to move and nothing could stop it."

Beccaria theorized in the first pages of *On Crimes and Punishments* that "neither eloquence, nor exhortations, not even the most sublime truths have been enough to hold back for long the [greedy] passions aroused by . . . objects which are close at hand."[15] In rational choice theories, the everyday world is a place in which the tug of wrongdoing is ever-present, with individuals purposefully choosing to break the law to further their own self-interests. Such decisions are darkly apparent as Neff and Dietrichson take steps to enact their murder plan.

Neff and Phyllis Dietrichson arrange for her husband to sign unwittingly his own accident policy. They make sure his daughter is present to witness the signing. They phone one another only from phone booths and meet only in public spaces such as a busy supermarket. They arrange for Dietrichson to take a railway business trip. Even when Dietrichson breaks his leg and then suddenly reschedules the trip, Walter and Phyllis move quickly to establish new alibis. Each step requires careful and deliberate decision making. At the moment of the murder, Walter, hiding on the backseat floor of the Dietrichson car, waits for a signal from Phyllis and then strangles her husband. He proceeds to assume Dietrichson's appearance: wearing a similar suit and walking with crutches, Neff poses as him on the train, jumping from the observation deck not long after the train's departure. In the process he makes sure he is observed by a witness, a businessman named Jackson. Phyllis meets

Figure 2.1. The flawed heroes, calculating dames, and dark visual style of Hollywood film noir bring a critical edge to the pessimistic vision of human nature that underlies rational choice theory. This criminological perspective depicts crime as the calculated choice of individuals who weigh crime's benefits against its costs in the pursuit of their own self-interests. In this scene from *Double Indemnity* (1944), antihero Walter Neff (Fred MacMurray) and seductive femme fatale Phyllis Dietrichson (Barbara Stanwyck) conspire to plan murder. Photo used by permission of Photofest.

Walter near the tracks; they drop the body at the jumping point and return home to carry on despite a brief suspenseful moment, a struggle to start the car again, that reveals the precariousness of their plan. But every step follows perfectly. That night, Neff feels their plan has been entirely successful—"not a miss." Yet, he becomes strangely apprehensive: "Suddenly it came over me that everything would go wrong. It sounds crazy, Keyes, but it's true, so help me. I couldn't hear my own footsteps. It was the walk of a dead man." This fatalistic sense of doom, typical of film noir, is *Double Indemnity*'s overarching theme and relates specifically to the issue of punishment in both popular and criminological discourses on rational choice.

It looks at first as if the film's protagonists have beaten the system. The case is ruled an accidental death. Not even the company's president, although he is anxious to avoid paying the double indemnity sum, can prove fraudulence. A variety of intervening figures, however, present obstacles to the crime's success and, in doing so, confirm the point of routine activities theorists who argue that for crime to occur, there must be a convergence of targets and motivated offenders with the absence of capable "guardians" who might prevent the crime or, at least, catch the perpetrator. In this case, there are several such guardians, and while they do not prevent the crime, they do help catch the murderers. One is Mr. Dietrichson's daughter, Lola, who, late in the film, reveals to Neff that she suspects that Phyllis has murdered her mother as well as her father. She also suspects that her boyfriend, Nino Zachetti, has been seeing Phyllis. Jackson, the eyewitness, testifies that the person he saw was much younger than the real Dietrichson. Finally, Barton Keyes (Edward G. Robinson), Neff's associate, friend, and recipient of his confession, simply cannot let the case go.

Keyes, a stand-in for Neff's conscience, shares Beccaria's dim view of human nature, although he is at first blinded to what is going on by his affection for his colleague. Nonetheless, Keyes views his job as a Pacific All-Risk claims adjustor as one similar to law enforcement in its deterrence function. The arbiter of right and wrong in the film, Keyes often refers to "the little man" inside him who can sniff out phony claims and knows when something is not quite right. Neff notes Keyes's location on the moral barometer a number of times, as, for example, when via dictating machine he tells Keyes at one point, "You're so darn conscientious, you're driving yourself crazy," and again later when he describes him as having "a heart as big as a house." As film scholar James Paris writes, Keyes "stands alone as a strict, yet kind[ly] and highly principled force."[16] Keyes's view of the dynamics of fraud echoes rational choice theory:

> To me, a claims man is a surgeon. That desk is an operating table. And those pencils are scalpels and bone chisels. And those papers are not just forms and statistics and claims for compensation, they're alive, they're packed with drama, with twisted hopes and crooked dreams. A claims man, Walter, is a doctor and a bloodhound . . . and a cop and a judge and a jury and a father-confessor all in one.

Throughout, it is Keyes's perpetual theorizing and problem solving that keep the plot in motion, as when, in a seemingly casual moment, he muses about the obstacles that the as-yet-unidentified murderers now face: "They've committed a murder and it's not like taking a trolley ride together where they can get off at different stops. They're stuck with each other and they've got to ride all the way to the end of the line and it's a one-way trip and the last stop is the cemetery." In the end, as Keyes surmises, it is because Neff and Dietrichson choose their own self-interests over mutual help that things end badly.

After the murder, Walter and Phyllis's secret relationship grows increasingly tense. They are nearly caught together on two occasions, one when Keyes sees Neff talking suspiciously on the office phone, the second when Keyes makes a surprise visit to Neff's apartment while Phyllis is there. Walter grows sympathetic to Lola's predicament, sparking an angry interaction in which he asks Phyllis to drop the double indemnity claim. Phyllis refuses, telling Neff: "I loved you, Walter, and I hated him, but I wasn't going to do anything about it, not until I met you. You planned the whole thing. I only wanted him dead." Realizing that Phyllis will try to pin the murder on him and that Keyes is building a case against Lola's boyfriend, Zachetti, Neff makes a decision that dramatically alters the film's trajectory. He arranges to meet with Phyllis one last time. When he arrives at her home, he finds they have identical plans—to murder the other. Phyllis shoots first but cannot follow through, claiming suddenly that she loves Neff. As she embraces him, he shoots and kills her. After providing Zachetti with an alibi, Neff makes his way to the office. Using the dictating machine, he relates his sorry tale to Keyes all night. As the morning dawns, Neff, now dying from Phyllis's first shot, turns and sees Keyes at the door. In the final scene, having decided that his only hope for escaping the gas chamber is to run for the border, Neff collapses at his office building's front door. Keyes calls an ambulance, and the police, we assume, are on their way. Keyes then waits with Neff, lighting what to all appearances looks to be his friend's last cigarette. The music rises, and the film concludes.

Few people know that a series of different endings was originally filmed for *Double Indemnity*. In the most extensive version, Neff is led to the gas chamber as Keyes and other witnesses look on. Once Neff enters the chamber, pellets are dropped, clouds of gas rise up, and then a doctor enters the room to pronounce Neff dead. Keyes exits the prison and enters the sunlight, lonely and forlorn. Billy Wilder went to great expense to film this scene, creating a shot-by-shot sequence of the execution that included an exact replica of California's gas chamber. But test audiences did not like the gas-chamber conclusion because they did not wish to see the film's protagonist, however morally ambiguous, killed.[17] Perhaps they were also reluctant to watch the infliction of the death penalty, a reluctance that recalls Beccaria's own opposition to capital punishment.

In *Double Indemnity*, Walter Neff engages in a cost-benefit calculation of crime, privileging his pursuit of pleasure (money and a woman) over the interests and safety of others. Capable of reasonable judgment with a clear understanding of the distinctions between right and wrong, Neff actively chooses crime. And true to the necessity of consequences that sits at the heart of Classical theory, Neff is unable to evade punishment and death. Finally, the film reflects the pessimistic vision of human nature that underlies Classical theory, one in which actors make dark decisions out of greedy self-interest—and the choices end badly.

Contemporary Challenges

Contemporary film explores rational choice perspectives in new and more complex ways. Many contemporary movies endorse the view that crime is a result of choice and free will, but they usually supplement rational choice explanations with others that are anarchistic or even nihilistic. Moreover, they lack characters who, like Barton Keyes, represent knowledge of good and evil and can right the moral order.

In Sidney Lumet's *Before the Devil Knows You're Dead* (2007), for example, two brothers (Philip Seymour Hoffman and Ethan Hawke), both in financial crisis, plan to rob their parents' jewelry store. But the plan goes awry, ending in two deaths, including that of their mother, and from that point on, the brothers find themselves caught in a downward spiral of crime. Their father (played by Albert Finney) at first takes the role of moral guardian, serving as a present-day incarnation of Barton Keyes. However, he too is pushed into rational but emotional choices that culminate in violence. As in most rational choice films, decisions are made, crimes occur and are eventually discovered, and punishment looms inevitably. However, in *Before the Devil Knows You're Dead*, that formula is troubled by the blatant irrationality of the "rational" choices—it makes little sense to go around robbing and killing family members. The traditional rational choice formula is also subverted by the fact that viewers are encouraged to sympathize with the criminals and the despair and alienation that define their lives. Amid failures of family, community, and traditional morality, the possibility of meaningful action at the individual level—the centerpiece of rational choice theory—falls apart.

Similarly, *Collateral* (2004), which chronicles a one-night killing spree by a contract killer (Vincent, played by Tom Cruise) who dragoons a hapless cabdriver (Max, played by Jamie Foxx) to drive him around Los Angeles in search of his targets, draws on the traditional rational choice formula while modifying and even undermining it. The basic premise is that of free choice: a hit man chooses to accept an assignment to knock off a series of victims in one twelve-hour period. However, in explaining why he makes this choice, Vincent excuses his behavior with overelaborate explanations. At first he tells the incredulous Max that most of his victims are bad anyway (for instance, some are informants from within a drug cartel). In the cosmic scheme of things, Vincent continues, murder and violence are meaningless; modern life lacks rationality, order, and any possibility of justice. After Vincent's first contract hit (the victim's body falls, crashing into the windshield of Max's cab), he reveals his existential alienation by chiding the cabdriver:

VINCENT: Max, six billion people on the planet, you're getting bent out of shape cause of one fat guy.
MAX: Well, who was he?
VINCENT: What do you care? Have you ever heard of Rwanda?
MAX: Yes, I know Rwanda.
VINCENT: Well, tens of thousands killed before sundown. Nobody's killed people that fast since Nagasaki and Hiroshima. Did you bat an eye, Max?
MAX: What?
VINCENT: Did you join Amnesty International, Oxfam, Save the Whales, Greenpeace, or something? No. I off one fat Angelino and you throw a hissy fit.
MAX: Man, I don't know any Rwandans.
VINCENT: You don't know the guy in the trunk, either.

As it turns out, under his carapace of bravado, Vincent is beset by anxiety and alienation. When the two first meet, Max asks Vincent, "First time in L.A.?" Vincent replies, "No. Tell you the truth, whenever I'm here I can't wait to leave. It's too sprawled out, disconnected." When Max comments, "It's my home," Vincent follows with, "Seventeen million people. This has got to be the fifth biggest economy in the world and nobody knows each other. I read about this guy who gets on the MTA [Metropolitan Transportation Authority] here, dies. Six hours he's riding the subway before anybody notices his corpse doing laps around L.A. People on and off sitting next to him. Nobody notices." In fact, this conversation forecasts Vincent's own ignominious and anonymous death .

The key scene in *Collateral* comes when Max's cab catches an extraordinary sight in its headlights: a coyote, beautiful and wild, trapped among the highways of L.A., out of place and bound to be killed. The coyote seems to symbolize both Max and Vincent—and all people caught in sordid urban worlds that will, one way or another, kill them. Here the film strikes a note of deep determinism. *Collateral* never fully resolves its tensions between free will and determinism, any more than, at the end, it settles its tensions between a tentative affirmation of the possibility of human relationships (Max gets the girl) and its unnerving impressions of desolation and loneliness. Furthermore, *Collateral*'s complex relationships of pleasure and pain, categories that are no longer discrete, fail to fit the simple utilitarian hedonistic calculations of early Enlightenment thinkers. Such films, in their presentation of crime, open up fundamental questions about the possibility of a meaningful social contract like the one envisioned by Beccaria; they interrogate the very terms of contemporary society and our relationships to one another.

Conclusion

Rational choice, one of the oldest explanations of crime, remains a staple in criminological theory and Hollywood cinema. Criminology continues to build theoretical perspectives that emphasize the role of opportunity, decision making, and deterrence. Hollywood cinema continues to present us with images of characters making poor decisions and facing stark outcomes. Increasingly, criminologists qualify Classical theory with the observation that criminal behavior is rarely, if ever, purely based upon free will and choice alone. It is always an act structured by social circumstance, contextualized through specific conditions and situations. Hollywood, even as it lovingly clings to the idea of individual blame, today actually undercuts that idea with exceptions, contradictions, and a nihilistic blankness that sometimes suggests crime has no explanation at all. Social forces and haunting shades of pathological monstrousness shape the behavior of even the most rational actors in much of contemporary crime cinema. In the next chapter, we turn toward some of these concerns, mapping the intersections of theory and film through the ever-popular lenses of biological and positivist accounts of crime.

Diabolique (1955)
Dog Day Afternoon (1975)
Heist (2001)
History of Violence, A (2005)
House of Games (1987)
Inside Man (2006)
The Killing (1956)
Out of Sight (1998)
A Place in the Sun (1951)
The Postman Always Rings Twice (1946)
Reservoir Dogs (1992)
To Die For (1995)
The Usual Suspects (1995)

———————————————————————————————— 3 ————

"He's Alive!"

Biological Theories and Frankenstein

The very first efforts to explain crime scientifically—those made in the 1870s by the Italian psychiatrist Cesare Lombroso—held that the causes of crime lie inside criminals themselves: in the inherited, primitive quality of their bodies and brains. Lombroso's theory of *criminal anthropology* caught the imagination of social reformers worldwide: it had a scientific ring at a time when people were turning to science for the answers to life's big questions; and it was literally spectacular, for Lombroso illustrated his books with grisly images of living and dead criminals whose twisted bodies seemed to mirror their twisted minds.

By the end of the nineteenth century, disenchantment set in, not with efforts to explain crime scientifically, for those persisted, but with the specific biological theory of Lombroso. Thereafter theorists devised other biocriminological explanations—the "feeblemindness" theory of the early twentieth century; Earnest Hooton's failed effort to resurrect criminal anthropology in the 1930s; William Sheldon's bodytyping theory of the 1940s and 1950s—but on the whole, sociological theories dominated throughout the twentieth century. Indeed, after World War II, when people learned what the Nazis had done in the name of biology, the revulsion against biological reasoning of all sorts was so strong that to many, it seemed inconceivable that anyone would ever again endorse a biological theory of crime. "Never again!"—the vow not to permit another Holocaust—became, in social science, the vow "Never again permit human problems to be blamed on bad biology."

However, out of sight of mainstream sociological criminology, in the 1960s some psychologists started to revive the idea of the criminal body—a body with abnormalities that encourage criminal behavior—and today, advances in genetics and neuroscience are again bringing biological explanations to the fore. While it seems unlikely that biological theories will ever again be taken as the *sole* explanation of criminality, as Lombroso's criminal anthropology and

Nazi biocriminology were, it seems very likely that as the twenty-first century progresses, biologists and sociologists will work out a *biosocial* explanation of crime tracing the origins of offending to an interplay of nature and nurture, biology and environment. Indeed, they are almost there already.[1]

The first of the following sections reviews biological theories of crime, from criminal anthropology through eugenic criminology to the emergence of biosocial explanations in the late twentieth century. The next section discusses the original *Frankenstein* (1931), the most successful depiction in film history of a biological theory of crime. It is followed by discussions of another film that draws on biological explanations, *The Bad Seed* (1956), and of a group of films that grew out of the feeblemindedness explanation of crime. In conclusion we point to several recent films, including *Minority Report* (2002) and *Monster* (2003), that reflect the genetic revolution in understandings of crime and crime control.

The Criminal Body

Lombroso's Criminal Anthropology

Criminal Man, whose first edition Lombroso published in 1876, argued that if criminology is to be a science, the object of study must be not criminal acts but criminals themselves. Criminals, Lombroso explained, are atavisms, throwbacks to an earlier evolutionary stage; they are more like dark-skinned "savages" than normal, law-abiding white people. "Primitive" in their bodies, minds, and morals, they can be identified by their physical and mental "anomalies" such as "low, sloping foreheads, . . . overdevelopment of the jaw and cheekbones, . . . oblique and large eye sockets, dark skin, thick and curly head hair, large or protuberant ears, . . . low sensitivity to pain, . . . laziness, absence of remorse and foresight, great vanity, and fleeting, violent passions."[2] The worst criminals—"born criminals"—are hopelessly criminalistic, Lombroso continued; they cannot stop themselves from offending time and again, from childhood through old age:

> Criminal anthropology, while not blaming the born criminal for his behavior, nevertheless prescribes for him a life sentence. We believe that those individuals least responsible for their behavior are most to be feared. Only sequestration can neutralize their innate, atavistic urge to crime.[3]

However, Lombroso maintained, there are also other categories—occasional criminals, political criminals, pseudocriminals, insane criminals—which taken together make up 60 percent of all offenders. In their cases, social as well as biological factors cause criminal behavior. They have few, if any, anomalies and enjoy some degree of free will. Because Lombroso studied the bodies and culture of criminals, and because he considered criminals to be close kin to the "savages" studied by contemporary anthropologists, he christened his science *criminal anthropology.*

The questions Lombroso asked about criminals' bodies and the ways he used science to answer them seem absurd today. What proportion of all criminals have red hair, compared with soldiers? Is the cranial circumference of criminal women larger or smaller than that of insane women and prostitutes? Do criminals' skulls resemble those of spider monkeys and lemurs? However, Lombroso's questions, research methods, and findings grew quite naturally out of the context in which he wrote.

Lombroso grew up in a period enamored with phrenology, the early science of the mind that pictured the brain as a group of independent "faculties" or abilities, each sited in a specific area of the brain. According to phrenologists, people who commit crime lack the faculty of benevolence, or they may have an overdeveloped faculty of acquisitiveness. Even though phrenology had passed out of fashion by the mid-nineteenth century, when Lombroso came to intellectual maturity, he retained its idea of crime as a result of some sort of physical brain abnormality, and all his life he kept on his desk an enormous model of a phrenological head, with the brain's faculties mapped out on it—a reminder of one of his inspirations for the notion that criminals' brains must differ from those of honest folk.

In addition, Lombroso found inspiration in anthropology, the popular nineteenth-century science that investigated "primitive" tribes in Africa and Australia and reported on their strange and seemingly backward customs. In fact, even before he published *Criminal Man* Lombroso had written a book on anthropology, a volume that shows him already fancying himself as an anthropologist (although his background was actually in medicine and psychiatry) and that includes ideas that later blossomed into his theory of criminal man.[4] Moreover, with anthropologists of his day Lombroso shared a belief in so-called *scientific racism,* the notion that mankind is organized into a hierarchy, with "civilized" white men at the top and "savage" black people at the bottom. Scientific racism shaped Lombroso's belief that criminals are closer to the primitive tribes of Africa than to "normal" whites, and he looked for similarities between actual "primitives" and the Italian criminals he studied. One was tattooing, a practice that he found among both "savages" and prisoners. Another was anomalies such as bumps and indentations in the skull; having itemized the "cranial abnormalities of criminals," he went on to point out "how closely they correspond to characteristics observed in normal skulls of the colored and inferior races."[5] In drawing on anthropology, Lombroso also drew on scientific racism, ensuring that scientific criminology began as a field heavily racist in content.

Of equal impact on Lombroso's theory of the criminal body was evolutionism—the various nineteenth-century explanations of natural change. From today's perspective, the most successful evolutionist was Charles Darwin, whose *Origin of Species* (1859) explained change in terms of natural selection—a struggle for existence in which the best adapted are most likely to survive and reproduce. Lombroso was impressed by Darwin's theory, for it seemed to explain why criminals resembled throwbacks to an earlier evolutionary stage—apparently they had not yet evolved from a primitive to a more civilized state. However, at the time, Darwin's theory was less popular than another explanation of natural change: degeneration theory, according to which criminals, together with other socially problematic groups, are degenerates, people who are evolving backward or devolving, losing their normal mental and physical health. As time went on, Lombroso incorporated degeneration theory into his idea of the criminal body, describing offenders as men and women who are deteriorated in body and mind. For example, of Marianna Kirtecen, "a clever swindler, although only twelve years old," he tells us that she

> was lame, squint-eyed, flat-skulled, and left-handed, her right arm being, indeed, almost paralyzed. . . . When she died of consumption, the autopsy revealed a longstanding porencephalia in the left hemisphere of the brain. The gyrus fornicatus was flattened in the middle portion, while the convexities of the pia mater and arachnoid enclosed a large number of pacchionian granulations such as are found in the aged.[6]

Just as degeneration theory predicted, a criminal like Marianna was abnormal in body and brain as well as morality.

Meshing so well with the sciences of its time—the recent fad for phrenology; the rise of anthropology and, with it, of "scientific" racism; and the period's obsession with evolution and degeneration—it is little wonder that Lombroso's biological theory of crime attracted widespread attention and enthusiasm. He took *Criminal Man* through five editions (the final edition alone comprised four volumes) and in addition wrote both *Criminal Woman* and a book on criminals' poetry and artwork.[7] In his home city of Turin, Italy, he founded a museum of criminal anthropology that was widely imitated in other European cities.[8]

Eugenic Criminology

Even before Lombroso's death in 1909, his theory of the anthropological born criminal was passé, done in by its lack of scientific sophistication. Biological theories entered a new stage of development. Over time, they have evolved from the original, Lombrosian emphasis on obvious physical defects to today's emphasis on microscopic genetic and neurological abnormalities that seem to be associated with criminal behavior.

The first step in this evolutionary process was the early twentieth-century "feeblemindedness" explanation of crime in terms of weak intelligence—a natural progression, really, in light of Lombroso's earlier interest in the criminal's mental as well as physical backwardness. According to the new theory, the "feebleminded" (meaning intellectually disabled people) are inherently criminalistic—too intellectually weak to control themselves—while, conversely, nearly all criminals are feebleminded. These claims were made even before Alfred Binet devised the first pen-and-paper tests of mental ability, but they were confirmed by the advent of intelligence testing, a science that was, at first, highly unreliable. Amateur psychologists marched into prisons and reformatories with sheaves of "Binet tests" under their arms, and they marched out with test scores proving that 90 percent or more of all the inmates were feebleminded.

At the same time, some of the first geneticists and their allies in social reform organizations were fashioning yet another new science—eugenics, a program for breeding better people (and preventing the breeding of inferior humans). In the early twentieth century eugenicists such as Henry H. Goddard, a psychologist and specialist in the care of the feebleminded, devised a method of tracing the family pedigrees of inmates in institutions for the mentally backward. Although his method relied on guesswork about the mental abilities of people long dead, it seemed to prove that feeblemindedness was an inherited trait, much like eye color, unchangeable by education or other environmental measures. Eugenicists, combining forces with the early intelligence testers, came up with a solution to crime as bold as it was simple: prevent the feebleminded from reproducing, through either sterilization or (the preferred solution) lifelong isolation, and crime rates would drop in the next generation. The feeblemindedness explanation of crime was much more than a theory of criminal behavior; it was a linchpin in the eugenics movement, the reform effort that swelled to a mighty crescendo about 1910. Institutions for the feebleminded expanded to embrace thousands of new commitments, while some states passed special "defective delinquent" laws enabling them to retain for life offenders who did poorly on intelligence tests.[9]

Feeblemindedness theory was probably the most universally acclaimed, if shortest-lived, explanation of crime in Anglo-American history. Why did it enjoy such popularity? Because it joined forces with the eugenics movement, an international effort replete with funding centers, thousands of volunteers, and social clubs in every major city and even small towns. Feeblemindedness theory was a part of a cause—the campaign to cleanse society of social problems.[10] Eugenics remained popular as an analysis of social problems even after the feeblemindedness theory of crime fell out of favor. Its popularity waned as intelligence testing improved, making it more difficult to show that criminals were feebleminded, and as reformers recognized the financial impossibility of institutionalizing all criminals for life.

In 1939, Earnest A. Hooton, an avid eugenicist and head of Harvard University's anthropology department, tried to revive criminal anthropology. Hooton thought Lombroso had probably been on the right track in his analysis of crime but that he had been ill-equipped methodologically. To test the idea of the anthropological criminal with up-to-date statistical methods, Hooton designed a multistate study of prisoners, reporting its results in two books—*The American Criminal* and *Crime and the Man*.[11] Not surprisingly, given his biases, both books concluded with eugenic recommendations.

> Criminals are organically inferior. Crime is the resultant of the impact of environment upon low grade human organisms. It follows that the elimination of crime can be effected only by the extirpation [elimination] of the physically, mentally, and morally unfit, or by their complete segregation in a socially aseptic environment [i.e., an institution where they could not reproduce].[12]

These policy recommendations did not follow from Hooton's data, however, and in any case, the books were so incoherent in their analyses that few people read past the first few chapters.

A decade later a friend of Hooton's, the eugenicist and psychologist William Sheldon, published *Varieties of Delinquent Youth*, reporting on his studies in "somatotyping"—efforts to classify people by their bodytypes and then find correlations between the bodytypes and personalities. Having identified three basic somatotypes (*endomorphic*, or soft and round; *mesomorphic*, or muscular and compact; and *ectomorphic*, or fragile and brainy), Sheldon found that delinquent boys tend to be mesomorphs. However, this finding was based on just sixteen cases, and even Sheldon himself was not impressed by it, partly because he recognized that these sixteen delinquents were physically superior to other youths in his sample, excelling in "general strength and general athletic ability"[13]—not what a eugenicist wanted to discover. He was far more interested in the "essential inadequacy"[14] of those youths characterized by "the spoor of insufficiency" (his unlovely term for various mental and physical weaknesses).[15] The worst "delinquents" are not those who commit crimes but those weaklings whose reproduction leads "toward biological catastrophe."[16] In conclusion, Sheldon recommends a vague set of eugenic measures to save mankind from "social chaos."

Are eugenic theories of crime dead and gone? Since the mid-twentieth century, only two halfhearted efforts have been made to revive them. The first appeared in *Crime and Human Nature* by Harvard professors James Q. Wilson and Richard Herrnstein; speaking warmly of research by Hooton and Sheldon, they hint at the possible efficacy of eugenics (without explicitly endorsing the doctrine).[17] The second effort appeared in *The Bell Curve*, in which Richard Herrnstein and political scientist Charles Murray put forth a modern version of feeblemindedness theory, again with eugenic undertones.[18] But although these two books attracted considerable attention among criminologists and lay readers alike, they failed to inspire eugenic policies; indeed, among other scholars, they inspired mainly criticism. (*The Bell Curve*, wrote evolutionary biologist Stephen Jay Gould, "presents no compelling data to support its anachronistic social Darwinism.")[19] Since the 1920s, outside of Nazi Germany few efforts have been made to control crime through eugenics. Nor is eugenics likely to be revived as a solution to crime, for the genetic assumptions on which it rested are no longer scientifically viable.

Biosocial Explanations

The twentieth century was the great era for purely sociological theories of crime. Sociocriminologists rejected biocriminologists' view of crime as a type of pathology or sickness, instead analyzing crime as an ordinary (indeed ubiquitous) phenomenon. Thus to some extent they "normalized" deviance. By 1950, Edwin Sutherland and other sociocriminologists so completely dominated the field that they were able to harden its boundaries and marginalize even respected researchers like Sheldon and Eleanor Glueck, who combined psychological and sociological approaches to crime.[20] Moreover, in reaction to the Holocaust, many prominent sociocriminologists considered it almost a political and moral duty to oppose psychologists or others who drew on traditions rooted in biological theories. Yet even during the heyday of sociocriminology, when nearly all the major theoretical disputes occurred *within* that realm, there appeared the first sign that biological theories would again claim a place at the criminological table. That event, in 1964, was the publication of Hans J. Eysenck's *Crime and Personality*.[21]

Eysenck, a German-born psychologist who fled the Nazis to live in England, developed a genetic and neurological theory that attributed criminal behavior to inherited personality factors. Some people, he explained, are born extraverts—partygoers and thrill seekers, drinkers and brawlers who crave stimulations that quieter introverts shun. Drawing on Ivan Pavlov's work on conditioning, Eysenck hypothesized that extraverts condition more slowly and weakly than introverts; they simply learn life's lessons more slowly, and some of them—the extreme extraverts known as psychopaths— never learn those lessons at all.[22]

In Eysenck's view, classical conditioning (a process involving involuntary behavior and the autonomic nervous system) accounts for moral behavior. Such conditioning occurs mainly in childhood, when parents and teachers punish children for negative behaviors and reinforce them for acceptable activities. Some children just never learn right from wrong; they never acquire a conscience. The degree to which one is conditionable—a person's location, so to speak, on the extraversion scale—is determined by "hereditary influences."[23] Psychopaths and other criminals are simply born that way.

Eysenck's biologism deeply offended sociologically oriented criminologists, but he did attract some followers among psychologists; they attracted yet others, and today, psychologists working on genetic and neurological influences on criminal behavior are again being taken seriously, even by sociocriminologists. Perhaps the best known of these psychologists is Terrie E. Moffitt of Duke University, who distinguishes between "adolescence-limited" offenders who outgrow delinquency and "life-course-persistent" offenders whose chronic criminality indicates biological deficits of various types.[24] Also well known in the field are David Farrington of Cambridge University in England and Adrian Raine, the latter a British psychologist who works in the United States.[25]

While the new biological research on criminal behavior does not yet play a central role in explaining crime, it is being developed in multiple ways and is likely to thrive in the decades ahead. Those who oppose it most vociferously often do not realize that today's biocriminologists reject the old-fashioned biological determinism of forerunners such as Lombroso and the false dichotomies of the old nurture-versus-nature debates. Instead, today's biocriminologists adopt a *biosocial* model, positing that people's behavior is a result of interactions between biology and environment, "nature" and "nurture," and while they hold that biological makeup affects the individual, they do not argue that biology operates in a vacuum to determine who we become. Nor do today's biocriminologists advocate eugenic measures—indeed, their biosocial model points toward social reforms.[26]

Biological theories of crime, then, have a long and, in some cases, disgraceful history. How do these theories show up in movies?

Frankenstein

Biological theories of crime achieved their most perfect realization in *Frankenstein*, director James Whale's horror film of 1931. The story begins with Henry Frankenstein, an ambitious young scientist, and Fritz, his hump-backed manservant, spying on a late-evening funeral from behind the iron fence of a cemetery. When the gravedigger completes the burial, Henry (played by Colin Clive) and Fritz unearth the body, carting it home along with another corpse they collect from a gibbet along the way to carve up and piece together into the body of a new creature. Normally Henry lives in the village with his grumpy old father, the Baron, but for his grisly experiments he has taken up residence in a medieval tower. Up the twisting staircase, on the second story, he has set up his laboratory.

When Henry sends Fritz to steal a brain from the nearby medical school, the dimwit returns not with the jar of formaldehyde containing a normal brain but with a jar marked "Abnormal Brain." (Earlier, a lecturer at the medical school, evidently a disciple of Lombroso, explained that the abnormal brain was that "of the typical criminal," and as such an organ with "degenerative characteristics.") Unaware of the mix-up, Henry transplants this brain into his new creature's skull.

All the important people in Henry's life—his father the Baron, his beautiful young fiancée Elizabeth, his old friend Victor, and his mentor, Dr. Waldman—beg him to give up his insane efforts to assume God's powers to create man, but Henry, increasingly feverish, refuses to listen. He chooses a wild night of thunder and lightning to complete his plan. Slowly elevating the table with the composite cadaver toward the tower's open parapet, he zaps his creature with a "great ray"; combining forces with the lightning, it does the job. When the table descends, the Monster (played by Boris Karloff) begins to move.

At first, Henry tries to train the Monster, but it turns vicious, and Dr. Waldman advises Henry to "kill it, as you would any savage animal." (Like

Lombroso, Dr. Waldman has decided that a criminal totally lacking responsibility should be permanently immobilized.) Henry weakly responds, "It's murder," but his fit of insanity has depleted him. Leaving Dr. Waldman to do the dirty work, he returns to his baronial home and the healing arms of Elizabeth. Later he is sufficiently strong to join the manhunt for the Monster, chasing it through rocky terrain until it captures him and takes him to an old mill. After a struggle, the Monster tosses Henry from the topmost platform of the wooden windmill; fortunately, Henry's falling body catches on one of the windmill's arms, from which he dangles until he plummets, injured but safe, into the arms of the mob below. At the film's conclusion, Henry prepares to marry Elizabeth. He has created a biological criminal—a true criminal man—and suffered a bout of insanity, but now, mad fantasies banished, he is ready to settle down to ordinary domestic pleasures.

Before he renounced his ambitions, Henry's approach to science was not unlike Lombroso's. Both Henry the mad scientist and Lombroso the criminal anthropologist were totally dedicated to the scientific pursuit of their goals and to pushing beyond the boundaries of the known into the mysterious unknowns of human nature. The research of both involved body parts and experimentation. Henry's laboratory is full of scientific trappings such as glass retorts and specimens in jars, just as Lombroso's books are full of tables, medical terminology, and diagrams of brains. Moreover, they share the scientistic belief that only natural science methods can yield knowledge about the causes of crime.

Although Fritz is but a minor character, he is key to both the plot and *Frankenstein*'s message about biological criminality. Amoral, animalistic, imbecilic, Fritz is a degenerate. With his hunched back, limp, and bulging eyes, he is also an atavism. He may slavishly follow Henry's orders, but otherwise he is malicious, governed by base and primitive instincts. It is Fritz who turns the initially docile Monster into a vicious killer: while Henry is upstairs working, Fritz corners the chained Monster in his basement cell, whipping him and tormenting him with a burning torch. To put an end to this torture, the Monster hangs Fritz from a beam—the first of his murders. The film presents a range of offenders, but Fritz is its purest criminal, and his criminality is biological. The Monster, too, is a biological criminal, but he, in contrast, is a kinder and more complex character.

The Monster makes his grand entrance as a living creature by walking backward into Henry's laboratory—he has not yet learned that forward is the way to walk. From head to toe he looks the part of the born criminal: ill-fitting black clothes leave his wrists and hands dangling; his eyes peer out, half lidded, under an overhanging brow; stitches and staples hold together the skin on his oversized head, while a bolt protrudes from his neck. He also acts the part of the primitive, poorly evolved born criminal, with his lurching movements and inability to communicate except through guttural moans. Yet, as we can tell from his soft, sad eyes, he is timid and scared, and anxious to cooperate. When Henry has him sit in a chair, the Monster looks up to the open parapet and, in an almost religious gesture, beatifically reaches toward the light. Immediately thereafter, like a trusting child, he reaches out to take Henry's hands; but Henry, caught up in his experiments, ignores the gesture. Indeed, he almost immediately decides that the Monster is dangerous, chaining him in the basement. Fritz's torments leave the Monster badly damaged, psychologically, and then Henry deserts him, leaving him in the clutches of Dr. Waldman, who stretches him out on the table to perform a live dissection before killing him outright. In self-defense, instinctively, the Monster wraps a hand around the neck of the unsuspecting Dr. Waldman and throttles him. Murder number 2.

Finding himself alone in the tower, the Monster escapes to roam the countryside. First he encounters an enchanting little girl playing in the sun beside an Alpine lake. Maria invites the Monster to join her; delighted, he watches her toss daisies into the water and then joins in. But when he runs out of daisies, he tosses Maria into the lake, where she drowns. Murder number 3.

Uncomprehending but appalled by the disappearance of his little playmate, the hapless Monster lumbers on. At the Baron's house, through an open window, he glimpses a spectacular sight: Elizabeth, in full bridal regalia, including an immense train of white gauze. The Monster clambers through the window, and it seems that he will rape or murder Elizabeth, perhaps both. However, noise from the rest of the house scares him off, and he leaves Elizabeth half dead on the bed. Almost murder number 4.

Hunted by braying dogs and a lynch mob, the Monster rushes crazily through the rocky mountainside. When he bumps into Henry, whom he now views as an enemy, he drags the scientist to the old mill, hauling him up ladders to the high platform where the arms of the windmill join at a large winch. They chase one another around the winch's drum until, in desperation, the Monster hurls Henry from the platform and then watches, distressed and horrified, as the villagers, after saving Henry, torch the mill and the flames leap toward him. A falling beam pins the Monster to the floor, and the flames consume him.

Most movies have heroes, and in a film about a biological criminal, in particular, we might expect a hero—a monster-destroyer. This is not the case

Figure 3.1. In his embodiment of Dr. Frankenstein's Monster, actor Boris Karloff created a template for the biological criminal: crude, primitive, menacing, mentally dim and yet physically powerful, born to kill, driven to violence by his criminal brain. From *Frankenstein* (1931). Photo used by permission of Photofest.

with *Frankenstein*, however. Egotistical and irresponsible, Henry cannot be the hero: he is a failed "parent" as well as a demented scientist. Willing to experiment with human life, he does not even respect the bodies of the dead. Nor does any other character fit the hero's mold. This film lacks not only a hero but also a central criminal. The bad guy might be Henry, who violates the laws of God and man; it might be Fritz, who is unadulterated evil and a biological criminal to boot; or it might be the Monster, who roams the countryside committing murders. However, the Monster is too much of a victim to be a full-blown villain. In *Frankenstein* we find a movie with a born criminal who is not clearly criminal, even though he looks and behaves like one.

The movie derives from one of the earliest Gothic novels, *Frankenstein, or the Modern Prometheus*, published in 1818 by Mary Shelley, when she was just twenty-one years old. Shelley tells how one Victor Frankenstein, a "pale student of unhallowed arts," is driven by an insane ambition to assemble a "hideous phantasm of a man," which he then brings to life, thus mocking "the stupendous mechanism of the Creator of the world."[27] Her monster, too, is lonely and at first innocent; but, mistreated by humans, he gradually realizes that he is revolting and sets out to avenge himself. Shelley's novel incorporates aspects of what today is termed *labeling theory*—the idea that negative labels drive people deeper into antisocial behavior (see chapter 8). "I am malicious because I am miserable," Shelley's monster tells Frankenstein. "Am I not shunned and hated by all mankind? You, my creator, would tear me to pieces, and triumph."[28] Shelley's Victor Frankenstein feels more guilt and remorse than does his movie counterpart—and with good reason, for in the original version, the Monster wipes out Victor's family, his best friend, and his bride, Elizabeth. At the end of Shelley's novel, both Victor and his monster die, done in by guilt and grief.

What makes James Whale's version of the story distinctive is its campiness—its quality of playful theatricality, its deliberate over-the-toppedness. Whale throws himself into the tale's Gothicism, but he does so with ironical amusement at its artifice and excess. That his version will be a campy interpretation is signaled by the opening graveyard scene, with its lamenting mourners, the large black cross on one nearby tomb, and a life-size, hooded skeleton on another. We see Fritz, peering with hungry fascination at the burial; we hear a clanging bell; and when the burial is complete and the gravedigger lights his pipe, we see the flash of fire against a forbidding sky, the film's recurrent symbol of life-in-death. Every detail signals sensationalism; we realize from the start that this film is having fun with the Gothic, hamming it up. The film goes beyond Lombroso, bringing a sophisticated amusement to bear on a theory that the Italian presented with grim seriousness.

Frankenstein goes beyond Lombroso's criminal anthropology in yet another way: it combines biological with sociological theories, pairing the two in perfect balance. Now, it is true that Lombroso himself investigated social as well as biological factors in criminality; in the case of criminals who are not born bad, he taught, sociological influences play a key role in pushing people into crime. However, Lombroso focused so dramatically on innate criminality that few readers paid attention to the sociological aspects of his work. *Frankenstein*, on the other hand, manages to illustrate biological and sociological explanations at the same time. Its Monster perfectly realizes the idea of the born criminal: he is hideous, his instincts are primitive, and he is clearly a born killer, since he does little else than murder. However (and this is why the contrast with Fritz is so important), the film's Monster is also born innocent and driven to crime through abuse, parental neglect, and the scientific mistake that gave him a criminal brain. Thus the film combines "nature" and "nurture" explanations, anticipating (however playfully) today's biosocial theories of crime.

Lombroso's criminal anthropology shows up in dozens of movies in addition to *Frankenstein*, including *The Bad Seed*, a mid-twentieth-century film that continues to attract enthusiastic audiences in television reruns. *The Bad Seed* portrays an unusual figure: the female born criminal. Although Lombroso wrote an entire book about female born criminals,[29] characters of this type, perhaps because they are so improbable, are seldom depicted in either criminology or movies.

Biological Psychiatry, the Fifties, and The Bad Seed

The 1950s were the high point for psychiatric and psychoanalytic explanations of behavior of all sorts, including criminal behavior. Psychiatrists and psychoanalysts, regarded by many as the ultimate authorities on deviant behavior, became almost cultural gods. Attributing criminal behavior to maladjustments, unconscious drives, inadequate socialization, irrational rages, and Oedipus complexes, they often linked such psychological causes to underlying biological defects. Nowhere in the cinema does this appear more vividly than in *The Bad Seed*. This film actually goes beyond Lombroso, who had only a vague notion of "heredity," to attribute the cause of crime to bad genes.

Rhoda (played by Patty McCormack) is a girl of eight years with preternaturally blond pigtails and saccharine temperament—until she is crossed. "Miss Uppity" is what LeRoy, the hired man, calls her, and with good reason, for she is the essence of the self-satisfied goody-goody. Invariably dressed in flouncy dresses, spotlessly clean and tidy ("Rhoda never gets anything dirty," her mother observes), Rhoda fawns on adults, flattering anyone who might be able to give her something she wants. Gradually, we become aware of just how manipulative appearances are in her case. Rhoda evidently killed several people in the film's backstory, before the tale that we see onscreen begins. In the latter, she first kills a classmate to get the gold penmanship award that she coveted for herself. Then she knocks off the hired man, LeRoy. Rhoda's mother, slowly realizing that her little darling is a psychopathic killer, consults with a psychiatrist who specializes in criminology. When the mother asks, "Do children ever commit murders?" he responds, "Oh yes. . . . Some murderers . . . start amazingly early." Disbelieving, the mother protests such killers must come from slums or other bad environments, but Dr. Tasker corrects her:

> Some fellow criminologists . . . have begun to make me believe we've all been putting too much emphasis on environment and too little on heredity. They cite a type of criminal born with no capacity for remorse or guilt, no feeling of right or wrong, born with the kind of brain that may have been normal in humans 50,000 years ago.

Later, Dr. Tasker explains that "it's as if these children were born blind, permanently, and you just couldn't expect them to see." Often they look normal, but "It's just that they are bad seeds, plain bad from the beginning, and nothing can change them."

From the start, characters in *The Bad Seed* refer to someone named Bessie Denker, "the most amazing woman in all the annals of homicide," as one describes her. "She was beautiful, she had brains, but she was ruthless," a born killer. In the course of the film Rhoda's mother discovers that she herself is the daughter of Bessie Denker. The bad seed must have skipped a generation, since the mother is the opposite of her daughter, but clearly it has taken root in Rhoda. Fortunately for all, Rhoda is finally struck down by lightning, thus terminating her line of bad genes. In *The Bad Seed*, the born criminal looks like a "little sweetheart." Innate criminality has moved inward in its expression. Gone are the twisted limbs and squinty eyes of Lombroso's born criminal; now we have an even more dangerous hereditary criminal—one who looks innocent.

Film and Feeblemindedness Theory

The feeblemindedness theory of criminal behavior inspired a number of memorable movies, but it also inspired a cinematic reaction against the theory—films that insist on the inherent innocence of people with mental disabilities. In both cases, we get stereotypes of people with intellectual impairments, flat depictions that assume such people are incapable of criminal responsibility. There is, however, yet a third type of film about people with intellectual disabilities: movies showing how easy it is for the criminal justice system to make mistakes, falsely accusing and punishing people who are intellectually unable to participate in their own defense.

At one end of the spectrum lie films that openly endorse feeblemindedness theory. *Of Mice and Men* (1939), based on a novel by John Steinbeck, was made at a moment when the theory had gone out of fashion with social scientists but retained widespread credibility with the general public. Starring Lon Chaney Jr. as Lennie, the sweet but imbecilic bumbler who cannot avoid harming pretty things, the film likens him in its very title to an animal—a mouse—and subsequent scenes strengthen this criminal association, showing that unlike a true adult, Lennie cannot control himself. Through overly enthusiastic patting, he kills first a puppy and then the overseer's wife, crimes for which he is not criminally responsible, the film tells us, because he did not understand what he was doing. George, Lennie's friend and protector, sadly concludes that he has to kill Lennie to protect him from the justice officials who are ready to lynch him. Lennie is simultaneously childlike, naive, animalistic, and criminalistic.

Sling Blade (1996) begins when a Lennie-like character, Carl Childers (played by Billy Bob Thornton) is released from the state mental hospital where he has been incarcerated since slashing his mother and her lover to death. We follow Carl's difficulties as he tries to support himself, make friends, and cope with hazing. While Carl is portrayed as intellectually limited and in some ways grotesque, his character also includes aspects of the childlike saint. He goes to live with a kindly young widow and her son, but when the widow's evil lover moves in as well, to protect her Carl kills again, this time with a sharpened lawnmower blade. The film interprets this murder, like the earlier ones, as an effect of his disability: Carl wants to help the widow but simply cannot figure out another way to handle the situation. However, because he does in fact save her, he becomes something of an avenging angel—or a Christ figure who purposefully sacrifices himself for someone in need. Unfortunately, *Sling Blade* is ultimately unsuccessful as a film because it tries to sustain two contradictory interpretations, showing Carl to have been both criminally responsible and criminally irresponsible for the slayings. It both illustrates and contradicts the feeblemindedness theory of crime.

At the other end of the spectrum are films that flat-out contradict feeblemindedness theory by portraying people with learning disabilities as essentially innocent, saintly, and incapable of evil. One of these improbable figures turns up in *The Hand That Rocks the Cradle* (1992), a thriller in which a large black handyman, Solomon (Ernie Hudson), saves a family from an evil nanny. Another shows up in *The Green Mile* (1999) in the form of John Coffey (Michael Clarke Duncan), another huge black man, this one with miraculous healing powers. John, although he is on death row for a crime he did not commit, is so kind that he even helps his own executioner (Tom Hanks) get through his dreadful task. Both of these films sentimentalize people with learning disabilities and rely on stereotyped racial imagery, all the while protecting themselves against charges of racism by attributing supernatural goodness to their large black male characters.

However, some films realistically portray cases in which people with mental retardation are unjustly convicted of crimes. One is *Brother's Keeper* (1992), a documentary about Delbert Ward, one of four elderly brothers, all backward and illiterate, who have spent their lives together on a hardscrabble farm. One of the brothers dies; Delbert is accused of killing him and is badgered into confessing. However, the local community comes to his aid, realizing that it is not difficult for sophisticated police officers to weasel a confession out of an elderly, slow-witted man. Similarly, *Let Him Have It* (1991) tells the real-life story of Derek Bentley, a brain-damaged young Englishman who was railroaded for a murder he did not commit and executed. When Derek yelled, "Let him have it," he was telling the actual killer to give his gun to the police, but the vindictive judge chose to interpret the phrase as "Shoot him"; Derek, unable to explain the real circumstances, receives and, in bewilderment, suffers a death sentence.

Biocriminology in Recent Movies

Some recent films—*Gattaca* (1997), *Minority Report*, *Monster*—are set against the intellectual backdrop of the ongoing revolutions in genetics and neuroscience. Without referring explicitly to those developments, they raise new issues about criminal responsibility and express new anxieties about how scientific advances might affect human rights. Directly or indirectly, they show an awareness of recent changes in the biological sciences and uneasiness about the possible consequences of those changes.

Gattaca—more of a sci-fi thriller than a crime film, although it does center on identity theft—is concerned with the return of eugenics policy and genetic discrimination. In a future world where everyone is ranked in terms of genetic makeup, there is no room for ambition or hard work to change the life one is assigned to. This kind of genetic hierarchy, in which low scores on intelligence tests would result in a lowly place in society, was the type of world projected by the first eugenicists for the "feebleminded." However, the film's plot proves that determination and ambition can overcome whatever genetic deficiencies one is born with.

Minority Report, starring Tom Cruise and directed by Steven Spielberg, is not directly concerned with genetic determinism, but it was made at a time when DNA testing was proving that many people on death row were in fact innocent. Set in the future, the film imagines the consequences of being able to detect a crime before it is committed. Policing, adjudicating guilt, and punishment would collapse into a single, preventative act: that of capturing the about-to-be criminal and immobilizing him or her for life. By implication, this sort of situation might prevail in the future if science were used to predict who would become criminal. A single person—the scientist—would serve as cop, judge, and punisher, just as John Anderton, Tom Cruise's character, does in the film. But, *Minority Report* shows, it is impossible to achieve such certainty about who will commit a crime in the future, and even to yearn for such a "scientific" solution to crime is to open government up to the dangers of demagoguery and dictatorship.

Monster, directed by Patty Jenkins and starring Charlize Theron as Aileen Wournos, a real-life prostitute who became a serial killer and was eventually executed in Florida, raises questions related to the new biosocial model of human development. In the film as in her actual life, Wournos suffered sexual abuse as a child, bore her first baby when she was barely a teenager, and experienced lifelong mental and physical abuse. Perhaps as a result of these environmental insults, she grew up to become slow-witted and, eventually, vicious. Disadvantaged by weak intelligence and other meager personal resources, she was unable to mount a defense that would have brought out her past and shown how it worked to diminish her criminal responsibility. As a result, she was executed—the film concludes with a view of Wournos being hurried into the death chamber.

Monster relates less to fears about what science will become than to what it has already demonstrated: that, because children's brains are molded by their environments, those who grow up in devastating circumstances may be saddled with emotional and intellectual deficits that eventually feed into crime. Of all the films discussed here, *Monster* is most successful at exposing the human rights issues of people with such deficits. Wournos's mental and emotional backwardness, combined with her alcoholism and brutalization by customers, pushed her into her killing spree. Without excusing Wuornos's crimes, *Monster* shows that they were not the acts of a person with full criminal responsibility.

Conclusion

Biological theories are among the most popular explanations of crime in moviedom, in large part because they are so photogenic, offering ample play for the grotesque or those devilishly pretty apparitions who, like little Rhoda, are not always what they seem. Since the earliest days of talkies, movies have proved adept at embodying biological theories and tracking their changes over time, from criminal anthropology through biological psychiatry into the present. Today, they serve as one of the most effective means of alerting publics to the dangers of biological determinism and genetic pigeonholing, even while, as in the case of *Monster*, they help demonstrate the legal implications of the biosocial model of criminal behavior.

FURTHER VIEWING

Deliverance (1972)
I, Robot (2004)
Murder, My Sweet (1944)
Scarface (1932)
Texas Chainsaw Massacre (1974)

4

"Blood, Mother, Blood!"

Psychological Theories and Psycho

The umbrella term *psychological theories of crime* covers explanations drawn from three "*psy*-sciences": psychology, psychoanalysis, and psychiatry. The three types of theory resemble one another in nomenclature and in subject matter, since all deal with mental phenomena and the causes of human behavior. Otherwise, however, they are often at odds.

Psychology as a field aims at creating a science of the mind and behavior, and it is itself multifaceted, including such diverse branches as applied, behavioral, clinical, and empirical psychology. As one historian explains, "Psychology occupies a peculiar place among the sciences, suspended between methodological orientations derived from the physical and biological sciences and a subject matter that extends into the social and human sciences."[1] Its terminal degree is a doctorate in psychology. *Psychoanalysis*, in contrast, is a body of thought developed in the early twentieth century by the Austrian physician Sigmund Freud; it includes a theory of how the mind works, an explanation of human behavior, and a method of treating emotional problems. Although Freud himself had a background in medicine, he insisted on the value of lay analysts, therapists trained in his theories who had themselves undergone psychoanalysis but did not necessarily have medical degrees. "As long as I live," Freud declared, "I shall balk at having psychoanalysis swallowed by medicine."[2] *Psychiatry*, the third member of the triad, is a medical specialty aimed at the treatment of mental disorders. Its analyses are sometimes more biological than those of psychology, and its treatments often involve pharmaceutical drugs.

Theories from these three overlapping areas of inquiry have frequently intersected with criminology, but among criminologists, interest in them is flagging. One recent textbook ignores psychological theories entirely on the grounds that crime is a sociological, not an individual, phenomenon.[3] Such dismissiveness reflects a larger struggle between sociology and psychology for sovereignty over criminology's domain. At the moment, sociologists are winning this competition, but psychologists are developing a biosocial model of explanation (see chapter 3) that promises to exercise increasing influence over the field in the years ahead. Moreover, psychological explanations offer perspectives on individuals' criminal behavior that sociology itself cannot provide.

This chapter first reviews psychological (including psychiatric and psychoanalytical) theories of crime, and then it discusses Alfred Hitchcock's *Psycho* (1960), a film that illustrates cinema's power to show how a number of psychological factors can operate simultaneously to produce criminal behavior. Next, focusing on the issue of criminal responsibility of the mentally ill, we analyze three additional films—*M* (1931), *The Boston Strangler* (1968), and *A Clockwork Orange* (1971)—that take various positions on this issue. In conclusion we argue that psychological theories of crime and the films that use them offer perspectives crucial to the understanding of criminal behavior.

The Psy-Sciences and Explanations of Crime
Behavioral Psychology

Of the numerous subspecialities of the field of psychology that have addressed issues relevant to criminology, behavioral psychology has inspired the most debate. A learning theory based on the concept of conditioning, behavioral psychology holds that the psychologist's sole concern should be with observable behavior—and not with mental states or anything else said to go on in the mind. Its fundamental premises appear in the famous "twelve infants" claim of the early behaviorist John Watson:

> Give me a dozen healthy infants, well-formed, and my own specified world to bring them up in and I'll guarantee to take any one at random and train him to become any type of specialist I might select—doctor, lawyer, artist, merchant-chief and, yes, even a beggar-man and thief, regardless of his talents, penchants, tendencies, abilities, vocations, and race of his ancestors.[4]

Watson, like other behavioral psychologists, viewed humans as blank slates whose behavior is formed solely through interactions with their environments. Dominant in the mid-twentieth century, largely through the work of B. F. Skinner (1904–90), behavioral psychology later fell from favor, eclipsed in part by neuroscientists' growing ability to study the inner workings of the brain.

Behavioral psychology's main criminological implication concerns the learning of law-abiding behaviors. In this respect, it begins with Ivan Pavlov's experiments with classical conditioning, in which the pioneering Russian psychologist fed hungry dogs while sounding a bell; in time, the dogs would salivate solely at the sound of bell, even if no food was present. Translated into human terms, the classical conditioning model looks like this: a child steals cookies, is punished, and feels uncomfortable and hurt; after several learning trials, the very *thought* of stealing a cookie will make the child unhappy.[5] The desire to steal is now inhibited, and the inhibition is a result not of a conscious, rational decision against cookie stealing but rather of conditioning, a largely involuntary process involving the autonomic nervous system. Building on Pavlov's work, the British psychologist Hans Eysenck argued that some people ("introverts") condition more easily than others ("extraverts" or potential criminals) and concluded that conscience—no matter how much we may admire those who seem highly ethical—is in fact no more than a conditioned reflex.[6] In theory at least, behaviorism can explain how we learn (or fail to learn) rules (for example, to keep our hands off that cookie).

In addition, behaviorism implies that through behavior modification, it may be possible to change lawbreakers into law-abiding citizens. One form of behavior modification—positive reinforcement—has been developed in the form of so-called token economies. Prisoners receive token rewards when they conform to the rules on the theory that eventually conformity will become habitual. A second type of behavior modification—aversive conditioning—uses loud noises, drugs that induce vomiting or paralysis, and electroshock to discourage prisoners' deviant behaviors. This is the type depicted in *A Clockwork Orange*.

Psychoanalysis

According to Freud, the human psyche has three parts, the ego, id, and superego, which constantly conflict with one another, not just in offenders but in all people. The ego, representing reason and deliberation, is the conscious aspect of the psyche. The superego or conscience constitutes one aspect of the unconscious, while the id or passions forms the other. The id, driven by the desire for pleasure, includes impulses, urges, and the libido or sexual energy. Iconoclastically, Freud maintained that even small children have sexual impulses and that everyone experiences a desire—the Oedipus complex—to partner with the opposite-sex parent and kill the same-sex parent. Trapped between the id and the superego, the ego is almost bound to feel guilty, for it is constantly bombarded by demands from the id, which the superego must then subdue. One result is defense mechanisms to which Freud gave names like repression, fixation, denial, and regression. His analysis provided filmmakers and other interpreters of human experience an arsenal of conceptual weapons for analyzing deviant behaviors.

Freud himself avoided theorizing about crime and wrote only one short article on the subject, "Criminals from a Sense of Guilt" (1916),[7] in which he speculates that some offenders, overwhelmed by a sense of guilt arising from the Oedipus complex, commit crimes in order to have something specific to feel guilty about:

> Paradoxical as it may sound, I must maintain that the sense of guilt was present before the misdeed [in the cases he had studied], that it did not arise from it, but conversely—the misdeed arose from the sense of guilt. These people might justly be described as criminals from a sense of guilt. . . . This obscure sense of guilt derived from the Oedipus complex and was a reaction to the two great criminal intentions of killing the father and having sexual relations with the mother. In comparison with these two, the crimes committed in order to fix the sense of guilt to something came as a relief to the sufferers.[8]

Freud did not claim that all criminals are driven by such self-punitive impulses, just that some are.

Although Freud showed little interest in the causes of specifically criminal behavior, followers enthusiastically applied his concepts to cases of crime and victimization, and some used Freud's ideas to treat delinquents and criminals. While they could not literally put criminals "on the couch" and let them free-associate, as Freud did with his patients, his followers generated a rich body of interpretive literature on crime, and some tried to work psychoanalytically with difficult children in group home settings.[9] Today, however, the enthusiasm for psychoanalytic interpretations of criminality has waned, partly because its treatment implications are impractical (how could governments possibly afford to psychoanalyze hundreds of thousands of lawbreakers?) and partly because psychoanalytic theory has not been validated scientifically. For social scientists, Freud's work is like a fine wine whose taste has soured: once it was in great demand, but today, few buy it.

Psychiatry

Psychiatry, the branch of medicine specializing in the diagnosis, treatment, and prevention of mental illness, took shape as a distinct profession in the early 1800s. Throughout the nineteenth century, psychiatrists ran lunatic asylums and testified in court when a defendant's sanity was in question. At the end of the nineteenth century, psychiatrists began to practice outside asylum walls, treating private patients in their offices and in some cases joining the mental hygiene movement to work for the prevention of mental disease, including delinquency, which they viewed as a type of maladjustment. As physicians, psychiatrists tended to locate the origins of mental illnesses in the brain, attributing them (at least during the nineteenth century) to abnormalities in the brain matter itself.[10] And due to this same interpretive framework, some twentieth-century psychiatrists experimented with physical treatments for criminality, including lobotomies, other forms of psychosurgery, and electroconvulsive "therapy."

Eventually reaction set in against psychiatrists' involvement in the diagnosis and treatment of criminality. After World War II, researchers discovered that Nazi psychiatrists had participated enthusiastically in Hitler's programs for elimination of "antisocials"; that American psychiatrists tended to overrecommend institutionalization as a solution to mental health and even political problems; and that treatment in hospitals for the criminally insane amounted to little less than torture (as revealed in the horrifying documentary *Titicut Follies* [1967]). The protest spilled over into *One Flew Over the Cuckoo's Nest*, a 1975 film starring Jack Nicholson as Randle Patrick McMurphy, leader of an antipsychiatry revolt in a mental institution who survives electroshock therapy only to be lobotomized, an operation that ends his insurrection against the authorities.

Cinematically, the most fertile psychiatric diagnosis is psychopathy, a supposed mental pathology defined in terms of subjects' inability to identify with others, remorseless cruelty, manipulativeness, deceitfulness, irresponsibility, constant search for stimulation, and criminal behavior. Although psychiatrists controlled the diagnosis of psychopaths for more than a century, recently psychologists have asserted expertise in this area,[11] and at the same time psychopathy has to an extent escaped even the authority of professional psychologists to lead a life of its own in popular psychology. Today, a key figure in pop psychology is the serial killer, a criminal type nearly always portrayed as a psychopath.

Psycho

One of most demented characters in cinema history—a figure whose mental quirks, twitches, and pathologies provide fodder for psychologists, psychoanalysts, and psychiatrists alike—is Norman Bates, the lead criminal in director Alfred Hitchcock's *Psycho*. Like a split personality, the film actually breaks into two distinct halves, the first devoted to a perfectly normal lawbreaker, Marion Crane (played by Janet Leigh), secretary to a Phoenix, Arizona, businessman. In the center of the film Marion crosses paths with Norman Bates (Anthony Perkins), at which point, in a symbolic rape, he stabs her to death and *Psycho* becomes the story of a mentally bizarre criminal. Criminal guilt is a central preoccupation of this film; Hitchcock explores it from various psychological angles.

Marion's minor waywardness demonstrates just how ordinary some forms of deviance can be. She is having an affair with Sam Loomis, whom she adores and wants to marry. However, Sam, who is struggling to make good on his father's debts while also paying alimony to his former wife, is too proud to marry Marion before he can get back on his feet financially. Soon after the film opens, in the office where Marion works, a businessman—tipsy, leering, and clearly involved in an unhealthy relationship with his adult daughter ("my baby")—turns $40,000 in cash over to Marion's boss, who asks her to deposit it in a bank on her way home. Instead, without ever making a firm decision to steal, she drifts into theft, absconding with the money and vaguely hoping that if she gives it to Sam, they will be able to marry.

Marion's misdeed immediately trips her up: her boss and the obnoxious client notice her as she is leaving town. A policeman catches her napping in her car, follows her, and looks on as, guiltily but pointlessly, she trades the car in for another. Rain drives Marion off the main highway into the Bates Motel, where she is the only guest. Norman Bates, the sensitive young man who runs the motel, hesitates momentarily before giving Marion the key to Cabin 1, next to the office. (Similarly, in the film's introductory scene, the camera hesitated momentarily as it sought out Marion and Sam's hotel room; in the motel office scene, the camera adopts Norman's point of view, luring us into his consciousness.) Sheepishly, Norman admits that "nobody ever stops here anymore" unless they wander off the new highway. He offers to bring Marion a sandwich for supper, a kindness she gratefully accepts. While she is unpacking, she hears an old woman's voice accusing Norman of wanting to do "disgusting things" with Marion; she also hears him explain that Marion is just a stranger in need of a bite to eat, but the old woman continues

Figure 4.1. More so than written texts, movies are capable of revealing the psychological pathologies that lead to crime. In *Psycho* (1960), director Alfred Hitchcock increasingly associates the nice young motel clerk Norman Bates (Tony Perkins) with birds of prey, foreshadowing the horrific murder to come. This studio portrait, like the film itself, suggests multiple facets of Norman's mental illness, including split personality, voyeurism, and sadism. Photo used by permission of Photofest.

to berate him ("as if men don't desire strangers"). These voices come from the decrepit Victorian mansion that rises on a hill just above the motel.

Returning with the sandwich, Norman invites Marion to eat in the parlor behind the office. There stuffed birds line the walls and perch on furniture—Norman is an amateur taxidermist. During this scene he gradually takes on the appearance of a birdlike predator, hard-eyed and hawk-beaked. When Marion asks about his friends, he replies, a trifle curtly, "A boy's best friend is his mother." "We're all in our private traps," he muses; "I was born in mine." He was just five when his father died, Norman explains; a few years ago Mother met a man who talked her into building the motel, but he died—horribly, it seems. Although Norman admits that "a son is a poor substitute for a lover," he feels he cannot leave his mother, and when Marion hints that he could put her in an old people's home, Norman angrily assumes she means a madhouse—a place with which he evidently has some familiarity.

During their conversation, Marion has a change of heart: she decides to return to Phoenix the next morning to restore the cash to her boss. Back in her room, she does some math in a notebook but tears the page up, flushing the pieces down the toilet. Meanwhile, in the adjacent parlor, Norman removes a print from the wall (an Old Master scene of a man attacking a woman) to uncover a peephole, through which he observes Marion undressing. Then comes the key scene—the most celebrated scene in cinematic history: the murder of Marion in the shower, with violins shrieking along with Marion and a knife stabbing her repeatedly, first slashing through the shower curtain, then sinking directly into her naked flesh. (For this scene Hitchcock used more than ninety shots and seventy different camera angles.)[12] Blood drips from the tile walls into the drain, swirling down, mixing with water from the showerhead. Through the shower curtain (the camera was in the tub with Marion at this crucial moment, looking out) we have caught a vague glimpse of the stabber, evidently someone in a long dress, but for the most part the camera focuses on Marion's agony as she collapses, half in and half out of the tub, dying with her head under the toilet. The camera lingers on one of her eyeballs, which echoes the shape of the drains in the tub and toilet.

Next the camera looks up to the mansion, where we hear Norman's voice, in great distress, crying, "Mother, oh God, Mother, blood! blood!" He runs back to Marion's cabin, discovers her body, and sets about the grisly task of tidying up, mopping the bathroom and putting Marion's body with her belongings in the trunk of her car. Behind the motel is a swamp, murky and mucky as a filthy toilet; Norman pushes the car into it, where it sinks from sight. Then he scans the horizon with a nervous but satisfied smile, again becoming hawklike, his eyes glinting and hard.

Marion's employer, anxious to retrieve his money (but not to prosecute her), hires a private detective, Mr. Arbogast. When Arbogast questions Norman, the motel keeper becomes defensive (just as Marion did when the cop questioned her); he tells minor lies and then trips over them, stuttering and nervously working his jaw, nibbling like a bird. Arbogast becomes convinced that Marion stayed at the Bates Motel the night she disappeared, probably in Cabin 1. When Arbogast notices a figure at a window of the mansion and asks Norman who lives there, Norman denies that anyone lives there aside from himself but then, under pressure, stammers, "Oh, that must be my mother." Later Arbogast goes into the house and climbs the stairs; he is about to enter Mrs. Bates's room when, to renewed violin shrieks, he is stabbed. He spirals backward down the stairs, at the bottom of which a figure in a dress continues stabbing him with a butcher knife. Next we see Norman, again gazing into the swamp (where, we assume, Arbogast in his car has gone to join Marion in hers).

Marion's sister, Lila Crane (Vera Miles), worried about Marion's disappearance, seeks out Sam, and together they start a search. The local sheriff tells them that Norman's mother died about ten years ago; she poisoned her lover when she discovered that he was married and then "took a helping of the same stuff herself—strychnine." Norman found them dead together, in bed. Back at the mansion, a worried Norman decides to hide Mother in the fruit cellar. We hear their voices, arguing. Tauntingly, she refuses to go, but he insists, and we watch him carry her down the stairs while she angrily objects.

Sam and Lila, pretending to be man and wife, take a room at the motel. Lila slips into Cabin 1, where behind the toilet she finds a fragment of the page that Marion flushed away; she recognizes Marion's handwriting. Next she slips into the old house, first touring Mrs. Bates's bedroom (where one side of the double bed is strangely sunken and twisted, as if someone had for decades been sleeping there with knees bent) and then looking around Norman's room, with its children's toys. Through a window, she sees Norman coming up the path and runs to hide in the cellar, where, horrifyingly, she finds Mrs. Bates in a rocking chair, stuffed. Someone dressed in women's clothes bursts into the fruit cellar, knife in hand, but Sam, close behind, tackles and disarms him. Off falls the wig, revealing Norman.

At the police station, a psychiatrist who has interviewed Norman reports that although for years the young man had a split personality, now his own identity has disappeared and he has, in effect, been taken over by his mother's persona. The final scene shows Norman alone, a blanket draped over his shoulders like a woman's shawl, speaking in Mother's voice, which predicts, "They'll put him away now." Then, in an unnerving shot, Norman smiles directly at us, breaking through the imaginary fourth wall between viewers and the viewed to engage the audience's gaze and smile at us in complicity, as if to say: "You and I, we know a lot more than we are letting on, right?" A double exposure merges Norman's face with the image of Mother's skull as the camera cuts to the swamp, where Marion's car is being hauled out of the muck.

At least five psychological themes come into play in *Psycho*: split personality, voyeurism, sadism, guilt and self-punishment, and anal fixation.

Split Personality

This, of course, is the psychiatrist's diagnosis of Norman's mental pathology. In his view, Norman was "dangerously disturbed ever since his father died," but for years he and his mother lived together "as though there was no one else in the world. Then she met a man, and . . . he killed them both." To erase the heavy guilt of matricide, Norman stole his mother's body from its coffin and preserved it as he did his birds; moreover, "he began to think and speak for her," developing a second personality.

Because Norman had been pathologically jealous of his mother (the psychiatrist continues), he assumed she felt the same way toward him. Thus, "if he felt a strong attraction to any other woman, the Mother-side of him would go wild." Over the years he (she?) killed two young girls (their bodies, too, the psychiatrist guesses, are down in the swamp), and when he encountered Marion, "he . . . was aroused by her. . . . Mother killed the girl," and Norman covered up her crime. Now, however, the struggle between the two sides of his personality has ceased; Norman has become his mother.

But is the psychiatrist's diagnosis to be trusted? He speaks glibly, and his answers to people's questions have a pat, textbook quality. It seems unlikely that this is just bad acting, given others' consummate performances in this film. It is far more likely that Hitchcock created a fatuous psychiatrist to encourage viewers to seek additional explanations for Norman's pathology.

Voyeurism

In the sexual disorder labeled *voyeurism*, someone derives erotic pleasure from secretly viewing others in intimate situations, including sexual activity. Voyeurism cannot be a onetime experience; to receive this diagnosis, the subject has to ogle repeatedly—to make a practice of sexual spying.

Psycho revels in voyeurism from its opening shot to the last. The film begins with the camera floating over the city of Phoenix, seeking exactly the right window through which to spy on a half-dressed woman—Marion— prone on a hotel room bed. Hitchcock links sex and peeking repeatedly but, with his usual drollery, suggests that viewers, too, make this association. The opening sequence establishes the equation of camera = voyeur = viewer. This equation is repeated when, with Norman, we peer through the peephole in the parlor wall to see Marion undressing. One may define voyeurism as a sexual deviation, but, Hitchcock reminds us, it is a deviation that we (and the film) share with Norman.

The voyeurism theme is echoed in *Psycho*'s many mirrors and mirror images, from the reflection with which Lila scares herself in Mrs. Bates's bedroom to the print in the parlor of Venus with a mirror. It helps explain the film's ending, in which Norman locks eyes with us, the audience, smiling over the secret he knows we share with him. We, too, are voyeurs; if we didn't enjoy peeking, we wouldn't still be watching.

Sadism

Sadism is the psychiatric term for sexual gratification obtained through hurting others, whether the hurt is physical or psychological. The term is often paired with *masochism*, meaning sexual gratification from pain; when a sadist's partner *consents* to the painful activity, he or she may be diagnosed as a masochist. The concept of masochism is an important tool for understanding the pleasure of movies. When viewers enjoy being terrified or take pleasure in watching pain inflicted on a character with whom they identify, their reactions may be described, figuratively, as masochistic.

In *Psycho*, we first identify with Marion, to whom Hitchcock devotes the entire first half of the film so we can develop this identification. She is killed by a sexual sadist who stabs her repeatedly. To some degree, we experience the stabbing as Marion does; the shower scene begins with viewers being (so to speak) in the tub with her as the camera first looks up at the showerhead, then out through the curtain to see the approaching figure. If Norman is the sadist, we are the masochists. This may be another reason why he smiles at us in the closing shot: he is on to our masochistic pleasure in vicariously experiencing harm.

Related but not identical to sadism is the sexual pleasure some people feel in viewing violence—or anticipating its appearance. The print on the parlor wall showing a male figure going after a naked woman alludes to this kind of gratification. When Marion first arrives at the motel and Norman opens the window in her room, the blackness outside and curtain blowing inward create a creepy sensation of danger and vulnerability (anyone could be looking in). The open window gives us a frisson of anticipation of the violence ahead. The stuffed birds, too, hint at violence, both the violence that was done to them when they were captured and the violence that they, with their sharp beaks, could inflict.

Guilt and Self-Punishment

Psycho offers a devastating, if playful, study of guilt and its repression. Evidence of guilt sinks into the bog behind the motel much as repressed memories sink into the subconscious. Guilt even has its own musical leitmotif: the opening theme, edgy, agitated, signaling dread. This guilt music recurs even when Marion simply feels guilty without good cause. The cop who awakens her in her car stares from behind black glasses; she cannot see his eyes to read what is the matter. His scrutiny, like that of a guilty conscience, makes her feel she has done something wrong by napping. (His hidden eyes, also evoking the predatory male who watches women sleep, will soon be repeated by the motel's open but black window and by Norman's secretive eye at the peephole.) The cop's gaze, penetrating Marion's soul, scouring it for guilt, links up visually with the gaze Norman exchanges with us in the final scene, when he suddenly sees into our souls, discovering our guilty secrets. Like Freud, Hitchcock was interested in free-floating feelings of guilt.

Furthermore, *Psycho* is a film about the human capacity for self-punishment. From the start, we sense that Marion will be punished, both for stealing the $40,000 and for extramarital sex in a hotel room in midday. She feels vulnerable to the cop because she knows it was wrong to steal the money—even though, as one critic points out, "It is Sam's fault that Marion steals the money, which has no importance for her. It is simply the means to an end."[13] During her parlor conversation with Norman about how people find themselves in traps, she observes, "Sometimes we deliberately step into those traps." Here she realizes that in fleeing with the money, she has set herself up for punishment—by herself, if not others. The theft was self-thwarting behavior. Similarly, Norman—punishing himself for the matricide, his Oedipal lusts, his more ordinary lusts, and his voyeurism—encourages his "mother" to berate and mistreat him. He feels so guilty that, as Freud would have predicted, he represses his knowledge of his murders, fashioning for himself a split personality that can punish him and from which it is impossible to escape.

Anal Fixation

The film's psychiatrist makes no mention of anal fixation as a cause of Norman's behavior, but *Psycho* does hint throughout at potty training gone amiss. According to Freud, humans go through stages of psychosexual development, first the oral stage (years 1 to 2, during which the child gains gratification from eating and drinking), next the anal stage, spanning the years 2 to 4, during which the child gains gratification from anal eroticism and toilet training. If the anal stage is not negotiated successfully, the child can end up fixated on defecation. Problems occur if the parent is punitive during toilet training—a response, one suspects, that may have come easily to the cranky Mrs. Bates. The anally fixated child, in Freudian theory, grows up to be compulsively neat and well organized (Norman changes the sheets in every cabin weekly, even if there have been no guests), obsessed with control, and (in some cases) strongly interested in collecting things—stuffed birds, for example.

When Norman first shows Marion around Cabin 1, he cannot bring himself to say the word *bathroom*—she has to complete his sentence for him. However, he does take pleasure in pushing and dropping things into the swamp behind the motel. The film constantly refers to toilets and to disposing things—blood, water, fragments of paper—down drains, a theme that Hitchcock ties in with voyeurism by comparing the structure of eyes to drains. Hinting at the notion of anal fixation, Hitchcock suggests yet another explanation for Norman's behavior.

Today the term *psycho* is almost synonymous with *psychopath*, but Hitchcock used it differently. *Psycho*'s title signifies crazy, totally mad. Hitchcock's interest lies in investigating how a sweet young man could wind up psychotic. While Norman does kill a string of people—Mother and her lover, two young girls, Marion, Arbogast—Hitchcock does not configure him as a serial killer, someone whose key trait is a compulsion to kill. Rather, the director is curious about the many dimensions of Norman's pathology, the psychical twists that have unhinged his mind. Norman's mind is like the old mansion in which he lives: multicompartmentalized and decaying. It is also like Mother's body, another rotting form in which his psyche is trapped.

But to dissect the film as we have done, identifying this aspect and that of Norman's mental illness, is ultimately to repeat the psychiatrist's mistake of reductionism. *Psycho* can be psychoanalyzed, but it is much greater than the sum of its parts, a monument to cinema's power to portray the depths of a diseased mind and force us to identify with it.

Criminal Responsibility

Psycho discusses the issue of criminal responsibility only briefly, but many films center on this topic. According to one of the most venerable principles in Western jurisprudence, people with severe mental illnesses should not be held fully responsible for committing crimes. But while the principle is clear, its implementation has been subject to endless debate. How should we determine whose sentence should be mitigated or waived entirely by reason of insanity? And who is qualified to make this determination? Courts are the ultimate arbiter, but court officials turn for guidance to psychiatrists and other mental health experts. Moreover, even when the courts and psychiatrists agree, the public may find their decisions outrageous, as happened in the case of John Hinkley Jr., the young man who tried to kill President Ronald Reagan in order to get the attention of the actor Jodie Foster, with whom he had fallen in love while viewing the film *Taxi Driver* (1976). Found not guilty by reason of insanity, Hinkley was confined to a mental hospital, but this disposition was so widely disputed that it precipitated a backlash against the use of expert psychological and psychiatric testimony in cases involving an insanity plea—and against the insanity plea itself. Ultimately, these cases are controversial because they raise issues about free will and determinism, helplessness and autonomy—matters that cannot be settled with finality.

Films that depict debates over criminal responsibility shape these discussions. Millions of people with no direct connection to a case of criminal responsibility nonetheless develop fierce opinions about the insanity defense through watching movies. In what follows, we examine three movies—*M*, *The Boston Strangler*, and *A Clockwork Orange*—that probe this issue from radically different angles.

M

Fritz Lang's celebrated *M*—the initial stands for *murderer*—tells a story embedded in actual events in 1920s Germany, where the film was made. The public was agitated about an apparent crime wave, which many attributed to governmental softness on crime, and some factions advocated a return to the death penalty. Executions, they argued, would deter would-be criminals as well as protect society against further misdeeds by the convicted.[14] Feelings ran high over a series of sex killings, particularly in the case of Fritz Haarmann, who had slain nearly thirty victims, most of them adolescent boys, between 1918 and 1924. (At trial it came out that Haarmann, after earlier sexual assaults on children, had been excused on grounds of mental illness and confined in an asylum, from which he escaped.) Not only does M's story echo that of Haarmann, it also—uncannily—resembles that of Peter Kürten, a child sex-murderer arrested just as the film was completed.

The character of M (he has no other name), played by Peter Lorre, lures little girls with toys, then rapes and murders them. With Berlin in an uproar, both the police and the underworld hunt for the killer. (Members of the underworld dislike the intensification of police surveillance; moreover, though criminals themselves, they are genuinely appalled by the killings.) The two groups hunt M through dark, winding streets that mirror his agonized mind. He is identified first by members of the underground, who take M to an abandoned warehouse to be "tried." He faces a self-appointed jury of hundreds of furious beggars and criminals, and he is given a "defense attorney"—a criminal experienced in legal matters. The criminals do not want to hand M over to police, their leader explains, because they fear he will plead insanity, as he did earlier, and end up in a state asylum, from which he will again be released, "free as air, with a law-protected pass because of mental illness, off again, chasing little girls."

Falling to his knees, M pleads, "I can't help what I do." The criminals respond that they all make that argument when they get caught, to which M retorts that they and others who break the law due to poverty and laziness have free will. "But I . . . I can't help myself! I have no control over this evil thing inside me, the fire, the voices, the torment!"

> LEADER: "You mean to say that you have to murder?"
> M: "It's there all the time, driving me out to wander the streets, following me, silently, but I can feel it there. It's me, pursuing myself. I want to escape, to escape from myself! But it's impossible. . . . I have to run . . . endless streets."

His face contorted with anguish, M explains that he never escapes the "ghosts" of the children he has killed and their mothers. "They are there, always there. . . . Always, except when I do it. Then I can't remember anything. And afterwards I see these posters and read what I've done."

The leader of the mob argues that it is just *because* M cannot help himself that he should be executed, but the "defense lawyer" maintains that irresistible impulse should serve as an excuse: "Nobody can be punished for something he can't help. . . . This man is sick. A sick man should be handed over not to the executioner, but to the doctor." The mob of criminals rejects this argument, however, crying, "Kill the brute." They rush forward, ready to tear M to pieces, but at just that minute the police break into the warehouse and take M away to be tried "in the name of the law." The official judges, too, decide on execution, but the movie is much less interested in their decision than in the laments with which the film ends: the mothers of the dead weeping, for an execution will not bring back their children.

Even though the circumstances portrayed in *M* were specific to their time and place, its central question is universal: When is mental illness sufficiently severe to spare from punishment someone who is clearly guilty of the most horrible crimes? *M* presents two opposed but equally energetic responses to this question: M's condemnation by the angry mob and Peter Lorre's brilliant portrayal of a man helpless to control his predations. Framing these two poles in the debate are the mothers—one from the beginning of the film who waited futilely for a child who never returned, and the three sobbing women at the conclusion—who demonstrate that no matter which position we take, there is nothing but tragedy in cases of criminal insanity.

The Boston Strangler

Whereas *M* examines both sides of the issue, *The Boston Strangler* argues strenuously for one position: allowing severe mental illness to serve as an excuse for crime. It retells the case of thirteen sexual assaults and murders of single women in Boston during the years 1962–64; eleven of the killings were attributed to "the Boston strangler," although it was never clear that a single person had killed all the victims. A workman, Albert DeSalvo, arrested for housebreaking and sex offenses in other cases, pleaded guilty to the stranglings, but many people doubted his confession: he evidently thought that by confessing, he could earn money to support his wife and children while in prison for the crimes for which he was arrested. Moreover, people who knew DeSalvo were convinced that he was incapable of such violence. Although a psychiatrist testified that DeSalvo was mentally ill, the jury found him guilty of the crimes for which he was arrested, and he was sentenced to Massachusetts's Walpole prison.[15]

The first half of *The Boston Strangler* focuses on the hunt for the killer, led by investigator John Bottomly (played by Henry Fonda). It uses a split-screen technique that enables viewers to watch several events simultaneously— for example, the arrest and questioning of several suspects. A newscaster, speaking generally of mentally ill criminals, announces, "There's a lot of talk about finding these demented people and treating them *before* they get to the point of killing"—the opinion the film endorses. Investigators question a series of "full-blown maniacs"—sex perverts, molesters, a cross-dresser who was kicked out of a monastery—before the film switches to the viewpoint of DeSalvo (Tony Curtis), watching television with his wife and two kids, a loving family man with a stable job as a furnace repairman. When he goes out we again get a split screen, one side showing him zeroing in on a victim, the other side showing the victim performing some daily routine before opening the door to a "repairman"—and her doom. But at one apartment a man is at home, and he chases DeSalvo for blocks before the police apprehend him. When questioned, DeSalvo even denies fleeing, and because he seems genuinely puzzled, he is sent to a hospital for a competency evaluation.

A psychiatrist concludes that DeSalvo has two separate personalities. Bottomly pushes him to confess, even though the psychiatrist objects that "this is a medical problem, not a legal one. . . . If you force Albert-the-family-man to acknowledge the existence of Albert-the-strangler, he'll go over the edge. . . . He could become catatonic, hide from himself, . . . withdraw totally." During Bottomly's questioning, the screen again splits; DeSalvo speaks in the present but remembers in the past. Gradually his resistance breaks down ("These things keep popping in and out of my head") as his repressed memories push through to the level of consciousness. At home, Bottomly confesses to his wife, "I'm enjoying this. It's a big-game hunt, and I don't like myself for it." Like DeSalvo, he too is finding that he is not what he thought he was, discovering a dark side that enjoys trapping prey.

Just as the psychiatrist foretold, DeSalvo's two personalities cannot coexist. Albert does indeed become catatonic, and we last see him standing in the corner of a starkly white room, unresponsive even to the calling of his name. Text on the screen tells us that "Albert DeSalvo, presently imprisoned in Walpole, Massachusetts, has never been indicted or tried for the Boston stranglings.[16] This film has ended, but the responsibility of society for the early recognition and treatment of the violent among us has yet to begin." Richard Fleischer, the director of *The Boston Strangler*, clearly did not doubt DeSalvo's guilt, but just as clearly, he did not believe in punishment of the mentally ill.

A Clockwork Orange

A unique perspective on the issue of criminal responsibility can be found in *A Clockwork Orange*, whose central character is "ultraviolent" but not mentally ill. Alex (played by Malcolm McDowell) lives in a dystopic England of the near future where the government is fascistic and everyone is half comatose, either wiped out by ennui and drugs (like Alex and his fellow hooligans) or deadened by television and government pacification programs. Alex, who narrates his own story, is reconditioned, from ultraviolent to ultragood; but as a result he becomes unable to choose his behavior, for his will has been destroyed by aversive conditioning. The film challenges the morality of such conditioning. The author of the book on which it was based, Anthony Burgess, and the cowriter and director of the film, Stanley Kubrick, make it understood that they would rather have a society in which even ultraviolent criminals have free will than one in which a government programs people's minds, turning them into automatons so that they behave like clockwork. Burgess formed the title from a combination of an old Cockney saying, "as queer as a clockwork orange," and a Malaysian word (*orang*) meaning "man." The title becomes a synonym for the "brainwashed man."

A Clockwork Orange starts with Alex and his droogs, or fellow delinquents, drugging themselves in preparation for an evening of recreational violence. They speak Nadsat, a futuristic combination of Slavic and English, and their interest lies in motiveless violence, including rapes and murders of strangers. Eventually Alex goes to prison; after two years, he volunteers for a government plan that guarantees release in a few weeks if he participates in a new rehabilitation program designed to reduce crime (and please voters). Only the prison chaplain has doubts: "If a man cannot choose," he observes, "he ceases to be a man."

In the mental hospital to which he is transferred, Alex is subjected to the "Ludovico technique." Doctors give him drugs to make him nauseous, after which they clamp his eyes open so he cannot avoid looking at the ultraviolent movies they show him. While forced to watch Hitler's troops marching, he also hears his favorite music, Beethoven's Ninth Symphony, the triumphalist sounds of which formerly inspired his most violent acts. Now its chords make him vomit. The music has become an analogue to the bell in Pavlov's experiments on dogs: the very notes make him nauseous.

When Alex is released and beaten up by former droogs and victims, he cannot fight back because he has been brainwashed. He ends up in the house of a writer, F. Alexander, whom he had earlier victimized while wearing a mask (Alexander is now in a wheelchair, and his wife, whom Alex raped, has died). Gradually Alexander realizes who Alex is and, to torture him, confines Alex in an upper room and loudly plays Beethoven's Ninth. Alex attempts suicide, jumping from the window; he awakes in a hospital in a body cast but with the effects of the Ludovico technique erased. He is again the great manipulator, ready for new orgies and more ultraviolence. But he can again choose between good and evil.[17] He has regained criminal responsibility, and such responsibility, Burgess and Kubrick show, is a necessary aspect of the human condition.

Conclusion

Psychological theories of crime have many critics. Sociologists object that psychologists ignore social processes, blaming individuals for what are in fact social problems. Some critics point to the unscientific origins of central psychological concepts (for instance, Freud arrived at his key notions through speculation, not data collection and testing); others questions whether childhood experiences—to which *psy*-professionals often look for explanations of abnormal behavior—really do exert strong influences into adulthood.

While the critiques cannot be ignored, it is also true that students of criminal behavior cannot merely dismiss the *psy*-sciences, for they provide perspectives that sociological theories cannot deliver. Crime occurs among individuals, and although social forces shape it, psychologists can address the motives of individual criminals and the emotional pain (sometimes pleasure) of victims and offenders alike. Moreover, with the swing today toward biosocial explanations of individuals' behavior, psychologists who study neurology and gene-environment interactions are likely to play increasingly influential roles in criminology as time goes on.

Movies, by embedding traditional psychological explanations of crime in their narratives and characters, help fill the vacuum left by criminology texts. Part of the work that movies do, socially, is to disseminate these theories for debate on a culturewide—indeed, cross-cultural—basis. Films become part of an international dialogue, conversations with people we will never meet but with whom we share the experience of having watched specific movies. They give us a common fund of information about certain issues. These issues have considerable social significance—the extent to which we should hold the mentally ill responsible for crime; the role that the *psy*-sciences should play in criminology and court processes; the advisability of behavioral methods of social control—and debating them is crucial to a society's vitality. People may disagree with a specific film's message (as surely many of today's viewers of *The Boston Strangler* do on account of its extreme pro-treatment, pro-psychiatry position), but through movies they learn to identify key issues and work out their own opinions.

Cinema's most significant contribution to psychological theories of crime lies in its ability to portray the simultaneous operation of a number of psychological forces. A psychologist analyzing criminal behavior on the page or in a talk must necessarily deal with one factor at a time, much as we did earlier in analyzing first Norman's split personality, then voyeurism, then sadism, and so on. A movie, in contrast, can depict the simultaneous interplay of multiple and sometimes contradictory psychological impulses, giving a fuller, deeper, and more complex view. Moreover, in daily life we can never see so clearly the tangle of interactions that lead to criminal behavior. Movies that explore criminal psychology enable us to go beyond our ordinary and necessarily limited perceptions to perceive the multiplicity of emotional currents and countercurrents that can lead to criminal behavior.

FURTHER VIEWING

Bad Lieutenant (1992)
Chinatown (1974)
Compulsion (1959)
Conversation, The (1974)
Dark Knight, The (2008)
Eye of God (1997)
Felicia's Journey (1999)
Gun Crazy (1950)
In the Cut (2003)
Kiss of Death (1947, 1995)
Let Him Have It (1991)
Se7en (1995)
Silence of the Lambs, The (1991)
10 Rillington Place (1971)
Vanishing, The (1988)
Woodsman, The (2004)

5

"You Talking to Me?"

Social Disorganization Theories and Taxi Driver

In recollecting his pioneering work in the formation of the Chicago school of sociology, W. I. Thomas recalled, "I explored the city."[1] Robert E. Park, another Chicago school founder, described his work this way:

> I wrote about all sorts of things and became in this way intimately acquainted with many different aspects of city life. I expect that I have actually covered more ground, tramping about in cities in different parts of the world, than any other living man. Out of all this I gained, among other things, a conception of the city, the community, and the region, not as a geographical phenomenon merely but as a kind of social organism.[2]

Explorations of the city lie at the heart of the theories, research questions, methods, and findings of the Chicago school, the community of scholars who, at the University of Chicago in the first half of the twentieth century, introduced social disorganization theories of crime. At a time when American cities were experiencing unprecedented growth, these sociologists were fascinated with the social changes that emerged out of this vast population shift. As the nation moved from rural, homogeneous, small towns to the complex, heterogeneous, industrial metropolis, new kinds of social problems bound up with poverty, immigration, and shifting values became apparent. The early Chicago school theorists laid the modern foundations for urban sociology and the study of social problems, including crime.

For these social scientists, the study of criminality was grounded in a theory of human ecology, according to which the dynamic social conditions of the city, marked by dramatic population shifts and waves of immigration, are the source of crime. Chicago was an exemplary research site, having experienced the most intensive urban population explosion in the United States. The city's population had shifted rapidly from thousands in the late 1800s to more than 2 million by the 1920s, with population influxes defined, as in most American cities, by waves of poor immigrants and the Great Migration north by recently freed slaves. The city was also experiencing a wave of crime and delinquency created by Prohibition, the period from 1919 to 1933 during which the sale, manufacture, and transportation of alcohol for consumption were illegal. Dramatic changes in norms, populations, and law often usher in new scientific paradigms, and the Chicago school brought with them a rigorous empirical approach to the collection of data and a qualitative emphasis that insisted people must be studied with close attention to their social settings. This research included deep observational studies and rich ethnographies of crime and delinquency that are used in criminology classes to this day.

This fascination with the city and its role in shaping social life sits at the heart of both social disorganization theories and popular culture. In this chapter, we explore how these theories mark a sharp turn away from the individual in their emphasis upon the role of the social environment and the city in shaping crime. After revisiting the central findings and perspectives of the Chicago school, we will turn to contemporary perspectives on social disorganization. Then, through the worldview of one of Hollywood's most troubled and complex characters, Travis Bickle, the antihero of Martin Scorsese's classic *Taxi Driver* (1976), we will illustrate some of the assumptions of social disorganization theories. More recent films, too, have also explored these perspectives, including Neil Jordan's *The Brave One* (2007), a film that, borrowing heavily from *Taxi Driver* and *Death Wish* (1974), traces the transformation of a traumatized New York woman, a victim of random violent crime.

Social Disorganization Theories

The Chicago School

At the end of the 1920s, a new major criminological tradition took hold, one that argued that the city, now central to American society, had become a criminogenic force in its own right. Chicago school sociologists argued that the key to understanding crime was found in its social roots, an explanatory framework that continues to play a primary role in criminological theory today. Contrary to biological and psychological theorists, social disorganization researchers perceived criminals and delinquents to be normal individuals whose criminal acts were stimulated by their environment, the ghettos and slums emerging at the centers of the metropolis. In this way, the city was

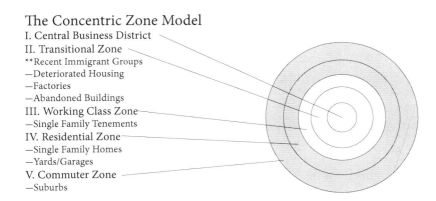

The Concentric Zone Model

I. Central Business District
II. Transitional Zone
**Recent Immigrant Groups
—Deteriorated Housing
—Factories
—Abandoned Buildings
III. Working Class Zone
—Single Family Tenements
IV. Residential Zone
—Single Family Homes
—Yards/Garages
V. Commuter Zone
—Suburbs

Figure 5.1. In *The City* (1925), the volume central to the social disorganization perspective, Robert Park and Ernest Burgess imagined the city as a series of concentric zones. Zone II, the transitional zone, characterized by population flux, conflict, and the breakdown of traditional beliefs, norms, and values, marked the area of most sociological interest for Chicago school theorists. The model pictured here continues to appear in teaching materials in sociology and criminology. Diagram courtesy of crimetheory.com.

constructed by Chicago school sociologists as a strategic research site—in fact, a laboratory for the study of social interaction.

According to these thinkers, the social structures and conditions of urban environments consist of dynamic social processes that resemble the ecosystems of the natural world. From this naturalist orientation developed one of the famous metaphors of the social disorganization perspective: *human ecology*.[3] As Chicago school theorists conceptualized it, human ecology was about the temporal and spatial relationships of human behaviors in urban contexts that were constantly in the process of change, "a ceaseless process of individual migrations."[4] Relying upon naturalistic terms, these researchers characterized these transitions and regional population shifts in terms of "invasion" and "succession," processes in which new groups moved into zones while previous residents migrated out. The central question for these researchers was why certain kinds of behaviors and social problems, including crime, remained constant in certain geographical spaces of the city, even while the city itself was characterized by radial expansion.

New questions raised new epistemological and methodological questions. The Chicago school took quite seriously the rethinking of what it meant to get at the meanings of other people's lives, asking how one might achieve "knowledge" as opposed to a superficial familiarity with the lives of others.

Robert Park spoke of "the blindness each of us is likely to have for the meaning of other people's lives," adding that "what sociologists most need to know is what goes on behind the faces of men. . . . Otherwise, we do not know the world in which we actually live."[5] Out of these guiding convictions, the notion that human behavior and social interaction could best be mapped up close and on the ground in the actual social settings of life emerged. Many of the classic studies of the Chicago school are immersions in the life of the city, ethnographic observations of some of the city's most troubled zones and inhabitants, including Polish immigrants, taxi dance halls,[6] Jewish ghettos, Italian slums, hobos, vice, and delinquency.[7] Their findings, the researchers argued, proved crime was not the product of individual actors but rather was structured by the surrounding environment and that it demonstrated consistent patterns across time and place. In this regard, Robert Park and Ernest Burgess's book *The City* remains the centerpiece of the Chicago school's work and deserves careful attention.

The diagram of zones represented the growth of the city as it radiated and extended outward. Researchers identified Zone I, the epicenter of the city, as the business district. They defined Zone II, the next ring out, as a transitional region. In these transitional neighborhoods, various cultural or ethnic groups would move in and then, over time, move out into more affluent areas of the city and its periphery. Meanwhile, another wave of immigrants would move into the transitional zone and begin these processes anew. Characterized by industry and temporary housing—often slums and ghettos—this transitional zone was the least desirable residential area of the city, defined by poverty, heterogeneity, transience, and disorder. Zones III, IV, and V were areas of gradually increasing affluence and single-family residences, petering out into the suburbs surrounding the city.

Zone II was most interesting for Chicago school theorists as an "interstitial area" (one that exists between more organized areas) characterized by social disorganization. Chronic transformation created the foundations for regions of rapid and constant transition, with groups of people moving in and out. In this context, residents had little incentive for identification with or commitment to neighborhood community. Such social relations made it difficult for people to establish clear norms or informal mechanisms for regulating, in particular, the behavior of youth. Delinquency posed a special problem and focal point for these early disorganization researchers. According to them, life experienced in a transition zone was defined by traumatic flux, conflict, and ultimately the breakdown of traditional beliefs, norms, and values—in short, a permanent sense of disorganization. There were empirical markers and "indexes," as Burgess called them, of disorganization, including "disease, crime, disorder, vice, insanity, and suicide."[8] Disorganization itself was conceptualized as a normal feature of city life. Burgess writes: "Disorganization as a preliminary to reorganization of attitudes and conduct is almost invariably the lot of the newcomer to the city, and the discarding of the habitual, and often of what has been to him the moral, is not infrequently accompanied by sharp mental conflict and a sense of loss."[9] Surrounded by condemned buildings and dilapidation, caught in contexts of transience, poverty, and high rates of illness, unemployment, and family disruption, urban populations in these regions were highly susceptible to criminogenic forces. Out of these conditions, researchers produced a theoretical explanation for the high rates of delinquency that prevailed in these areas.

Densely populated with high concentrations of immigrants and African American residents, these transitional areas were also defined by heterogeneity. One of the most important findings of the Chicago school researchers demonstrated that delinquency rates were associated with population density and transition, not race, ethnicity, or any specific group or individual characteristic.[10] Sociologists Clifford Shaw and Henry McKay, early proponents of social disorganization theory, found that despite total and continuous turnovers in population (a process they termed *residential succession*), these neighborhoods retained high and consistent rates of delinquency, a direct challenge to the popular assumption that delinquency must be associated with the physical constitution or cultural features of immigrants and blacks. This perspective emphasized instead that delinquency rates must be connected to their environment.

Another set of findings emphasized the role of stable, inclusive institutions in mitigating disorganization amid transformation and transition by maintaining a sense of constancy. For instance, family, communal spaces, synagogues, even gangs facilitated the ability of some groups to maintain cohesiveness and withstand radical transitions. Alternatively, settings where markers of urban decay—mobility, transience, anonymity, and inequality—predominated were characterized by delinquency and crime. Criminologist Walter Reckless referred to Zone II dwellings as "immoral flats,"[11] and Paul Cressey described these neighborhoods as subject to the "triumph of the impersonal in social relations."[12] This realization that often isolation and alienation are found in socially disorganized areas deeply affected later criminological research.

In these early days, one of the central concerns of the Chicago school was the question of how to study such quickly evolving and transitioning social settings. The far-ranging and meticulous methods of the Chicago school are, consequently, among the many celebrated innovations they bring to criminology. These advances include an emphasis upon case studies and field research methods by way of life histories and ethnographic techniques, attention to the role of documentary sources and institutional records (newspapers; work, court, medical, and school records) as well as statistical maps and analyses of crime data (arrest, truancy, and divorce rates) across time and place. These methods made large contributions to urban research.

In the end, the Chicago school research fundamentally reshaped methodological inquiry to introduce a multimethod approach, relying on a combination of research methods to build an empirical picture of everyday life in the new urban centers. Contextual, observational, exhaustive, qualitative, and quantitative, Chicago school methodologies always measured the role of social forces in community life. These researchers saw life histories and statistical pursuits as complementary, and their findings exactingly mapped the role of social forces and factors in their subjects' lives. Volumes like Clifford Shaw's *Jack-Roller* (1930) and *The Natural History of a Delinquent Career* (1931), through a careful analysis of the life experiences and personal narratives of their research subjects, established delinquents as normal in their intelligence, psychology, and physical conditions; however, in the neighborhoods where these individuals lived, conventional institutions and norms had broken down, erasing meaningful opportunities for a law-abiding life and replacing them with occasions for delinquent and illegal activities. In fact, these researchers found that training in delinquency began early while opportunities for successful employment were all but missing. Over time, the individual's identity came to be associated with criminality, a worldview and orientation that dominated his or her peer groups and neighborhood.

Not surprisingly, out of these new pursuits came entirely new policy implications. Chicago school researchers found that efforts to deal with social problems via the criminal justice system often failed in that they rarely addressed the social conditions and processes of the neighborhood. Their own policy recommendations centered upon building programs that would actually change the conditions of life in disorganized communities; they designed strategies to foster circumstances for the development of informal social control by strengthening the old ties maintained by family, church, and cultural traditions that social disorganization had damaged. Shaw launched the Chicago Area Project, establishing twenty-two neighborhood centers across the city. These centers were managed and staffed by local residents, in an effort to build better social conditions from the ground up and direct neighborhood commitment and experience into social reform. This project operated for twenty-five years, until Shaw's death in 1957.

Contemporary Social Disorganization Perspectives

> I believe that social processes should be at the heart of sociological inquiry. . . . To get at the major unanswered questions in the study of crime . . . requires a renewed focus on the unfolding of social action, process, and change within both individuals and communities. Such a focus is, of course, foundational to the sociological imagination—Chicago-School style.[13]
>
> —Robert Sampson

Although many subsequent criminologists were profoundly influenced by the Chicago school and its theory of crime as a consequence of social disorganization, in this section we will focus on the school's most prominent heir: sociologist Robert Sampson of Harvard University. Sampson's work, grounded in criminology and urban sociology, examines community-level social processes, including the formation of concentrated inequality, the social meanings of "disorder," and the possibilities of collective civic engagement. At the heart of his work, like that of the Chicago school theorists, is an interest in the social structure of the city and neighborhood effects. His research has extended social disorganization theory by focusing on the variables that lie at the heart of the perspective. One of the continuing debates that flow from the work of the Chicago school centers upon how to define and measure notions of order and disorder, organization and disorganization. Sampson and others have developed new terms, such as *social capital* and *collective efficacy*, to explicate more thoroughly dimensions of social disorganization.

One way to think about the term *social capital* is simply as the ability of communities to organize collectively for positive purposes.[14] Sampson argues social capital to be a useful measure of the capacity of social relationships among people to facilitate common actions and realize common goals, including crime control. Social capital is one of the positive by-products of social relationships, allowing for collective understanding and action. It may also be thought of as "a byproduct of social relationships that provides the capacity for collective understanding and action." *Collective efficacy*, a term that often accompanies the study of social disorganization, refers to the ability of actors in neighborhoods to build social capital. Sampson defines it as "the social cohesion among neighbors combined with their willingness to intervene on behalf of the common good," a definition that emphasizes the role of informal social control.[15]

The meanings of these present-day analytical concepts build upon the central ideas of the Chicago school. "Social and organizational characteristics of neighborhoods," write Sampson and his colleagues, "explain variations in crime rates that are not solely attributable to the aggregated demographic characteristics of individuals."[16] Poverty combined with residential mobility and population density may lead to higher rates of crime. With a focus upon the ways in which residents achieve public order and maintain informal social control, contemporary scholars insist that phenomena like social capital and collective efficacy should be considered part of larger systems of stratification and inequality beyond the neighborhood. In other words, in keeping with the move away from individualist perspectives, they argue that the individuals in neighborhoods lacking social capital and collective efficacy should not be held responsible for their own damaging contexts.

Despite the work of Sampson and other heirs of the Chicago school, many members of the public continue to associate disorder with cultural values, and racial hierarchies continue to define the segregated spatial order of U.S. cities. Moreover, even some criminologists take a simplistic approach to issues of community disorder, arguing that if a neighborhood cleans up its "broken windows" and other signs of disorder, crime rates will go down.[17] Sampson's research has consistently held that "broken windows" are not indicators of victimization or crime.[18] Rather, he argues that the idea of cleaning up disorder through crackdowns on panhandlers, loiterers, and vandals is an unsophisticated solution that overlooks the broader conditions necessary for building social capital and collective efficacy in neighborhoods where patterns of a "durable inequality" persist.

The majority of contemporary criminological perspectives are indebted to some degree to the early social disorganization theorists. As Sampson has argued, the value of the Chicago school perspectives is found in their reaffirmation of "the importance of thinking about social ways to approach social problems"[19] and the idea that

> the good community, at least with respect to public safety, is one that is created not through marginalization, exclusion of outsiders, and the singular reliance on threat by agencies of formal control. Rather, the good community is one where the legitimacy of social order comes in part from the mutual engagement and negotiation among residents, mediating institutions, and agencies of law enforcement.[20]

Taxi Driver

Taxi Driver is the story of a twenty-six-year-old Vietnam veteran and former U.S. Marine, Travis Bickle (Robert De Niro), who spends his nights driving the streets of New York City. The opening sequence begins with the slow-motion movement of traffic through the neon-lit, rainy streets of the city at night. Travis takes the job of taxi driver because he has insomnia, wants to work long hours, and already spends most of his nights aimlessly riding around on buses and subways. Living in a dilapidated, one-room apartment, he leads a life of solitary acts. He does not follow politics or music and is severely out of touch with the world around him. Travis's journal, which forms the basis for the film's voice-over narration, constitutes his main form of communication. Through his narration, we can construct his perception of the city. Travis's views from his taxi serve as another window into the city: bright lights and neon signs, flashing words like *Fascination* that materialize in the darkness; sirens screaming through the night; people in constant motion; and steam pouring hellishly from manholes in the dirty city streets. Moving amid the litter and people, Travis observes early in the film:

> All the animals come out at night — whores, skunk pussies, buggers, queens, fairies, dopers, junkies, sick, venal. Someday a real rain will come and wash all this scum off the streets. I go all over. I take people to the Bronx, Brooklyn, I take 'em to Harlem. I don't care. Don't make no difference to me.

Travis hates the city, which contradicts his beliefs about how people should live. Moreover, his perceptions of the city are distorted by his naive ideas about class, race, and gender. His urban experience is shaped by the value conflicts, fraying of social ties, and absence of family and other stabilizing social institutions that Chicago school theorists wrote about. Even so, Travis seems compulsively attracted to the most troubled sections of New York City. He tries to make a place for himself in the social order even as he deteriorates, popping pills, experiencing headaches, pouring whiskey on his breakfast cereal, and taking Alka-Seltzer with dinner. The film chronicles Travis's failure to make sense of a world from which he is increasingly cut off.

In an early scene, Travis attempts to strike up a conversation with a woman selling candy at a porn theater, but she threatens to call the manager. Later, he writes in his diary, "The days go on and on . . . they don't end. All my life needed was a sense of some place to go. I don't believe that one should devote his life to morbid self-attention. I believe that one should become a person like other people." The routine loneliness of Travis's life is altered only when he becomes attracted to a political campaign worker, Betsy (Cybil Shepherd), whom he describes as an "angel" emerging "out of this filthy mess." Eventually Travis asks Betsy out for a cup of coffee. During their conversation, he tells her that she too is "lonely" and "not a happy person." He senses that there are "connections" between them. Betsy responds with interest and tells Travis that he reminds her of lines from a song: "'He's a prophet . . . he's a prophet and a pusher, partly truth, partly fiction. A walking contradiction.'" Their conversation leads to a date, but the encounter goes awry when Travis takes her to a porn theater and Betsy, suspecting that she is dealing with someone who is psychotic, refuses his awkward efforts to make amends.

Travis's small circle of fellow cabbies provides another avenue for social interaction. Travis meets them periodically for coffee and food at diners when taking breaks from his shifts. They discuss sexual exploits and confrontations with passengers, their conversations reflecting the turbulence and normlessness of their world. Travis has difficulty interacting and finding a place among them. It is also increasingly evident that he strongly associates blacks and Hispanics with violence. In one diner scene, Travis and a black male dressed like a flashy pimp gaze hostilely at one another. Travis then relates a story he heard on the radio about someone "getting all cut up."

Forming the backdrop of Travis's experiences is a presidential political campaign that Betsy works for. The candidate, Charles Palantine, eventually shows up in Travis's cab and asks, inauthentically, what Travis thinks is the biggest problem the country faces. Travis replies that he is not sure but that

> whatever it is, you should clean up this city here, because this city here is like an open sewer, you know? It's full of filth and scum. And sometimes I can hardly take it. Whatever—whoever becomes the president should just *[Travis honks the horn]* really clean it up. You know what I mean? Sometimes I go out and I smell it, I get headaches it's so bad, you know. . . .They [the headaches] just never go away you know. . . .It's like, . . .I think that the president should just clean up this whole mess here. You should just flush it right down the fuckin' toilet.

Later, a twelve-year-old runaway, Iris (Jodie Foster), shows up in his cab, trying to get away from her pimp, Sport (Harvey Keitel). Sport eventually forces her out of the cab while Travis watches. Travis's rejection by Betsy and encounter with Iris are followed by a disturbing encounter with another fare. The man in the backseat in this instance (Martin Scorsese in a cameo appearance) is disgruntled because his wife is having an affair with an African American man. In fact, he is stalking her from Travis's cab, which he has Travis park outside the man's apartment window. He tells Travis of his plan to kill his wife, a misogynist fantasy that involves shooting her with a .44 Magnum in the head and crotch, a graphic image of the potential for violence that haunts the city. Travis listens silently and intently to the man.

With no viable social supports, Travis moves steadily toward mental breakdown. He tells the Wizard (Peter Boyle), his friend and fellow cabbie: "I'm real down. Just want to go out and really do something." He stammers and repeats to himself: "I got some bad ideas in my head." The Wizard advises him that a job is an anchor for identity as it constitutes "who you are." Nonetheless, Travis's headaches worsen, as do his stomach pains. Finally he arrives at a plan, writing in his journal:

> Loneliness has followed me my whole life. Everywhere. In bars, in cars, sidewalks, stores, everywhere. There's no escape. I'm God's lonely man. . . . June 8th. My life has taken another turn again. The days can go on with regularity over and over, one day indistinguishable from the next. A long continuous chain. Then suddenly, there is a change.

Travis decides to get "organized": he purchases multiple firearms, practices at shooting ranges, and attends Palantine's campaign rallies. Across city loudspeakers, Palantine's unctuous voice asserts: "We Are the People. We suffered. We were there. We the People suffered in Vietnam. We the People suffered. We still suffer from unemployment, inflation, crime and corruption." This hypocritical rhetoric contrasts strikingly with Travis's real suffering. He starts plotting Palantine's death. In one of the film's most famous scenes, he practices his shooting reflexes in front of a mirror. "You talkin' to me?" he asks his reflection. "You talkin' to me? You talkin' to me? Then who the hell else are you talking to. . . .You talking to me? Well I'm the only one here. Who the fuck do you think you're talking to? Oh yeah? OK." And then he draws his weapon. This monologue quickly develops into a diatribe with Travis addressing the unlistening world around him: "Listen, you fuckers, you screwheads. Here is a man who would not take it anymore. A man who stood up against the scum, the cunts, the dogs, the filth, the shit. Here is a man who stood up."

Later, in a routine convenience store visit, Travis shoots and kills a robber, a young black male. As Travis's instability deepens, Iris reappears in his world.

This time, Travis, in his new vigilante mode, decides to pose as a potential client and, once alone with her, to refuse her sexual services and instead offer to pay for her way out of the city. Iris, who has no interest in being saved, rejects Travis's efforts but humors him by joining him for a cup of coffee.

In the film's climactic moments, after Secret Service agents foil Travis's plan to assassinate Palantine, he returns to Iris's neighborhood and massacres Sport and two other men. Travis is also badly injured in the exchange. The aftermath, filmed from an aerial perspective, is a bloodbath. *Taxi Driver* concludes with a disturbing irony. Newspaper cutouts on Travis's apartment walls hail him as a hero: he has saved Iris. There is also a letter from Iris's parents thanking him for the safe return of their daughter. They write, "The transition has been very hard for her, as well you can imagine, but we have taken steps to see she has never cause to run away again." Travis returns to the night and his taxi driving, and when Betsy reappears as a fare, now curious after his sudden celebrity, he treats her like any other fare, and the film ends much as it began—bright lights, wet streets, endless night driving. There are hints, however, that Travis remains just as psychotic as when the film began.

Taxi Driver is an exemplary text from which to explore social disorganization theories. Such an analysis naturally begins with the depiction of the city itself, given its primary place in Chicago school perspectives. The film treats New York in its entirely as what the Chicago school termed an interstitial zone—a place of corruption, value conflict, and isolation. For Travis, the question is how to find an identity within such a context, what Burgess called "a place and role in the total organization of city life."[21] His taxi is one such site, as Travis lives out his life behind the wheel, always mobile, gliding among areas of vice and anonymity. The indices of social disorganization appear as fleeting images throughout *Taxi Driver*: juvenile delinquents, transients, gangs, crime, poverty, infidelity, abandonment, mental illness, and prostitution are routine elements of Travis's world.

Behind social disorganization theories lie not only a fascination with the city but also a suspicion that it is a dangerous, criminogenic force in its own right. Travis came from a rural midwestern town. For him, the encounter with New York City, even though it followed a tour in Vietnam, constituted cultural conflict, the value clash out of which his subjective vision of disorder, tinged by racial and sexist stereotypes, emerges. The Chicago school sought to study and change processes of disorganization in order to understand crime and other social problems. However, unlike Travis, these theorists saw criminality as a normal component of transitional urban environments, one grounded in social conditions themselves. Travis's worldview, a

Figure 5.2. Traversing the mean streets of New York City's red-light district, Travis Bickle (Robert De Niro) stands out as "God's lonely man." In *Taxi Driver* (1976), director Martin Scorsese uses elements of social disorganization in city life to accentuate Travis's alienation. In this scene, signs of one-way streets, tow zones, porn theaters, and dilapidated buildings capture the chronic normlessness that characterizes Travis's existence. Photo used by permission of Photofest.

distortion of Chicago school focal points, misses the ways in which his social surroundings contribute to his own pathology. The film emphasizes the distortions in his perceptions through optical motifs—images through windshields and rearview mirrors, his suicidal hectorinig in his mirror—lenses through which Travis views the world.

Travis's approach to the city mimics the methods of social disorganization theory. Circling New York in his taxi, he explores the city with ethnographic detail (literally, taking notes in his journal) and assesses its night life as if he were in a laboratory, observing the good and evil of human nature. Immersed in the most troubled zones of the city, Travis does get his "pants dirty," as Park recommended, but he has so little perspective that his experiences only exacerbate his suffering. Travis's efforts to "become a person" end up further disturbing the city's fabric—his assassination attempt is deflected but becomes an act of child saving that is actually multiple murder.

Jodie Foster's memorable performance as the child prostitute, Iris, also echoes many of the Chicago school themes. In a series of scenes, we see Iris being trained by both Sport, her pimp, and her fellow prostitutes. Chicago school theorists argued that delinquency was a product of the breakdown of conventional norms and institutions through which opportunities for crime emerged. According to this perspective, opportunities for delinquency begin early and become more persistent and durable across time as individuals age into crime. Iris is a classic example of a conventional youth whose criminality is embedded in social context. Travis's preoccupation with saving her is bound up with his interpretation of the city's effects upon her behavior. Like the child-saving reformers active in late nineteenth-century Chicago, he actively seeks to return Iris to her parents and small-town life in order to offset the city's malign influence.[22] Much like the early theories of social disorganization, Travis's perspective arises out of a particular sociohistorical context. The fact that he is a Vietnam War veteran returning to radical changes at home figures prominently in the film. His relationships with Betsy and Iris are marked by a gap between his primitive ideas about gender and sexuality and the shifting role of women in the 1970s. Travis embodies in many ways the disenfranchised white male, popularized by law-and-order backlash movements in response to the civil rights and countercultural movements of the 1960s. Palantine's slogan "We the People" further exacerbates the emptiness of Travis's existence. An era marked by the breakdown of conventional norms, values, and traditions, the sociohistorical context of *Taxi Driver* pushes the notion of zones of transition well beyond the transitional zones of New York City. Rather, in *Taxi Driver*, it is U.S. society that has now entered into a period of seemingly chronic normlessness, with Travis Bickle its antihero.

Other Social Disorganization Films

Films that pay strong attention to crime, time, and place often recall the central concerns of social disorganization theory. John Singleton's classic *Boyz n the Hood* (1991) was the first film to examine how the lives of black youths are defined by drugs, gangs, and violence, in this case elements of social disorganization characteristic of the early 1990s in South Central Los Angeles. The film's hero, Tre Styles (Cuba Gooding Jr.), is a seventeen-year-old whose parents try desperately to insulate him away from the gang life. However, it is impossible for him to avoid violence, drugs, alcohol, guns, and police for they are ubiquitous in his neighborhood. In the course of the film, Tre is confronted with choices that test his relationships to his girlfriend, father, friends, and future. *Boyz n the Hood* initiated a wave of "hood" films focused on the intersections of poverty, race, drugs, and violence in African American urban neighborhoods. This category includes films like *New Jack City* (1991), *Menace II Society* (1993), and *Clockers* (1995), which chronicle how drug use and the war on drugs left American urban centers in a perpetual criminogenic crisis.

A very different kind of film, Neil Jordan's psychological thriller *The Brave One* (2007), is also infused with themes that tie it to Chicago school theory. *The Brave One* draws heavily on three earlier movies, *Taxi Driver, Ms. 45* (1981), and *Death Wish* (1974). The latter starred Charles Bronson in the story of a New Yorker who engages in a series of vigilante killings after his daughter is raped and his wife killed. *The Brave One* begins by showing successful radio show host Erica Bain (Jodie Foster) as she moves through New York City, observing the passing scenes, a little like Travis Bickle and Chicago school researchers, but in this case recording its sounds for her radio program. She states on air, "I walk and watch and listen, a witness to all the beauty and ugliness that is disappearing from our beloved city." Waxing nostalgic, Eric asks, "Are we going to have to construct an imaginary city to house our memories? Because when you love something, every time a bit goes, you lose a piece of yourself." These words turn prophetic when Erica is brutally beaten and her fiancé murdered at Stranger's Gate, one of the entrances to New York City's Central Park. Erica's overwhelming loss leaves her isolated and afraid due to the unresponsiveness of the police. In her intense grief and fear, Erica obtains a gun and commits a series of vigilante acts that culminate in a killing spree across the city: she intervenes in every act of male violence against women that she sees. In the absence of effective social institutions, Erica, like Travis and the Bronson character, takes it upon herself to bring justice. She is eventually befriended by a detective who understands her anguish and reasons for killing. Erica is eventually caught; however, her fate ends with an irony similar to the conclusions of *Taxi Driver* and *Death Wish*. Her actions are covered up, and her vigilante acts are reconstructed as self-defense.

Conclusion

Chicago school theorists, although fascinated with urban centers and their new place in American social life, expressed concern with the ability of communities and individuals to sustain themselves in contexts defined by disorganization. They identified what the city or community could not provide and opened up possibilities for criminologists to think through alternatives to formal social control, including ways to assist the most troubled neighborhoods in developing the capacity for collective action and the achievement of community goals. At the heart of their work lies a question about what occurs in settings where the idea of a public or common good has been lost. Consequently, they directed many of their efforts toward what today would be called community organizing. Social disorganization scholars over time have shared the assumption that central to the process of reform is improvement in the social conditions that drive action, process, and change. When resources are absent in contexts of durable poverty and persistent inequality, when the city cannot or will not provide, then actors look elsewhere, including to crime, to organize their lives and opportunities.

Theories linking crime to disorganization in urban centers developed against the backdrop of the isolation and alienation of migrants and immigrants who participated in the birth of the American city. These perspectives echo throughout popular culture. "Hood" films concentrate on social disorganization itself. Films like *Taxi Driver* and *The Brave One* are more interested in the dynamics of exclusion and the failure of social institutions to address social suffering. At such moments, the ways in which social conditions structure such isolation are less apparent than the virulent pathology of exclusion. In *Taxi* Driver and *The Brave One*, Hollywood shows how sympathetic but troubled actors, left alone, cut off, and powerless, attempt to salvage their lives through violence.

FURTHER VIEWING

Angels with Dirty Faces (1938)
Batman Begins (2005)
Boys Town (1938)
City of God (2002)
Clockers (1995)
Crash (2004)
Menace II Society (1993)
New Jack City (1991)

6

"You're Giving Me a Nervous Breakdown"

Strain Theories and Traffic

This chapter deals with strain theories—explanations arguing that individuals turn to crime when they cannot cope with the strains and stresses of life through legitimate means. We begin with *Traffic* (2000), Steven Soderbergh's celebrated film about the effects of drugs trafficking. Then we turn to strain theories, showing how they inform *Traffic* and other movies.

Traffic

Traffic deals with the drug trade on three levels: the national level, where it explores trafficking relationships between the United States and Mexico; an intermediate level, where it focuses on midlevel drug distribution and U.S. government efforts to curb it; and the individual level, where it shows the impact of drugs on characters whose lives are in one way or another transformed by them. The movie weaves together three different plots; like other films that disrupt and fragment narrative lines, *Traffic* is less interested in telling a single coherent story than in juxtaposing bits of multiple stories to see what the contrasts and echoes will reveal. Yet despite its fragmentation, *Traffic* makes an impression of profound unity, partly because the three plots deal with aspects of a single phenomenon—the drug trade—and partly because it uses the same type of explanation (strain theory) for the film's numerous crimes, ranging from prostitution to murder, illegal surveillance to smuggling, freebasing to torture. Viewing the film, one is unaware that the plots share this single criminological viewpoint—indeed, Soderbergh himself may not have been familiar with strain theory in any formal sense. Yet the single interpretation of crime that cuts across the plots unifies the film despite its initially puzzling fragmentation and its quick leaps among plotlines. *Traffic* is a tour de force in which strain theory accounts for the drug trade and drug use on all levels.

Plot 1, the most complicated of the three narrative lines, is where the movie starts. Set in Mexico, its scenes are overlaid with a golden-sepia color that invokes not only the sand of the desert and dust of Tijuana, where many of the scenes take place, but also the skin color of its characters, all of whom are Mexican.[1] These characters speak only Spanish to one another (their words are subtitled in English)—a sign of Soderbergh's determination to maintain an authenticity of place and be as respectful of the Mexican as of the American settings. The central figure in this plot is Javier Rodriguez (played by Benicio Del Toro), one of two police officers who intercept a truck full of cocaine and arrest the smugglers, only to be stopped themselves by a high-ranking official, General Salazar (Tomás Milián). Announcing that he will now take over, Salazar dismisses the two officers but later asks Javier, who has impressed him, to capture Francisco Flores ("Frankie Flowers"), a hit man for the Tijuana drug cartel lead by the Obregón brothers. Javier dutifully brings in Francisco and passes him over to Salazar; later, he hears Salazar's men torturing Francisco, who gives up the names of key figures in the Tijuana cartel. Salazar arrests them and as a reward for his apparently vigorous clampdown on the narcotics trade, he is named Mexico's drug czar. However, Javier, already troubled by Salazar's use of torture, now learns that the general himself is working for the rival Juárez cartel. This was his underlying motive for seizing the truck full of cocaine and making war on the Obregón brothers.

Javier is at first an ambiguous character, perhaps shady, perhaps tolerant of the corruption he sees around him,[2] but he is also charming, relaxed, and reliable, and as the film goes on we discover he is a gentle, altruistic man. It is significant that Javier, the film's hero, is Mexican: *Traffic* is a film about not only the drug trade but also racial and ethnic stereotypes of those involved in the drug trade. Throughout, the film makes a point of contradicting these stereotypes. When Javier's partner, Manolo Sanchez (Jacob Vargas) is killed by drug lords for selling information to the U.S. Drug Enforcement Administration, Javier decides to cut a deal with the FBI, which is also trying to interdict drug smuggling from Mexico. What does Javier ask for in return for risking his life to wear a wire and pass on his insider's information on the Juárez cartel? Electricity in his neighborhood so local kids can play baseball at night and thus have a legitimate activity to keep them away from drugs.

Francisco Flores is assassinated for betraying the Obregón cartel; Salazar's true identity as a drug lord is exposed (presumably through information that

Javier gave the American authorities), and he is tortured and killed. The film ends with Javier watching kids play nighttime baseball under lights in the local stadium. His story provides the framework for the other three plots, and his unassuming courage becomes a yardstick for measuring the integrity of other characters. However, the other characters are not condemned for falling short of this ideal; like Javier, Soderbergh remains nonjudgmental and at times amused by human folly.

Plot 2, set almost entirely in Cincinnati and Washington, D.C., was shot with a type of film filter that bathed the scenes in cold blue, a frigid light corresponding to the nature of its characters: chilly, affluent whites. Chief among them is Robert Wakefield (Michael Douglas), a conservative Ohio judge who is appointed U.S. drug czar. This plot belongs to him and his sixteen-year-old daughter, Caroline (Erika Christensen). Although other officials warn Wakefield that the war on drugs cannot be won in the short run, Wakefield, naively hoping to succeed where others have failed, starts out energetically. Beneath his veneer of modest competence lurk self-satisfaction and hubris. Robert is gratified to attend parties with influential politicians (Senators Barbara Boxer, Orin Hatch, and Harry Reid have bit parts, as does former Massachusetts governor William Weld), and his sense of self-importance is encouraged by the promise of "face time" with the president.

Unbeknownst to Wakefield, however, Caroline—blond-haired and blue-eyed, an honors student at a private school, a girl with every advantage—is heavily into drug use, having been introduced to progressively stronger drugs by her boyfriend, Seth. She is arrested when she and friends dump an overdosed schoolmate at the door of an emergency room. Although her parents try to halt Caroline's addiction, she spirals downward, lying to them and stealing her mother's jewelry. She runs away from a residential rehabilitation facility to return to the city streets, where she links up with a pimp who is also a drug dealer and therefore able to keep her supplied. Robert and his wife, Barbara (Amy Irving), blame one another, with him taunting her about her youthful drug use and her accusing him of caring more about his job than his daughter.

Despite his increasing concern about Caroline, Robert flies to Mexico, where he is easily led to think that Salazar is heroically fighting the narcotics trade. (It is through Wakefield's intervention, the movie implies, that Salazar is appointed to be Mexico's drug czar.) Meanwhile, Caroline is half conscious in a sleazy hotel with a naked black man. Here *Traffic* reproduces an old myth, depicted in numerous early movies, according to which men of color kidnap young white girls to induct them into "white slavery."[3]

Returning to Washington, Wakefield starts to deliver his first important speech as leader of the National Office for Drug Control, a talk setting forth his ten-point plan for combating drugs, but he cannot get through it, breaking down in the middle. "I can't do this," he says. "There is a war on drugs, and many of our family members are the enemy. I don't know how you wage war on your own family." Quitting his post, Robert returns home, tracks Caroline down, and rescues her from prostitution. Near the film's end we see him and Barbara attending a Narcotics Anonymous meeting with Caroline; to identify himself, he says, "My name is Robert, and my wife Barbara and I are here to support our daughter Caroline, and we're here to listen." Robert has evidently become less self-important, more truly responsible, ready to listen rather than tell other people what to do. However, the hint of smugness in Michael Douglas's delivery of that line makes one wonder how much Robert has really changed.

Plot 3 is set in sunny San Diego, where midlevel drug smugglers try to evade federal investigators. For these scenes, Soderbergh used overexposure and special filters to intensify Technicolor's warmth,[4] reflecting the affluent life of the family on whom this plot focuses. DEA investigators Montel Gordon (Don Cheadle) and Ray Castro (Luiz Guzmán) are trying to collect evidence against Carlos Ayala, a man of considerable wealth who distributes drugs for the Obregón brothers. They arrest Eduardo Ruiz (Miguel Ferrer), a midlevel distributor who works for Ayala, and persuade him to testify against Ayala in return for leniency in his own prosecution. To keep Ruiz safe until Ayala comes to trial, they put him up in a seedy hotel. Judge Wakefield appoints an especially tough prosecutor to go after Ayala, whose conviction, he hopes, will send a stern message to other drug dealers. (Here as elsewhere, the plots overlap on their edges.)

This third story belongs principally to Ayala's trophy wife, Helena, played by Catherine Zeta-Jones. Before her husband's arrest, Helena has no idea of how he earns his income; she spends her time enjoying life on her estate, meeting country-club friends for lunch, and caring for her young son. But when Carlos ends up in jail, awaiting trial, Helena figures out where the money comes from—or rather came from, for her bank accounts are running dry—and without blinking, she hires Flores to assassinate Ruiz, the chief witness against her husband; his death would derail Carlos's trial. Helena has several motives for jumping in to perpetuate and even fortify her husband's business: she fears falling back into the poverty in which she grew up; someone to whom Carlos owes money almost kidnaps her child; and she realizes that Carlos may spend decades in prison, leaving her alone to raise their son and the second child who is on the way. Helena has what film critic Manohla Dargis describes as "an almost feral will to survive."[5] When Ruiz escapes her attempt to have him shot, Helena has him poisoned. In a subplot, she eludes the advances of Arnie Metzger (Dennis Quaid), Carlos's slimy lawyer and partner in the drug business. Carlos is released, and it looks like the Ayalas will resume business as usual; however, near the film's end, Montel surreptitiously plants a surveillance device beneath Carlos's desk. There is hope, then, that eventually the government investigators will win a round.

In what follows, we outline the origins and early development of strain theory, using *Traffic* to illustrate its key points and, at the same time, using strain theory to illuminate the film.

Classic Strain Theory

Origins of Strain Theory

The origins of strain theory lie in the concept of *anomie* formulated in the 1890s by the French sociologist Émile Durkheim.[6] *Anomie* literally means "without law" (*a* + *nomos* in Greek); Durkheim used the term to denote a social condition in which individuals are no longer fully governed by the unwritten social norms for their group's behavior. Historical changes cause disjunctions between the society's culturally approved goals and its legitimate means for achieving them. Under the pressure of change, a group's norms erode, so that people can no longer be sure that others think as they do or have the same morality. Left normless, either fully or in part, individuals become anxious or depressed; they feel "anomic"—alienated and powerless. In *Traffic*, Caroline, the young crack addict, provides an example of anomie: While she seems to have everything anyone could want in life, Caroline is actually frightened and lost. Feeling unloved by her parents and adrift in a society in which no one is genuine ("It never seems that anyone says anything that matters to them"), she is alienated from the world about her. Her achievements seem purposeless. Encouraged by Seth, she turns to drugs; and while he is able to control his drug use, she is one of those people who, once started, is unable to stop. Durkheim did not condemn anomic individuals for their condition; rather, he was analyzing effects of historical, social-structural shifts of which an individual might be only dimly aware.

In the same decade during which Durkheim developed the concept of anomie, the American sociologist W. E. B. DuBois inaugurated what became a tradition within strain theory: attempting to explain why crime is more prevalent among the poor and disenfranchised than among middle- and upper-class groups. White Philadelphians, worried about black crime rates in their city, hired DuBois, a well-credentialed sociologist who was himself black, to explain those rates. His comprehensive study, published as *The Philadelphia Negro*, concluded that the causes of Negro crime were threefold. First, after long enslavement, the black population had experienced the "sudden social revolution" of emancipation, an enormous change that strained their personal and collective resources. Second, after the Civil War, newly emancipated blacks had begun migrating north, where they "precipitated themselves upon the Negroes" already established in cities like Philadelphia, depending on them for sustenance and depleting meager resources while all tried to assimilate into new ways of life. And third, they experienced color prejudice, "the widespread feeling all over the land, in Philadelphia as well as in Boston and New Orleans, that the Negro is something less than an American."[7]

Although DuBois did not use Durkheim's term *anomie*, he was identifying three sources of strain that would be almost certain to induce anomie; in such strains DuBois found the cause of differential crime rates. *Traffic* points to analogous phenomena to explain the Mexican narcotics trade and American attitudes toward it. Like the Philadelphians for whom DuBois conducted his study in the 1890s, many present-day Americans view a dark-skinned group—in this case, Mexicans—as criminals, stereotyping them as drug smugglers and dealers. They fail to recognize that poverty, racism, and rapid economic change push Mexicans into drug trafficking and that trafficking victimizes Mexicans as well as Americans.

Robert K. Merton's Analysis of Social Strains

A few years after DuBois published *The Philadelphia Negro*, in another run-down section of Philadelphia, Robert King Merton (né Meyer R. Schkolnick) was born to Eastern European immigrants.[8] As a young Harvard professor, Merton published "Social Structure and Anomie" (1938), a milestone in the development of strain theory. In this article Merton observed that while all Americans aspire to economic success and the power and status that go with it, many are unable to achieve success through legitimate means such as a college education and family connections; these limitations particularly affect members of the lower classes, who have fewer resources. As a result, some lower-class people turn to illegitimate means in their quest for success. But not all illegitimate means are alike; in his famous typology, Merton described five possible modes of adaptation, using a plus sign (+)

TABLE 6.1
Merton's Modes of Adaptation

Mode of Adaptation	Cultural Goals	Institutionalized Means
Conformity	+	+
Innovation	+	-
Ritualism	-	+
Retreatism	-	-
Rebellion	+	+

to indicate acceptance, a minus sign (–) to indicate elimination, and a joint plus-and-minus sign to signify "rejection and substitution of new goals and standards."[9]

Each mode of adaptation can be illustrated with a character in *Traffic*. Conformity, the legitimate adaptation in which the individual accepts both the group's goals and its normative means for achieving them, can be represented by Ana Sanchez (Marisol Padilla Sanchez), Manolo's girlfriend. Decent, hardworking, and poor, Ana adores Manolo; when he disappears for a night, she comes to Javier for reassurance. We last see her preparing to burn Manolo's clothes, since she now knows he is dead. Despite her poverty and stunning loss, she attempts nothing illegal; she is almost faceless in her conformity and acceptance of her plight. Ana's American counterpart is Barbara Wakefield, Robert's wife; after a brief period of youthful high jinks, she settled down, somewhat grimly, into the prescribed role of housewife. That is the goal that society set for her, and she uses conventional means to achieve it. Conformity heads Merton's list because it is the usual adaptation, typical of the vast majority of people; they do not experience anomie because they accept both their society's goals for success and its means for achieving it. Their behavior is legitimate.

The other four adaptations, on the other hand, represent various ways of coping with disjunctures between goals and means. Merton's second mode of adaptation, innovation, or "the illegitimacy adjustment,"[10] describes those who accept traditional definitions of success but, finding themselves strained by inability to achieve success legitimately, turn instead to illegitimate means. A number of *Traffic*'s characters illustrate this adaptation, including Helena and Salazar. Helena has already achieved success through traditional means—she married into wealth, but when it threatens to evaporate, she has not a moment's hesitation in taking over the family drug-smuggling business. With equal adaptability, Salazar adopts a range of illegitimate means to achieve success, from torture to deceptive identity. Seth, Caroline's boy-friend, describes something very like Merton's innovation adaptation when he angrily explains to Robert Wakefield why desire for money leads to drug selling. Wakefield, dragging Seth along in his hunt through slums for Caroline, says, "I can't believe you brought my daughter to this place," to which Seth replies:

> Whoa. Why don't you just back the fuck up, man. "To this place"? What is that shit? OK, right now, all over this great nation of ours, a hundred thousand white people from the suburbs are cruisin' around downtown asking every black person they see, "You got any drugs? You know where I can score some drugs?" . . . I—God, I guarantee you bring a hundred thousand black people into your neighborhood, into fuckin' Indian Hills, and they're asking every white person they see, "You got any drugs? You know where I can score some drugs?" within a *day* everyone would be selling. Your friends. Their kids. Here's why: It's an unbeatable market force, man. It's a three-hundred percent markup value. You can go out on the street and make five-hundred dollars in two hours, come back and do whatever you want to do with the rest of your day and, I'm sorry, you're telling me that— you're telling me that white people would still be going to law school?

Merton felt that most crime could be classified as innovation (in *Traffic*, too, the majority of crime falls into the innovation category). He also believed that disjunctions between the "success-goal" and the means used to achieve it would snowball, becoming increasingly frequent over time and breeding ever more anomie.[11]

Merton's third adaptation, ritualism, is the one eventually adopted by Robert Wakefield, who wholeheartedly embraces traditional definitions of success—and revels in achieving them—only to find that he must reject them if he is to keep faith with his wife and daughter. At the pinnacle of his Washington success, Robert quits his job and settles for attending his daughter's Narcotics Anonymous meetings in Cincinnati. (Merton pointed out that people may move from one adaptation to another as their circumstances change.)[12] Retreatism, Merton's fourth adaptation, which he characterized in terms of alcoholism, drug addition, and mental illness, is illustrated by Caroline. She is a particularly interesting example as she contradicts Merton's assumption that retreatism will be the mode of adaptation for those who are "*in* the society but not *of* it."[13] Caroline is very much "of" the society when we first meet her, a girl with prime access to worldly success, yet she rejects both the success-goal and the legitimate means that, so far, she has used to reach it. She turns her back on all that she has, in terms of worldly goods and status, becoming addicted to crack cocaine.

As for Merton's fifth adaptation, rebellion, in which individuals not only reject normative definitions of success but also try to replace them with something better, the perfect illustration is Javier. He rejects the worldly success that motivates Salazar (for example) but has his own goals, which he achieves through his own means: getting the FBI to provide electricity for the kids' baseball stadium.[14] In a world where many people are willing to sacrifice everything in a frantic struggle for money and fame, Javier's fundamental decency is a form of rebellion. He is the only major character who is not afflicted by anomie.[15]

Strain and Delinquency Theory

Strain theory took another leap forward in the mid-twentieth century, spurred on by two developments. First, a youth culture flourished, one that cut across social classes to affect a majority of adolescents. Prosperity made it possible for young people to earn their own money; becoming relatively independent of their parents, they could reject the older generation's goals and prescribed means for achieving them. Sometimes frightening their elders, young people developed their own subcultures, dress codes, jargon, and gestures. (The British film *Let Him Have It* [1991], based on a true story, vividly dramatizes the terror inspired in stuffy elders by post–World War II youth culture—and a tragic result of this social-structural disturbance.) Some lower-class youths joined gangs and engaged in criminal activity. Strain theorists, like other criminologists of the time, recognized that they needed to explain delinquent subcultures, particularly those of gangs.

Second, strain theory developed in this period because in it, Americans and other Westerners discovered intractable poverty. Partly thanks to the civil rights movement, they became able to see that poverty might be the result of not just laziness or fiscal irresponsibility but something in the social system that maintained and reproduced it. Marking this realization, in 1964 President Lyndon Johnson signed legislation declaring a War on Poverty. Criminology now had something else to explain: poverty's persistence and its relation to crime. (These developments in strain theory, although they fall outside the scope of *Traffic*, are widely reflected in other movies, some of which we mention later in this chapter and in chapter 7.)

In 1955, in *Delinquent Boys*, sociologist Albert Cohen extended strain theory by bringing Merton's insights to bear on the special problems of boys from impoverished families. Such youths, he argued, are often unable to achieve success and status in conventional institutions, especially schools. Their families may not have raised them to value school success or may have lacked the resources to instill the sorts of skills that schooling requires. As a result (Cohen continued), lower-class boys go through a process of "reaction-formation," vehemently rejecting the school and all it represents, at the same time developing oppositional values such as irresponsibility, rudeness, maliciousness, and aggression. Cohen was thus able to account for seemingly gratuitous crime like destruction of school property. Alienated from mainstream society, lower-class boys form gangs with their own subcultural values, which they may transmit to the next generation of youths. Cohen's *Delinquent Boys*, one of the most successful criminological texts of its day, streamlined strain theory to address the concerns of the moment. (In chapter 7 we explain how Cohen, together with the theorists discussed in the next paragraph, were also influenced by subcultural theory, with the two types of explanation converging in their works.)

Another mid-twentieth-century refinement in strain theory, addressing those same issues, appeared in Richard Cloward's and Lloyd Ohlin's *Delinquency and Opportunity* (1960). Like Cohen, Cloward and Ohlin began with Merton's ideas (Cloward in fact had been a student of Merton's, and at the time the book was written, all three men were associated with Columbia University). They agreed with Cohen that impoverished youths, strained by their lack of legitimate opportunities for success, may turn to illegitimate means instead. But a problem remained: slum kids seemed to have *differential* access to illegitimate opportunities. Those growing up in areas with well-organized criminal subcultures had role models and older criminals to train them in illegal enterprises. But other disadvantaged kids, growing up in disorganized slums, lacked these supports. According to Cloward and Ohlin, members of this second group are more likely to use violence to establish themselves; they belong to not "criminal subcultures" but "conflict subcultures." The authors also identified a third, "retreatist subculture" of "double failures," kids who, unable to achieve through either criminal or conflict subcultures, turned to heavy drug use. Thus Cloward and Ohlin supplemented Merton's and Cohen's ideas about the social origins of strain, anomie, and deviance with the notion of differential access to illegitimate opportunities.[16] Because their book appeared when the John F. Kennedy administration and then Lyndon Johnson's administration began funding antipoverty and antidelinquency programs, *Delinquency and Opportunity* had considerable impact on public policy.[17]

Classic Strain Theory in the Movies

In addition to *Traffic*, what other films illustrate strain theory as it was formulated during this classic period? Oddly, few delinquent gang movies illustrate strain theory, despite Cohen's and Cloward and Ohlin's strong interest in the subject; rather, gang films tend to illustrate the social learning and subcultural theories outlined in chapter 7. However, Stanley Kubrick's *Clockwork Orange* (1971), portraying gang activity in a futuristic England, does provide an excellent illustration of Cohen's concept of reaction-formation, formulated to account for the pointless violence of some gang behavior. Alex, the lead delinquent of *A Clockwork Orange*, and his gang find their evening amusement in beating up the elderly and raping women. Their violence flows from a refusal to accept the values of the faceless, banal world about them; in their eyes, it is better to be violent than to be nothing at all.

Cloward and Ohlin's criminal subcultures, which are stable through the generations, providing opportunities for older criminals to tutor youngsters in their trades, fit with depictions in *Angels with Dirty Faces* (1938), *Goodfellas* (1990), and even *The Godfather* (1972), although in these cases, strain theory overlaps with social learning and subcultural explanations. *A Clockwork Orange* can again be invoked to illustrate Cloward and Ohlin's disorganized and violent conflict subcultures, and while it is difficult to find a gang movie to illustrate these authors' retreatist subcultures, several films do portray adolescent retreatism per se. For example, *Requiem for a Dream* (2000) depicts the downfall of anomic, addicted youths, setting it in the context of Coney Island decay, while *Badlands* (1973) literally depicts a retreat as Kit (Martin Sheen) and Holly (Sissy Spacek), hands-down winners of an award for Cinema's Most Anomic Characters, retreat from life as well as the police through the South Dakota Badlands, killing as they go.

Merton's deviant adaptations have already been illustrated with *Traffic*, but it is noteworthy that just as Merton found innovation to be the most common nonconformist adaptation in real life, so too is innovation a commonly depicted adaptation in crime movies. It turns up in films about immigrants to America and other poor people who, unable to achieve success and status by traditional means, turn to crime (*Public Enemy* [1931]); *Scarface* [1932; remade in 1983 starring Al Pacino]; *Bonnie and Clyde* [1967]; *American Gangster* [2007]). It provides the theme for *The Bicycle Thief* (1948), considered by many critics to be one of the best films of all time; set in postwar Rome, this movie tells the story of a very poor man whose income depends on getting around the city by bicycle, only to have his bicycle stolen.[18] More recently, the innovation adaptation informed the plotline of *Fargo* (1996), in which a hapless car dealer (played by William H. Macy) tries to solve his financial problems by having his wife kidnapped for a ransom that will, in theory, be paid by her rich father and eventually make its way back into his pocket.

General Strain Theory

Whereas classic strain theory focused on social structure, interpreting crime as a function of disjunctions between socially approved goals and the means to achieve them, *general strain theory* (GST), developed by Robert Agnew of Emory University, is a social-psychological theory. Agnew takes little interest in social-structural issues; for example, in a book-length exposition of GST published in 2005, he mentions neither anomie nor Merton.[19] GST is less an extension of classic strain theory than an attempt to explain "why some *individuals* are more likely than others to engage in *behaviors that are generally condemned* and that *carry a significant risk of sanction* by the state if detected."[20] For Agnew, strain and stress occur at the personal, not the social-structural, level.

Agnew argues that "a major motivation for crime is negative treatment by others."[21] Strains include not only blocked goals but also a sense of unfairness, removal of things of value, and threats. Strain leads to frustration and anger, which in turn may lead to crime (you hit those who mistreat you, steal money from the employer who fired you, or use drugs to forget the teacher who flunked you). Not every mistreated person responds with crime, however; those most likely to break the law are people with few external constraints (such as watchful parents when one is a teenager and watchful cops later in life) and few internal constraints (such as well-developed coping skills or the belief that one should not hit others, or steal, or use drugs). In addition, people are more likely to react criminally when the adverse effects are strong in magnitude, long in duration, or clustered in time.[22] Moreover, certain personality traits, especially irritability and impulsivity (which may have a biological basis, according to Agnew), and certain family factors, such as inconsistent parental discipline, may promote one's likelihood of responding to negative treatment with criminal behavior.[23]

Readers familiar with other criminological theories will have already realized that Agnew's GST incorporates aspects of current biological explanations and of Gottfredson and Hirschi's so-called general theory of crime.[24] GST's broad embrace further includes many hypotheses not covered by our brief summary, going beyond classic strain theory to specify more sources of strain, address constraining and predisposing factors, and cover more types of deviant behavior.[25] Critics, however, maintain that GTS is so broad—indeed, so "general"—as to be almost untestable; that Agnew does not successfully explain why some people but not others respond to strain with crime;[26] and that he needs to show why the causal direction goes from strain to crime rather than crime to strain.[27]

Because it is a notably commonsensical theory of crime, GST often turns up in movies. Take, for example, Agnew's proposition that mistreatment leads to anger, which leads in turn to crime. An example appears near the end of *Traffic*, when after his mistrial Carlos is back on his estate, reunited with Helena and resuming his drug business. He phones his partner, Arnie: "Let me ask you something. When were you going to tell me about the $3 million we got in from San Francisco two days after I was arrested? . . . You had it all figured out, didn't you? You were going to move into my house, raise my kids, sleep in my bed, with my wife. Sounds like a nice plan." Carlos hangs up, but the camera remains on Arnie as he becomes aware of men moving in to kill him. Carlos got annoyed and had him murdered.

Agnew identifies revenge as a motivator for crime, and nearly all the revenge films in the cinematic repertoire can be used to exemplify the theory. Some are rape-revenge films: director Abel Ferrara's droll and ferocious *Ms. 45* (1981); Clint Eastwood's *Sudden Impact* (1983), one of the Dirty Harry sequence; and Barry Levinson's *Sleepers* (1996), in which the avengers were raped as boys in reform school. Other film avengers have different motives: mistreatment in prison (*The Shawshank Redemption* [1994]); an attempted lynching (*Fury* [1936]); a sister's death (*Coffy* [1973]); the murder of a loved one (*Death Wish* [1974]; *The Brave One* [2007]); false imprisonment and a hunger for redemption (*Sympathy for Lady Vengeance* [2005]). However, while these films exemplify GST, they do little to illuminate it, just as the theory does little to illuminate the films, for we already know that when people get angry, they sometimes retaliate. More revealing, perhaps, are films that indicate the explanatory limitations of GST—*Serpico* (1973), for instance, and *The Woodsman* (2004), in which the protagonist undergoes immense, repeated strain without resorting to crime. Similarly, in *L.A. Confidential* (1997), a movie about a corrupt police department, three officers are tempted, in different ways, to put their own interests before those of the department. However, all three resist, and the two survivors (Bud White, played by Russell Crowe, and Ed Exley, played by Guy Pearce) become avenging angels, purifying the department of its depravity. Their strains are no lighter than those of their more deeply corrupt fellow officers, but degree of strain seems irrelevant to the final outcome. If cinema could rank criminological theories, it would relegate GST to near the bottom of the list.

The American Dream and Institutional Strain Theory

The most recent innovation in strain theory began in 1994, when Steven Messner of the State University of New York–Albany and Richard Rosenfeld of the University of Missouri–St. Louis published the first edition of *Crime and the American Dream*, setting forth what they would eventually name *institutional anomie theory* (IAT). With the IAT explanation, strain theory found its sociological groove again, for Messner and Rosenfeld have returned to the tradition of locating the ultimate causes of crime in the social structure, specifically in *imbalances* in the social structure. They are especially concerned with imbalances in the power of various "institutions," by which they mean not organizations such as insane asylums and universities but rather the broad systems of regulatory norms established by the economy, education, the family, government, and religion.[28] "*Social institutions*," Messner and Rosenfeld explain, "are complexes of particular elements of culture and social structure that perform . . . basic functions of adaptation, goal attainment, integration, and pattern maintenance. . . . The interrelations among these institutions constitute a society as an ongoing concern and distinguish it from other societies."[29]

It is typical, Messner and Rosenfeld continue, for a society to be dominated by one institution more than others. American society is dominated by the free-market economy: the American Dream of fortune and fame for anyone who works hard enough to achieve it. Other institutions "'bend' to the economy as plants to sunlight. . . . Think of the accommodations families make to economic requirements. . . . Think of how competition for grades in school mimics the competition for income in the labor market."[30] The result is an anomic society that values material success more than the legitimate means of achieving it. Such a society can be expected to have high crime rates; it is "a society organized for crime."[31] Another type of society, for example, one dominated by religion, might have less crime but "excessive social control and human rights abuses."[32]

Certain policy recommendations flow from the IAT analysis. Messner and Rosenfeld note that countries with strong social welfare systems that protect citizens from market forces have lower crime rates than those where social welfare is minimal. Paid family leave when a new child arrives or someone gets sick would help restore the balance among social institutions, as would "universal national service, which would protect families from the full brunt of market forces and socialize the young in the obligations and responsibilities of adulthood."[33] Similarly, criminal justice systems that aim at reintegration of offenders and minimize the destruction of families would reduce crime. To reduce crime, Americans would have to shift their priorities away from free-market competition, developing a new American Dream with a better balance between economic success and other institutions such as the family and education.

The most typical exemplar of IAT theory would be an extremely rich person who killed and pillaged with impunity, such as Daniel Plainview, the California oil man of *There Will Be Blood* (2007), who is driven by greed, rivalry, and sadistic pleasure in causing others to fail. With variations, illustrations of IAT turn up in *Traffic* as well. *Traffic* shows how the domination of economic success throws other institutions out of balance. In fact, it has thrown a whole society out of balance, leaving Mexico crippled by the drug trade. In Cincinnati, a different version of success dominates the Wakefields, creating an imbalance that drains the life out of their marriage and family. A third variation on the theme of institutional imbalance is afforded by the character of Helena, the pregnant housewife who is so determined to maintain her financial security and prestige that she thinks nothing of ordering murder. Although she remains devoted to her family, otherwise Helena is almost empty, her flat affect and emotional deadness signaling anomie. Javier, however, ignores the lure of the dominant institution—the economy—instead continuing to value friendship and community. At peace with himself, he is able to live with the institutional stresses and corruption that surround him.

Falling Down, Joel Schumacher's 1993 film, focuses on a character who, although he is the polar opposite of *There Will Be Blood*'s Daniel Plainview, nevertheless provides another outstanding example of IAT. William "D-FENS" Foster (played by Michael Douglas) is a milquetoast, a nonentity who is in many ways fundamentally decent, devoted to playing by the rules and in tune with normative means although his society's institutional systems are collapsing around him. In a single day—the day of his death—he endures failures in the economy, government, and family. *Falling Down* begins with a breakdown in the Los Angeles transportation system: caught in a traffic jam on a very hot day, Foster eventually abandons his car, with its D-FENS license plate, wandering off into the nearest neighborhood. In a convenience store, he asks the Korean owner for change to make a phone call, but the man refuses to give change without a purchase, and when D-FENS buys a

Figure 6.1. According to strain theories, personal and institutional strains can lead to crime. In *Falling Down* (1993), the nonentity William "D-FENS" Foster (Michael Douglas) succumbs to violence as his society's institutional systems and his personal world disintegrate around him. Here we see him starting to become unhinged; his previous vision of the world is literally shattered. Photo used by permission of Photofest.

can of soda, he feels the price is too high. Already on edge, he starts yelling about foreigners coming to the United States and charging unreasonable prices when they can't even pronounce English properly ("You come to my country, you take my money, and you don't even have the grace to learn how to speak my language?"). Grabbing the Korean's baseball bat, he slams into the shelves holding merchandise he considers overpriced, destroying half the store. Next he encounters Hispanic gang members who harass and then try to shoot him. ("You missed," he observes with a smile. "Take some shooting lessons, asshole"). When he tries to buy breakfast in a fast-food restaurant, he is told he is two minutes too late—it is now lunchtime, and he must order a Whammy Burger. These incivilities, or what he sees as incivilities, culminate in his ex-wife's refusal to let him visit his daughter on her birthday.

On the other hand, D-FENS himself clearly precipitates or exacerbates many of these institutional failures. He abandons his car in the middle of the road during the traffic jam. Feeling like a beleaguered white man whose country is being ruined by foreigners, he grossly overreacts in the convenience store and later is so violent with the gang members that they flee in terror. (Later still, surviving their retaliatory drive-by shooting, he captures their satchel of guns.) A scene at the home where he lives with his mother reveals that he was fired from his job over a month ago. He is not as extreme a right-winger as the homophobic neo-Nazi from whom he buys boots ("I'm not a vigilante"), but he does kill the neo-Nazi when the latter becomes violent, and he re-outfits himself in army fatigues. Dressed like a survivalist and toting automatic weapons, he treks toward "home," the Venice Beach cottage where his ex-wife and daughter live. He phones his former wife repeatedly, sometimes hanging up; suspecting that he is coming to kill her and the little girl, she asks for police protection, only to be brushed off.

However, while it seems that the criminal justice system is yet another institutional failure, an about-to-retire cop, Martin Prendergast (Robert Duvall), puts together the reports from the Korean, witnesses to the drive-by shooting, discoverers of the knifed neo-Nazi, and so on to realize that a psychotic killer is making his way toward Venice Beach. Prendergast himself is the victim of failing institutional systems, in his case, the family (his little girl died, and his infantile wife has badgered him into early retirement) and work (his boss and fellow cops treat him like a failure). But, rising to the occasion, Prendergast saves D-FENS's wife and daughter, reverses his decision to retire, reasserts dominance over his wife, and restores his reputation with his fellow detectives. He also shoots D-FENS, who by this point is begging for suicide-by-cop. Thus while D-FENS follows a falling trajectory, undermining institutional systems even as they fail him, Prendergast finds ways to strengthen the institutional systems that, partly through his own passivity, have been failing him.

Conclusion

For well over a century, the strain explanation has proved itself a remarkably resilient and vigorous theory, originating in 1890s with Durkheim's concept of anomie, informing DuBois's account of Negro crime and poverty, made famous by Merton's 1938 article, and in the mid-twentieth century not only developed by Cohen, Cloward, and Ohlin but also applied by government antidelinquency programs. Even though strain theory then faded from the criminological scene for several decades, it was revivified in the 1990s by Agnew's general strain theory and Messner and Rosenfeld's institutional anomie theory, both of which have attracted international attention and are being tested worldwide.[34] As other countries increasingly adopt the capitalist model, embracing the American Dream with all its promise and costs,

IAT is likely to become an ever-more-popular explanation for the relationship between social-structural strain and crime. Indeed, we can even detect something resembling IAT theory in Muslim purists' rejection of the American Dream, which in their view undermines social cohesion by valuing financial success over religion and family.

To see strain theory through the lens of a film that exemplifies it, such as *Traffic*, is to appreciate its complexity and its richness of meaning. In her review of *Traffic*, *New York Times* critic Manohla Dargis writes, "In one respect, *Traffic* is essentially about borders and what it means for an individual to cross borders that are legal and geographic, emotional and psychological, real and imagined."[35] To that we would add that *Traffic* also shows what it means to cross the boundaries between the normative and socially illegitimate, even when no formal laws are broken. A visionary film like *Traffic* can show these crossings and violations on multiple levels simultaneously, so that entire countries become characters, and it can show how a social structure dominated by economic concerns shapes the nature of both other institutional systems and personal lives. Using handheld cameras to create a sense of immediacy, juxtaposing multiple story lines, and handling narrative elliptically, *Traffic* forces the viewer to participate in the unfolding of the story and brings strain theory alive.

FURTHER VIEWING

American Psycho (2000)
Boyz n the Hood (1991)
Bully (2001)
Catch Me If You Can (2002)
Collateral (2004)
Dirty Harry (1971)
Kids (1995)
Negotiator, The (1998)
River's Edge (1986)
Wall Street (1987)
Wire, The (Home Box Office television series, 2002–8)

7

Getting the Drift

Social Learning Theories and Mystic River

Social learning theorists argue that crime is the result of the same learning processes that are involved in all types of behavior. In their view, criminal values are learned mainly through associations with others, especially those who belong to deviant subcultures, groups that transmit criminal values across generations. This chapter focuses on both social learning and subcultural theories of crime, in particular on the work of Edwin Sutherland, the dominant figure in twentieth-century criminology and a man whose work profoundly shaped both types of explanation.

Sutherland, who earned his doctorate from the University of Chicago's sociology department during its early twentieth-century "golden era," put forth a social learning type of explanation of crime that he termed *differential association theory* and claimed could account for every sort of offending. In this chapter we show how he came to develop this theory, what the theory said, and why it was criminologically significant. Then we turn to subcultural theories of crime, illustrating them and demonstrating how films have frequently repeated their key ideas. Our central example is *Mystic River* (2003), Clint Eastwood's somber tale of a tightly knit working-class community, part of Boston but geographically and culturally isolated from it, where the abduction and serial rape of a child lead to a kind of fratricidal murder. We also include a section on Sutherland and cinema, showing how movies have echoed his work on professional and white-collar crime. In conclusion, we assess the current status of social learning and subcultural theories.

Edwin Sutherland and Differential Association Theory

Edwin H. Sutherland (1883–1950) received his doctorate in 1913, just as the Chicago school of urban sociology, with its ecological analysis of social disorganization (discussed here in chapter 5), was taking shape. Sutherland later honed the Chicago school's concept of social disorganization into a more specific, but still thoroughly sociological, explanation of crime. Without Sutherland, the nascent field of criminology might not have become a sociological speciality. After teaching elsewhere for a number of years, Sutherland returned in the early 1930s to teach in the Chicago sociology department, now one of the most powerful and creative groups of sociologists in the country. However, he was denied tenure, possibly because of a falling-out with the department's chair,[1] and left to head the sociology department at Indiana University, where he taught for the rest of his life. Under him the Indiana department became a national leader in criminological theory.

In his account of the origins of differential association theory, Sutherland explains that after graduation from Chicago, he sometimes taught a criminology course but was primarily interested in labor issues until a publisher asked him to write a criminology textbook. For the first edition (1924), he drew on sociological principles but in an ad hoc fashion, without trying "to extend these sociological concepts to explain all criminal behavior." When he published the second edition (1934), now titled *Principles of Criminology*, his friend Henry McKay "referred to my theory of criminal behavior, and I asked him what my theory was. He referred me to pages 51—52 of my book. . . . I assure you that I was surprised to learn that I had stated a general hypothesis regarding criminal behavior."[2]

As Sutherland mulled the possibility of elaborating a general theory of crime, he became increasingly interested in the phenomenon of clashing cultural values. He was impressed by a student's dissertation on crime in China, which "had the thesis that crime is due to cultural conflict." About the same time Sutherland and his friend Thorsten Sellin of the University of Pennsylvania were asked to write a report on a key criminological issue of their choice. During a weeklong visit of the Sutherland family to Sellin's farm in Vermont, Sellin recalled, "We selected culture conflict as the problem and spent considerable time organizing the data and problems of criminal behavior around that concept." In retrospect, Sutherland saw this work on conflicting social norms as a prelude to his theory of differential association.[3]

By the time he prepared the 1939 edition of *Principles of Criminology*, Sutherland was ready to put forth his differential association hypothesis, but "I was reluctant to make the hypothesis explicit and prominent . . . for I knew that every criminological theory which had lifted its head had been cracked down by everyone except its author." Not until the 1947 edition—published when he was sixty-four years old—did he present his full-blown theory. "It seemed to me that learning, interaction, and communication were the processes around which a theory of criminal behavior should be developed. The theory of differential association was an attempt to explain criminal behavior in that manner."[4]

Differential Association Theory

What, then, *was* Sutherland's theory of crime causation? It consists of nine propositions. The first, "*Criminal behavior is learned*," eliminates psychological and biological explanations, announcing that this will be a social theory of crime causation. The second and third propositions, maintaining that "*criminal behavior is learned in interaction with other persons in a process of communication*" and that "*the principal part of the learning of criminal behavior occurs within intimate personal groups*," claim that people learn criminal behavior mainly through face-to-face interactions. (In view of the topic of the present book, we should note that Sutherland explicitly excluded "picture shows," newspapers, and other media as influences on criminal behavior. Today, criminologists are more open to the possibility that media may affect behavior.)[5] Propositions 4 and 5 state that the learning includes not only techniques of crime commission but also attitudes toward legal codes.[6] Here Sutherland was thinking of culture conflicts over the worthiness of legal codes, the topic on which he had worked with Sellin.

Proposition 6 sets forth Sutherland's core idea: "*A person becomes delinquent because of an excess of definitions favorable to violation of law over definitions unfavorable to violations of law.* This is the principle of differential association. It refers to both criminal and anti-criminal associations. . . ." There has been a good deal of discussion about what Sutherland meant by "definitions," but clearly he had in mind something like attitudes and values. Note that his underlying comparison here is to a balance scale that tips toward criminal behavior when one pan becomes fuller than the other with definitions favorable to law violation. Sutherland is here offering a model of not only learning but also decision making. Proposition 7 claims, "*Differential associations may vary in frequency, duration, priority, and intensity*,"[7] while proposition 8 asserts, "*The process of learning criminal behavior by association with criminal and anti-criminal patterns involves all of the mechanisms that are involved in any other learning*," a statement that makes criminal behavior entirely normal—and endeared Sutherland to generations of liberals. Ninth and finally: "*While criminal behavior is an expression of general needs and values, it is not explained by those general needs and values since non-criminal behavior is an expression of the same needs and values.*

Thieves generally steal in order to secure money, but likewise honest laborers work in order to secure money. . . ."[8] This too is a normalizing claim. It throws the weight of explanation away from psychological factors such as needs and motives and back onto "definitions" favorable or unfavorable to law violation.

At the end of his list of propositions Sutherland put distance between himself and the Chicago school's notion of *social disorganization*. Agreeing that we need *some* term to explain why crime rates vary by group and over time, he states a preference for the term *differential social organization*—a less judgmental label (and one that, in the view of some scholars, signaled abandonment of the social-structural concerns of Chicago school theorists).[9] However, he concludes that "regardless of the name," his key point is that "crime is rooted in the social organization and is an expression of that social organization."[10] In sum, Sutherland's theory is one of social learning under varying group conditions.

Significance of Differential Association Theory

All of the key concepts in Sutherland's differential association theory were sociological—cultural learning, culture conflict, social organization, differential access to attitudes and values—and his textbook strongly endorsed sociological methods. Sutherland helped establish the parameters of criminology, voicing firm opinions about what criminologists should and should not do in his books, his governmental work, his reports to private foundations, and his waspish reviews of books and theories that strayed from what he considered the true path.[11] Generations of criminology students formed their ideas about the field through reading *Principles of Criminology*. Moreover, Sutherland's students—including Albert Cohen, Donald Cressey, and Lloyd Ohlin—became giants in the next generation of theorists. As criminological historian John Laub explains, "Sutherland clearly touched all those involved in the formation of criminology as a distinct intellectual discipline."[12]

Over time, however, Sutherland's thesis lost its allure. Donald Cressey, who worked closely with Sutherland over the years and even coauthored later editions of *Principles of Criminology*, observed that "the statement of the differential association process is not precise enough to stimulate vigorous empirical test, and it therefore has not been proved or disproved."[13] Albert Cohen pointed out that although Sutherland explained how people acquire criminal culture through associations, he failed to explain where the culture came from in the first place—another way of saying that Sutherland ignored social structure.[14] Assumptions that seemed sound in the mid-twentieth century—Sutherland's blank-slate belief that humans are shaped almost entirely by social factors, and his confidence in social determinism—have been shaken or rejected. Indeed, the last decades of the twentieth century saw something like a Sutherland backlash, with one set of critics arguing that Sutherland's theory rejects "healthy empiricism in favor of a pre-scientific mode of thought"[15] and another that Sutherland's commitment to a sociological model and analytic induction may have damaged the field's development.[16]

Although Sutherland's theory no longer seems the breakthrough it once did, his influence in the field remains strong and pervasive. Nowhere is this better seen than in the area of subcultural explanations of criminal behavior—theories that flowed from Sutherland's differential association theory.

Subcultural Theories of Crime

Interest in delinquent and criminal subcultures ballooned in the mid-twentieth century, swelled by the post–World War II rise of American youth subcultures.[17] For the first time in history, adolescents had disposable incomes, which they spent on clothes (for guys, tight blue jeans and a white T-shirt, preferably with a pack of cigarettes tucked into a rolled-up sleeve), transportation (souped-up convertibles), music (rock 'n' roll), activities (drag racing, jitterbugging), and imitating icons such as Elvis and the live-fast-die-young movie star James Dean. Older generations watched with puzzlement and alarm as adolescents developed their own subcultures, especially when those subcultures became the equivalent of gangs.

In criminology, two traditions converged to explain gang subcultures. The first flowed from the Chicago school and its "golden age" work on urban diversity, social disorganization, differential association, cultural transmission, and pockets of cultural difference within the society as a whole. The second tradition flowed from Merton's strain theory, with its concept of varying adaptations to blocked access to wealth and status (see chapter 6). While Merton's analysis explained generally why segments of the population adapted differently to economic strain, it did not explain why various people *within* a particular adaptation committed different deviant acts. Nor did Merton's famous chart (page 89) account for the collective, gang nature of some criminal behavior, particularly that committed by lower-class males.

Subcultures and Delinquency

With these two theoretical traditions—differential social organization and social strain—converging on the hottest criminological issue of the day, it is little wonder that the era's first major book on delinquent subcultures, *Delinquent Boys* (1955), would be the work of a man who had studied with both Sutherland and Merton: Albert Cohen. This was the work that introduced the term *delinquent subcultures*.[18] Cohen disagreed with Sutherland's idea that the difference between becoming a delinquent and (as he put it) "a Boy Scout" lay "only in the cultural pattern with which the child associates."[19] He wanted to know why and how delinquent subcultures came into being in the first place, so that they existed for youngsters to differentially associate *with*. He also wanted to know why members of delinquent subcultures were so often working-class boys and why their activities tended to be malicious, aggressive, and destructive.[20]

Cohen's answer to these questions was that the subculture offers solutions to the working-class boy's "status problems"—his inability to achieve middle-class goals due to "class-linked handicaps."[21] Through a process of *reaction-formation*, some working-class boys adopt subcultural values that "make nonconformity with the expectations of the outsiders a positive criterion of status within the group."[22] Reaction-formation represents not a total repudiation of middle-class cultural values but a process of turning those values on their head through hostility, nonutilitarian acquisition, and aggression. That these behaviors are congruent with masculine but not feminine roles explains the gender differences in gang delinquency. In sum, "It is in the male working-class sector that there exists a *common core* of motivation, more specifically, of status discontent, to which the delinquent subculture is an appropriate solution."[23]

The next major contribution to delinquency theory was made by Richard Cloward and Lloyd Ohlin in *Delinquency and Opportunity: A Theory of Delinquent Gangs* (1960). Ohlin, too, had studied with Sutherland, and he did his graduate work at the University of Chicago.[24] Cloward was a student of Merton. Thus again the two potent sociological traditions, social disorganization and strain, converged in a theory of delinquent subcultures. But unlike Cohen, who wrote of an undifferentiated delinquent subculture,[25] Cloward and Ohlin identified three specific types: the *criminal subculture*, populated by boys growing up in areas with well-organized adult criminal groups; the *conflict subculture*, populated by disadvantaged youth growing up in disorganized slum areas that offered no stable adult role models, criminal or otherwise; and the *retreatist subculture*, populated by "double failures," youngsters who, unable to achieve goals through organized criminal groups *or* conflict subcultures, retreated into drug use. Like Cohen, Cloward and Ohlin wanted to know where subcultures "come from"—to explain their origins as well as their nature. Ohlin described their work as "really a theory of subcultural formation."[26]

Subcultures Go to the Movies

The middle decades of the twentieth century were glory days for research on subcultures—not only delinquent subcultures but also police subcultures, inmate subcultures, subcultures of violence, drug subcultures, organized crime subcultures, and the so-called culture of poverty.[27] This outpouring of interest, while stimulated by the convergence of two authoritative sociological traditions, as outlined earlier, was also kindled by films. In fact, the phenomenon of subcultural analysis was to a large extent *preceded* by films and nourished by them.

Albert Cohen was still in grade school when Hollywood released its first high-impact gangster movies—*Little Caesar* (1930), *Public Enemy* (1931), and *Scarface* (1932)—depicting (in *Scarface*'s opening words) "gang life in America" and showing lower-class men, crude and uneducated, shooting their way to riches, fame, and misfortune. Their images of social disorganization and subcultural life are pure Chicago school; they are also perfect examples—before the fact—of Merton's "innovation" adaptation to strain.[28] Equally galvanizing were films on juvenile delinquency such as *Blackboard Jungle* (1955) and the James Dean classic *Rebel without a Cause* (1955), both released in the same year as Cohen published *Delinquent Boys* and depicting something very like Cohen's reaction-formation. Inmate subcultures were depicted in dozens of prison films starting in the 1930s; not until decades later were they analyzed by authors such as Donald Clemmer (*The Prison Community* [1958]), Gresham Sykes (*The Society of Captives* [1958]), and Rose Giallombardo (*Society of Women* [1966]).[29]

Why did *movies* depicting subcultures and *criminological theory* about subcultures flourish simultaneously in the mid-twentieth century? Did the first lead to the second, or did some third factor encourage both? The answer lies in a remark made Albert Cohen when, looking back on midcentury delinquency research, he observed that at the time studying subcultures was "normal science"—everyone was doing it. "'It may have been, like so many other things, "in the air." . . . I don't know how much to attribute it [all the subcultural theorizing] to *Delinquent Boys* or to what extent *Delinquent Boys* and Cloward and Ohlin and so on were sort of expressions of the same phenomena."[30] To judge from cinematic evidence, that interest in subcultures was indeed "in the air," part of a Zeitgeist or a broader cultural phenomenon manifesting itself in *both* movies and scholarly work.

While the scholarly study of subcultures faded, subcultural analyses remained movie staples. Few police films failed to portray a knot of bad officers, members of a corrupt cop subculture, and in some police films (for example, *Serpico* [1973]), the subculture became the main theme. Prison films such as *The Shawshank Redemption* (1994) and *American History X* (1998) integrated inmate subcultures into their plots, while addiction movies such as *Trainspotting* (1996) and *Requiem for a Dream* (2000) threw the blame on drug subcultures. *The Godfather* (1972), *The Godfather II* (1974), *Goodfellas* (1990), *New Jack City* (1991), and countless other organized crime movies depicted subcultural organizations.

One of the most original representations of a criminalistic subculture appears in director Clint Eastwood's award-winning *Mystic River* (2003). The next section examines *Mystic River*'s exploration of the geographical, psychological, and sociological dimensions of the subcultural idea.

Mystic River

Mystic River takes place just north of Boston, in a working-class enclave of closely set triple-decker homes where the Mystic River flows into Boston harbor. The film begins with a view out into the harbor, toward the more lively, urbanized areas beyond. Slicing horizontally across the screen, the Mystic River Bridge divides these two sectors, emphasizing the community's geographical—almost metaphysical—isolation. Laundry hangs on backyard lines and over porch railings, paint peels from wooden doorways, some windows are boarded up. The area is Irish, Catholic, and poor, part of the larger city yet separate, with its own history, codes, and sorrows. Working from a novel by Dennis Lehane, who grew up in one of Boston's working-class Irish neighborhoods, Eastwood creates a world as closed as the insular communities studied by early subcultural theorists.

The film's claustrophobic atmosphere underscores its message about the nature of this subculture. Many of the scenes were shot in semidarkness, within apartments lacking light and air. The characters, hardscrabble and minimally educated, lead constricted lives. Their community is one of tough women and hard-drinking, sometimes violent men. Progress—or at least

Figure 7.1. In *Mystic River* (2003), director Clint Eastwood takes us into a working-class community, cut off from the larger city by the bridge in this shot's background; it is a hardscrabble community of triple-deckers whose inhabitants have their own subcultural value system. Sean Penn plays Jimmy Markum, the epitome of this subculture—angry, hard-drinking, and ready to bypass the law to extract his own vengeance. Film can vividly indicate the importance of place and subcultural values in crime. Photo used by permission of Photofest.

change—nibbles around the margins: one character remarks that "yuppies are coming," driving up housing prices, and the cost of take-out coffee is rising as well. But otherwise, the modern world is held at bay, and although the action takes place around the year 2000, the streets are as empty of cars as in the 1940s.

In the opening scene, three eleven-year-old boys—Dave Boyle, Jimmy Markum, and Sean Devine—are playing street hockey when two men posing as cops drive up in a black car and abduct Dave. They hold him for four days in a cellar, raping him repeatedly before he escapes. Then *Mystic River* skips ahead to the present day to investigate what happened to the three boys when they grew up.

Dave Boyle (Tim Robbins) is married and has a small son; fearfully, he sticks close to the boy when they are outside. Unable to escape his trauma, a permanent victim, Dave walks and talks distractedly. Jimmy Markum (Sean Penn), owner of a mom-and-pop market, has a nineteen-year-daughter by a woman who died many years ago and two younger daughters by his current wife. Sean Devine (Kevin Bacon), a cop, is also married, but his pregnant wife disappeared six months ago, and although she phones him, trying to speak, she cannot even utter the name of the child she has now borne. The three men seldom see one another these days, but Dave's abduction is seldom far from their minds. Without consciously realizing it, they are inextricably linked, knotted to one another by horrific memories. The past keeps intruding, silently, just as Sean's alienated wife keeps phoning without speaking.

Unknown to Jimmy, his beloved oldest daughter, Katie, is about to elope with a neighborhood kid, Brendan Harris. Her good-bye party with girlfriends ends with them dancing on top of the bar where Dave sits nursing a beer. The next morning Jimmy discovers that Katie is missing, but instead of eloping to Los Vegas with Brendan, she has been beaten, shot to death, and tossed in an old bear pit in a nearby park. (A carving on the pit's wall of two bears embracing in a fight becomes an emblem of the film's near-fratricidal violence.) Jimmy's grief—"a world of hurt"—is almost unbearable; he swears to kill those who murdered "my Katie." Meanwhile, we learn that the night before, Dave did not get home till 3:00 a.m., when he stumbled in, his hand bloody, to tell his wife a confused story of being jumped by a guy in a parking lot. Maybe he killed the guy. "Makes you feel alone, y' know, hurting somebody."

In bits and pieces, we learn that Jimmy is part of a crime gang that includes the thuggish Savage brothers and used to include Brendan's father, Just-Ray Harris. Decades earlier, when Jimmy and Just-Ray committed a robbery,

Just-Ray "rolled" on Jimmy, testifying against him, and while Jimmy was serving his two-year sentence, his first and greatest love, Maria, died, leaving the infant Katie. For years after he got out, it was just the two of them, Jimmy and Katie, talking late at night in the kitchen, alone together with their loss.

Not long after Jimmy's release from prison, Just-Ray disappeared; his wife and two sons, who since then have regularly received a $500 monthly check postmarked Brooklyn, assume that he simply ran out on them. Thus they too are alone, another fractured family. In truth, Jimmy, consumed with guilt and rage at being in prison when Maria lay dying, blamed Just-Ray, and on release from prison, killed him, shooting him at night on the water's edge.

Sean and his partner are assigned to investigate Katie's brutal murder. Dave, increasingly unhinged, keeps changing his story about how he hurt his hand, saying he injured it fighting a mugger, fixing a garbage disposal, beating up a child molester whom he saw in a car with a kid late on the night Katie died. Even his own wife begins to suspect him of killing Katie, and she confides her suspicions to Jimmy. In a scene paralleling the original abduction, the Savage brothers lure Dave into a bar; when he is almost too drunk to stand, Jimmy appears, taking him out on a tiny strip of beach where he beats and shoots him. Once again, Dave is brutalized and made to disappear.

The scene of Dave's murder is intercut with a simultaneous scene between Brendan, his mute brother Silent Ray, and a friend. Silent Ray's inability (or refusal) to speak is another of this film's signs of isolation and the impossibility of communication in this subcultural world. The boys fight, almost to the death. It turns out that Silent Ray and his friend killed Katie when she noticed they had a gun—the gun that Just-Ray had hidden in his house before Jimmy killed him. The cops find a dead pedophile in the bushes, confirming Dave's innocence. "Sometimes I think . . . all three of us got in that car," Sean remarks, "and all this is just a dream, you know? In reality we're eleven-year-old boys, locked in a cellar, imagining what our lives would've been if we'd escaped." But from the geographical and psychological circumstances of this film, there is no escape. Violence will continue as long as the culprits in Dave's victimizations remain unidentified.

When Jimmy confesses to his wife, Annabeth (Laura Linney), that he has murdered Dave but now realizes that Dave was not Katie's killer, she seizes on the event as a way to increase their power in the neighborhood, assuring him that it is "never wrong" to do something to help those you love. "A king knows what to do. You're going to rule this town." The entire neighborhood spills out on the street to observe a parade. For once the day is sunny, and Sean has reconciled with his wife—a hint that healing is possible. For the most part, however, communication remains impossible. Annabeth, triumphant, stares down Dave's cowering widow. The widow waves frantically to her son on a float, but he doesn't notice her. Jimmy and Sean lock eyes, both knowing that Jimmy murdered Dave—but aware that there is no proof. Some day, Sean may break open the closed circle of silence to reveal the truth, but at the moment, Jimmy and Annabeth are too strong to let the secret out; their iron determination binds the secret in its cask of memory. The camera reminds us of the origins of all this pain—the three boys' names in the sidewalk pavement, scratched there in newly poured concrete just before the abduction—and then again shows the Mystic River Bridge, but this time from the other side of the harbor, looking back toward the small community where dark secrets and violence, like Just-Ray's hidden gun, pass from generation to generation.

In this subculture as in those studied by Chicago school sociologists, people absorb deviant norms from their environments. From their social surroundings they pick up their values, including the conviction that to respond to injustice, one must take the law into one's own hands. They *learn* to remain inarticulate and stay apart. Katie tried to escape, but she was killed for her presumptuousness. Trapped in a cul-de-sac, just as the bears were trapped in the pit, members of this community have figured out that to survive, they must fight one another. There is no way out. Suspicion and guilt are the norm, as are lost childhoods, lost children, parentless children, and death. *Mystic River* is a dark and somber film, a tale of a subculture's perpetuation of loneliness, grief, and desolation.

Sutherland and the Cinema: Life Histories and White-Collar Crime

We have been discussing cinematic examples of subcultural theory, movies that extend the work of Sutherland and other Chicago school scholars. In the next section we discuss ways in which film has extended two other aspects of Sutherland's research, his life-history approach to the study of crime and his innovative research on white-collar offending.

Criminal Life Histories

The life-history approach to understanding criminal behavior began in 1930, when Clifford Shaw, a leader of the Chicago school, published *The Jack-Roller*, the biography of a young parolee (called Stanley in the book).[31] Delinquency specialists had been collecting case histories for many years, but *The*

Jack-Roller was a unique and riveting work. It validated a new method in criminological research—the "own story" approach to the study of delinquency—and it was inherently sensational: a jack roller supports himself by assaulting homosexual men and stealing their money. Stanley had been arrested twenty-six times by the age of ten for offenses including truancy, begging, "bad sex habits," and shoplifting as well as jack rolling. *The Jack-Roller* offered what came to be dubbed "sociology noir," a work of gritty immediacy and underworld allure.[32] Shaw saw a number of advantages to the life-history approach, including the light it could throw on the causes of delinquency and the guidance it could provide for individualizing treatment.[33] *The Jack-Roller* remains a high-profile memoir; in 2007 the journal *Theoretical Criminology* ran an entire issue of articles on Shaw's classic.[34]

Seven years later, Sutherland published *The Professional Thief: By a Professional Thief*—Broadway Jones, to whom Sutherland gave the pseudonym Chic Conwell.[35] Although *The Jack-Roller* doubtless gave Sutherland a sense of direction, he was less concerned to produce a biography than to study the phenomenon of professional theft (highly polished stealing by expert thieves) per se. Conwell's story comprises part I of *The Professional Thief*, but it was edited and annotated by Sutherland, and part II, "Interpretation and Conclusion," is entirely Sutherland's work. *The Professional Thief* inaugurated the behavior-system approach to the study of specific offense types that persists unabated today. It also influenced later work on career criminals and life-course criminology.

Sutherland builds *The Professional Thief* on his usual assumption that criminal behavior is normal, a type of activity that, like all behaviors, is learned in interaction with others. "Differential association," he writes, "is characteristic of the professional thieves, as of all other groups."[36] He also shows that professional thieves constitute a subculture: "The thief is a part of the underworld and in certain respects is segregated from the rest of society."[37] Sutherland maintains that Conwell came from a middle-class background ("his family was in comfortable circumstances"),[38] a claim that reinforces Sutherland's contention that poverty does not cause crime. And in showing how Conwell learned to be a professional thief, Sutherland supports what he came to call his differential social organization thesis.[39] A critic has questioned some of *The Professional Thief*'s data, arguing, for instance, that Jones/Conwell was probably working-class in origin.[40] Moreover, despite Sutherland's claim that "the thief wrote approximately two-thirds" of the book "on topics and questions prepared by me,"[41] Conwell writes (and thinks) suspiciously like Sutherland himself. However, the details are less important here than the fact that, with Shaw, Sutherland launched the criminal life-history approach,[42] a true-crime genre that has also played an important role in cinema.

In fact, the life-history approach has proved far more popular in film than in criminology. Following the careers of lawbreakers who pursue a goal and partially succeed, only to be caught in the end, the life history has a built-in story line of rise and fall, together with a built-in moral. Frequently, life-history films draw material from the careers of actual criminals—folk heroes whom viewers admire because they took risks that the rest of us only fantasize about, or scandalous figures who somehow take hold of the public imagination.

"My mother died of pneumonia when I was just a kid," explains Holly at the beginning of *Badlands* (1973), the tale of two teenagers on a killing spree. This celebrated movie by the director Terrence Malick re-creates, in fictionalized form, the history of Caril Ann Fugate ("Holly") and her boyfriend, Charlie Starkweather ("Kit"), lovers-on-the-lam who in the 1950s mesmerized the country as they fled through the South Dakota Badlands in an orgy of violence. After she and Kit are captured, Holly wraps up the narration by reporting, dispassionately, that "I got off with probation and a lot of nasty looks. I married the son of the lawyer who defended me. Kit was sentenced to die in the electric chair, . . . and he did." That five other movies have also retold the Fugate-Starkweather tale is a testimony not only to its grip on the American imagination but also to the life-history film's capacity to capitalize on that fascination.

Another true criminal life-history forms the basis for *Goodfellas* (1990), director Martin Scorsese's film about the career of mobster Henry Hill. *Goodfellas* begins with Henry reminiscing about his youthful admiration for organized crime figures in his neighborhood:

> To me, being a gangster was better than being the president of the United States. . . . I knew I wanted to be a part of [the mob]. To me it meant being somebody in a neighborhood that was full of nobodies. They did what they wanted; they parked in front of a fire hydrant and nobody ever gave them a ticket. . . . People like my father could never understand, but I belonged, I was treated like a grown-up. Every day I was learning to score.

Scorsese's criminological sensibility is not much different from Sutherland's: both see crime as a normal outcome of subcultural learning, and both refuse to moralize.[43]

Scorsese again uses the life-history approach in *The Departed* (2006), a film about police corruption, the activity of a specific mob during the 1980s, and a cop who goes undercover to penetrate the mob. In other words, it is a complex story. To ease us into it, Scorsese begins as though this is going to be a life-history narrative, with mob boss Frank Costello (played by Jack Nicholson) drily asserting, "I don't want to be a product of my environment; I want my environment to be a product of *me*." Frank's narration peters out after a while, and he is eventually shot; but by that point we are far enough into the plot that the life-history device is no longer needed.[44]

The dozens—perhaps hundreds—of other films in which a first-person narrator relates his or her criminal life history include *Double Indemnity* (1944) (discussed in chapter 2) and *Fight Club* (1999), in which the narrator is mentally ill and thus unreliable, giving viewers an extra plot twist to unravel. Movies use first-person narratives to relate criminal life histories for the same reason Shaw gave his jack roller a pen and paper and Sutherland transcribed Broadway Jones's replies to his questions about the routines of a professional thief: the technique, with its persuasive intimacy, gives the story the ring of authenticity.

White-Collar Crime

Late in life Sutherland published *White Collar Crime*, the first systematic study of upper-class offending. White-collar offenses are crimes, he argued, even if they do not result in criminal convictions. As in his other work, he tried to show that crime is the result of, not psychological illness or poverty, but social learning.[45]

For *White Collar Crime*, on which he worked for decades, Sutherland collected records on law violations by America's seventy largest industrial and commercial organizations, documenting a total of 980 "adverse decisions" against these companies, only a small proportion of them reached by criminal courts. In business, the offenses included fixing books, manipulating the stock market, bribing public officials, tax fraud, and embezzlement; in medicine, they included giving false testimony in accident cases, performing illegal operations, supplying narcotics, and fee splitting; in politics, they encompassed bribery and graft. So long as the behavior involved a violation of the criminal law—so long as it *could* have been prosecuted as a crime— it should count as a white-collar crime, Sutherland insisted, even if it was in fact prosecuted in a civil court. Prosecutors often show leniency to the upper-class perpetrators of white-collar offenses, Sutherland observed, and yet white-collar crime is more costly than street crime, not just financially but also socially, because it damages personal relationships through violations of trust.

Sutherland's analysis of upper-class crime was integral to his theory of offending. In an early version of his *White Collar Crime* thesis, he claimed

> that white-collar criminality, just as other systematic criminality, is learned; that it is learned in direct or indirect association with those who already practice criminal behavior; and that those who learn this criminal behavior are segregated from frequent and intimate contacts with law-abiding behavior. Whether a person becomes a criminal or not is determined largely by the comparative frequency and intimacy of his contacts with the two types of behavior [lawful and unlawful].[46]

Massive in detail and iconoclastic in import, *White Collar Crime* added a phrase—its title—to the English language,[47] initiated an important line of criminological research, opened up debate on the definition of "criminal" and the validity of crime statistics based solely on criminal-court convictions, and drew attention to social-class differences in offending and punishment. It was one of the most influential criminological studies ever published.

White-collar crime is difficult to portray in narrative film.[48] Offenses of this type tend to be invisible and undramatic, involving no gunshots, car chases, or bedroom scenes. To inject excitement into movies about white-collar crime, filmmakers either fictionalize real events, making them more hair-raising than they were in real life, or they forget verisimilitude entirely, making up the plots from scratch. (An example of the latter approach can be found in *Michael Clayton* [2007], starring George Clooney as a law firm "fixer" who manages to pin environmental pollution on a large chemical company.) In addition, filmmakers focus less on the offense itself than on the person who uncovers it, creating characters who develop into heroes. Movies based on real-life cases of white-collar crime include *A Civil Action* (1998), starring John Travolta; *The Insider* (1999), starring Russell Crowe and Al Pacino; and *Erin Brockovich* (2000), starring Julia Roberts.

Social Learning and Subcultural Theories Today

Attacks on Sutherland and other Chicago school criminologists started in 1978 with publication of Ruth Kornhauser's *Social Sources of Delinquency* and continued with salvos from Travis Hirschi, Michael Gottfredson, and others interested in redirecting criminology toward control theories of crime causation.[49] Like pirates, these rivals scaled the criminological ship that had long been skippered by Sutherland and manned by other Chicago school affiliates. The control-theory invaders went after the view of human nature embedded in social learning and subcultural theories, arguing that it wrongly assumes that humans are born as blank slates on which culture inscribes values and beliefs. (In contrast, control theorists espouse a view of human nature as inherently selfish and predatory—a position that makes it easier to explain criminal behavior.)[50] Control theorists also went after the determinism inherent in Sutherland's and related work. If the behavior of individuals is inevitably dictated by the values and beliefs of their cultural environment, as Sutherland seemed to argue, what role does that leave for human agency? Why do most residents of a high-crime area remain law-abiding? Why do some youths in a no-crime environment violate laws?

Additionally, the invaders took aim at the very idea of subcultures, asking whether groups whose values, beliefs, and so on are antithetical to those of the broader society really do exist. Surveys demonstrate that most people, even those who live in apparent subcultures, condemn murder, assault, and other serious crimes. No one, not even burglars, enjoys having their closets rifled. How, then, are we to identify delinquent subcultures and measure whether individuals have "an excess of definitions favorable to violation of law over definitions unfavorable to violations of law"? In fact, in *The Professional Thief* Sutherland himself recognized that Chic Conwell held many conventional values and disliked being "antisocial."[51] However, Sutherland was not clear as to why, despite this dislike, subcultural values won Conwell's allegiance.

The major counterattack against the invaders was led by criminologist Ronald L. Akers, who since 1966 has attempted to update and revitalize differential association theory by combining it with psychological learning theories that specify how criminal "definitions" are acquired.[52] He published his definitive statement on the topic, *Social Learning and Social Structure*, in 2009, yet even here, Akers continues to use Sutherland's underlying metaphor of balance pans: scales tip in favor of criminal behavior (that is, criminal behavior is more likely to be learned) when there are more criminal than noncriminal associations, definitions, exposures, and reinforcements. Unfortunately, the balance-pan metaphor is incapable of accounting for the complexities of human learning. Despite Akers and other defenders,[53] social learning theories have become criminological wallflowers, watching from the sidelines as control and life-course theories boogie in the limelight.

Today, some criminology textbooks bypass social learning and subcultural theories almost entirely.[54]

Despite the ascendancy of control theories, however, Sutherland remains a towering figure in the history of criminology, one who would be attacked less vigorously had he not reached a pinnacle where later criminologists would now like to sit. Not only did he develop a theory that changed criminological history and gave birth to subcultural theories; he also elaborated the life-history approach and almost single-handedly put white-collar crime on criminological and political agendas. Movies about deviant subcultures, criminal life histories, and even white-collar crime keep the Sutherland tradition alive.

FURTHER VIEWING

Blackboard Jungle (1955)
Civil Action, A (1998)
Eastern Promises (2007)
Few Good Men, A (1992)
Fight Club (1999)
Firm, The (1993)
Godfather, The (1972)
Insider, The (1999)
Oz (Home Box Office Television Series, 1997–2003)
Rebel without a Cause (1955)

8

"Pornography in Foot-High Stacks"

Labeling Theory and Capturing the Friedmans

One of criminology's theoretical assumptions is the idea that the causes of crime precede criminal justice interventions. Labeling theory counters this perspective, arguing instead that social responses to deviance, including defining individuals as "criminals" or "labeling" them, may worsen criminality. One of the foundational tenets of this perspective is that society is narrow in its understandings of deviance and that the criminal justice system, in particular, is limited in its capacity to restrain crime. Worse, state intervention may intensify the deviant acts and criminal behavior it had hoped to stop, anchoring individuals in these identities. At a moment when the United States leads the world in unprecedented incarceration rates, 2.3 million in prison with another 6 million on probation or parole, the costs and effects of state intervention assume a high level of priority for criminologists. Unlike previous criminologists and most policy makers, labeling theorists view this kind of intervention as criminogenic.

This chapter identifies the main principles of labeling theories, describes how these perspectives developed, and explores their meanings in popular cinema. The main film we will examine is Andrew Jarecki's documentary *Capturing the Friedmans* (2003), a riveting and disturbing look at the complex interpretations that underlie labeling processes. An intimate portrayal of a middle-class family in a suburban New York community, largely through their own home movies, *Capturing the Friedmans* depicts a family ripped apart when the father and his eighteen-year-old son are accused of molesting dozens of young boys in the basement of their home. To its credit, the film offers no clear answers or easy resolutions, thus forcing us to work through the ways in which the Friedmans are rendered deviant and criminal, processes that ultimately result in the destruction of the family.

Labeling Theory

Labeling theory, also known as the *societal reaction* approach, marks an important turn in the understanding of crime whereby labeling theorists insist that crime is "socially constructed": what constitutes crime changes across time, societies, and contexts. Consequently, these theorists argue that criminologists must address the social conditions that determine which behaviors are criminalized, the processes by which individuals are labeled criminals, and the consequences of that label. This approach assumes that no behavior is inherently criminal. For instance, killing, although recognizably injurious, is not defined as criminal because of the harm it incurs but rather by the process of state intervention—whether the act is defined by law as criminal. Killing during wartime or as an act of self-defense is often not criminalized but rather justified by the state.

Labeling theorists provide an alternative starting point in the search for the causes of crime, one that moves beyond individual motives or social environments, and points instead toward the social reactions that others have toward deviant behaviors—and the role of those reactions in the construction of crime. Sociologist Howard Becker, trained at the University of Chicago after World War II, eventually becoming the central proponent of labeling theory, famously wrote that "deviance is *not* a quality of the act the person commits, but rather a consequence of the application by others of rules and sanctions to an 'offender.' The deviant is one to whom that label has successfully been applied; deviant behavior is behavior that people so label."[1] His research reflects the influence of early labeling theorists such as Frank Tannenbaum and Edwin Lemert and, more broadly, the *symbolic interactionist* approaches of sociologists Charles Cooley and George Mead. For these theorists, crime is best understood in terms of the meanings those actions have for the actor rather than biological, psychological, or social factors. Labeling perspectives, consequently, derive from *symbolic interactionist* traditions that assert the individual's self-image is constructed primarily through interactions with others. Labeling theorists are especially concerned with the impact that defining an individual as a criminal has upon his or her behavior; the meaning of crime to criminals; and the processes by which categories of behavior are defined as crimes. This labeling process extends beyond the state to parents, peers, educators, employers, and the media.

Becker's career reflects these commitments. His early work focused upon the occupational worlds of schoolteachers and jazz musicians, which led him to develop an interest in the study of recreational drug use. In 1953, he published a widely read and influential article, "Becoming a Marihuana User," in the *American Journal of Sociology*. In 1961, he became the editor of the journal *Social Problems*, published by the Society for the Study of Social Problems, a professional organization dedicated to critical sociology and established in response to the more dominant, conservative American Sociological Association. Becker's research and professional service foreground the study of deviance with a labeling emphasis. Labels, Becker argued, risked becoming self-fulfilling prophecies, forging criminal identities by making conformity difficult through processes of exclusion and isolation.

Marking a radical shift in understandings of crime, this approach reframed questions about the causes of crime by considering the ways in which particular acts come to be labeled or defined as criminal or deviant. As a result, labeling theorists used qualitative methodologies, often historical or ethnographic in their techniques. This orientation reflects a fundamental methodological challenge that figures at the heart of labeling enterprises—a perspective both skeptical and critical of a mainstream reliance in criminology on crime rates and other official statistics. Labeling studies tend to question the nature and legitimacy of authority, viewing criminals and deviants as oppressed by state intervention, often sympathetic to the plight of offenders. These processes are described in a series of monographs from the 1960s that reflect many of labeling's theoretical concerns.[2] In *Asylums* (1961) and *Stigma* (1963), Erving Goffman draws attention to the ways in which institutions and social response negatively shape identities of ex-prisoners, the mentally ill, homosexuals, and the physically disabled. Joseph Gusfield's *Symbolic Crusade* (1963) maps how the American temperance movement led to Prohibition and the creation of a vast category of alcohol offenses that otherwise might not have existed. Kai Erikson's *Wayward Puritans* (1966), still considered a classic study of deviance in its examination of the social construction of witchcraft in colonial New England, depicts how the religious worldview of early Puritans in Massachusetts Bay led to processes for identifying and sanctioning deviants, especially women who stepped outside conventional gender roles.

In *Outsiders* (1963), the central theoretical statement of the era, Becker explored how categories of *primary* and *secondary* deviance develop, as well as how those in positions of power and authority make and enforce rules that culminate in new groups of outsiders. *Primary* deviance (criminal behavior that originates in the context of a noncriminal self-image) occurs when an individual engages in initial acts of crime or deviance with no prior stigmatization. At this initial stage, the offender often views his or her behavior as temporary or part of an otherwise socially acceptable role. An individual might engage in a small act of theft or recreational drug use but then return to his or her previous law-abiding role. More commonly, teens experiment with alcohol and drugs throughout high school and college, but few become alcoholics or addicts. In fact, primary deviance is not rooted in character or lifestyle and is likely to be transitory. However, any act of criminal behavior that is formally or officially acknowledged generates a negative social reaction, thereby weakening the individual's noncriminal, conformist self-image. This may lead to further acts of deviant or criminal behavior. *Secondary deviance* is driven by the responses of others to the initial behavior. With the reactions to each act of primary deviance, the offender becomes stigmatized through labeling and stereotyping. This is a complex process that involves more than simply being processed by the criminal justice system; rather, in an encounter made up of degradation and moral judgment, one's worth and identity are redefined by a variety of external agents in a manner that defines the individual (not the behaviors) as criminal.

Through an internalization of this stigmatized identity, actors begin to adhere to their deviant status and organize their lives around this identity. In this way, labeling processes create a self-fulfilling prophecy. Most consequentially, labeling may solidify one's identity as deviant. At the heart of labeling theory is social reaction and the (often misguided or misinformed) assumptions that people make about offenders and their likelihood to recidivate, leaving individuals fixed permanently in status positions such as that of the addict, gangster, or sexual predator. These reactions, Becker and others argued, have the power to set in motion the very behavior that was the target of reaction.

In this pursuit, Becker focused not only on the processes by which actors were acculturated into deviance but also on the nature of social reaction itself. His most famous studies are of the recreational use of marijuana and how the rise of "moral entrepreneurs" culminated in campaigns to outlaw the drug. He chronicles the role of Harry Anslinger, the commissioner of the Federal Bureau of Narcotics (which later became the Drug Enforcement Administration), in the creation of a new category of drug offender through his campaign to outlaw marijuana and introduce the Marihuana Tax Act of 1937. Films of the era also reflect these concerns. *Reefer Madness* (1936), now treated as one of the classic camp cult films in American history because of the drug misinformation it contains, portrays teenagers in small-town America who are lured into marijuana use and then caught up in a series of tragic events, including manslaughter, suicide, and rape.

The scope of the labeling perspective extends well beyond crime; in fact, as should be evident, labeling theory was essential in the rise of deviance as an area of historical and sociological study. The field has historically focused on four primary domains: drug use, juvenile delinquency, mental illness, and sexual behavior are all categories where what is designated by the state as criminal is not constant but rather a process made up of efforts by powerful groups and individuals to construct different crime realities. Labeling theorists point, then, to the necessity of understanding the origins of labels. More controversially, they follow this presupposition with the notion that the process of labeling individuals as criminals, social reaction itself, exacerbates crime, leading to chronic involvement in illegal behavior. This claim poses an interesting and original problem in criminology. If social reaction is the source of criminality, then state intervention and efforts to label lawbreakers as criminal have the ironic and unanticipated consequence of creating the very behaviors they were meant to prevent.

The labeling theorists of the 1960s echo the arguments of many criminologists across time, particularly those sociologists of punishment who, from the birth of the penitentiary, pointed out the negative effects of incarceration. The early labeling theorist Frank Tannenbaum argued that the most formative influence upon a juvenile's criminal behavior is separating the child from society and placing him or her within the criminal justice system, what he described as "a process of tagging, defining, identifying, segregating, describing, emphasizing, and evoking the very traits that are complained of. . . . The person becomes the thing he is described as being."[3] Numerous prison memoirs document these kinds of processes, including Jack Henry Abbott's *In the Belly of the Beast*; George Jackson's *Soledad Brother*; and Sanyika Shakur's *Monster*, an L.A. gang member's memoir of gang life. The offender becomes, as Becker writes, "one who is different from the rest of us, who cannot or will not act as a moral human being,"[4] and who consequently assumes the "master status"—or identity—of criminal. Social rejection and public scrutiny all further undermine the positive, conformist influences in the offender's life, loosening his or her stakes in conventional life. Offenders' identities as spouse, parent, and professional are supplanted by their criminal identities and negative self-perception. Ties with friends, family, and institutions are weakened. All of this builds up pressure for further criminal activity and criminal associations.

A final break with ties to conventional society, labeling theorists argue, is most probable when state intervention involves institutionalization. Imprisonment severs many conventional ties (employment, education, etc.), strains relationships with friends and family, and provides opportunities for association with other criminals. Finally, stigma follows offenders from prison as they reenter society and attempt to find employment, access education, and rebuild their relationships. Consequently, ex-offenders face lower wages, limited access to education, higher divorce rates, and limited opportunities for participation in civic life, all of which, in true labeling theory form, increases the likelihood of a return to crime.[5] Classic Hollywood punishment films, ranging from *I Am a Fugitive from a Chain Gang* (1932) to *I Want to Live* (1958), have long depicted the complex effects of labeling and institutionalization. In the 1992 film *American Me*, Edward James Olmos directs and stars as Montoya Santana, a Chicano youth who enters the California penal system while a juvenile and is caught in a lifelong trajectory of crime, in and out of prison. Loosely based on the rise of the Mexican Mafia, *American Me* chronicles how mass, racialized incarceration leads to the formation of powerful gangs in the California prison system, leaving Santana, a gang leader, caught in a permanent and institutionalized criminal identity, incapable of functioning in the free world upon his release.

The Context of Labeling Theory

A theoretical perspective that achieved popularity in the 1960s, labeling theory made sense in its identification of state intervention as the cause of the crime problem rather than its solution. Against persistent patterns of racism, sexism, and class inequality, the civil rights movement pointed directly at the unwillingness of government and political officials to address long-standing injustices. The growing unpopularity of the Vietnam War and disturbing police and military responses to social and political protest—across the South, at Kent State University, and in American prisons—all revealed a crisis of legitimacy for U.S. government and legal institutions. Simultaneously, the boundaries between normalcy and deviance blurred with the open celebration of recreational drug use, sex, antiwar sentiment, and countercultural lifestyles. In this context, it made sense that state intervention and social reality were perhaps more complex and problematic than previous criminological theories had conceded.

For these reasons, labeling theorists tended to embrace policies directed at decriminalization, diversion, due process, and deinstitutionalization—all of which experienced uneven application across the era and resulted in complex and, in some cases, far worse outcomes. Decriminalization favored the legalization of a wide variety of offenses, including recreational drug use and gambling, arguing that criminalization created more contexts for criminal behavior than legal regulation. The policy with the most dramatic long-term effect, deinstitutionalization, resulted in the movement of large numbers of youth and mentally ill out of institutional environments and into the community. Recidivism rates among youth remained low or comparable to rates under formal social control. However, deinstitutionalization left many people homeless and ultimately culminated in the incarceration of vast numbers of the mentally ill and retarded in today's contemporary prison system.[6]

Critiques and Contemporary Trajectories

Critics have had much to say in response to labeling theory. Since its inception, some have countered that labeling never fully accounts for the primary act of deviance and has resisted careful empirical testing. Although labeling theory emphasizes the role of social reaction in response to crime and deviance, in fact, the focus of most of the classic studies on labeling is directed at the process of becoming deviant, works more in line with subcultural studies (see chapter 7). Such a tendency may represent, in part, an effort to build greater identification and empathy with individuals and communities on the margins of society, those who are most often targeted by state intervention. Even here, critics have pointed at the ways in which labeling theorists have overemphasized the importance that official labeling processes can have. Most criminologists point toward social conditions, like poverty or high-crime neighborhoods, as being more influential than the act of criminal sanctioning. Others invoke a wave of empirical research that finds that extra-legal variables exert only a weak effect on labeling, with the seriousness of the crime (not the offender's background) serving as the largest determinant of state intervention. As well, there may be cases in which the individual is not as resistant to the deviant or criminal label as labeling theory suggests. Some argue gang identity and ex-con labels have become status symbols in communities hard hit by crime and mass incarceration.

A variety of camps within criminology have also critiqued labeling's foundations. Feminist and left realist theorists who focus on women's victimization counter the constructionist approach of labeling, arguing that the problem of rape required state recognition and formal intervention in order to shed light on the reality of violence against women. Many feminists found labeling's alliance and empathy with the offender misplaced and called for tough, aggressive laws and crime policies to protect women. Also, groups that had come to be defined as deviant in the 1950s and 1960s now refused the labels of the labeling theorists, insisting that they, as gays, lesbians, individuals with physical or mental disabilities, and so forth, were important members of larger communities whose identities should not be reduced to categories of deviance. Here, actors attempted to reappropriate their identities as viable, positive, and respectable in their own right.

Conflict or radical criminologists launched one of the strongest critiques. They agreed that crime was socially constructed but argued the source of differential treatment of rich and poor offenders was found in the distribution of power and the underlying economic order—encouraging a move beyond a focus upon the law and criminal justice system.[7] As sociologist Joel Best writes, "The conflict theorists agreed with labeling's critique of mainstream ideas, but they charged that the labeling interpretation was halfhearted, that labeling theory, which billed itself as critical of agencies of social control, failed to provide a truly meaningful critique, because it took for granted the social arrangements within which labeling occurred."[8] For conflict theorists, labeling theories failed to provide a serious political critique of social control institutions, instead focusing upon subjects who were relatively powerless in rejecting their deviant labels, subjects whom sociologist Alexander Liazos famously characterized as "nuts, sluts, and preverts."[9]

In spite of its many critiques, labeling theory still plays a powerful role in many contemporary criminological approaches,[10] including life-course theories, shaming perspectives, and, as discussed previously, accounts that attempt to make sense of mass incarceration. Life-course theorists, with their emphasis on trajectories or pathways of development over the life course, provide an important way in which to measure the effects of labeling across time. Through an examination of critical "turning point" events and experiences in childhood and adulthood, researchers have a better perspective into incremental changes in life trajectories, including the times of decision or opportunity that culminate in law-abiding or lawbreaking behavior. Robert Sampson and John Laub, key proponents of life-course perspectives, argue that labeling theory has an overlooked but nonetheless "obvious affinity to a life course, developmental framework."[11] They have found that the stability of behavior (its persistence, whether positive or negative) may be bound up with the stability of social response. Certain kinds of persistent stigmatizing processes in criminal justice and negative responses by other social institutions may make secondary deviance a likelihood. Given that one of the major criticisms of labeling perspectives is the inability to test them, life-course researchers provide an important context in which to conduct this research, although few studies have been done to date.

Some contemporary researchers have given careful attention to the conditions under which societal reaction increases or decreases crime. Criminologist John Braithwaite argues in his volume *Crime, Shame, and Reintegration* that social reaction often takes the form of two kinds of shaming: *disintegrative* and *reintegrative*. Disintegrative shaming, like most forms of reaction studied by labeling theorists, excludes and stigmatizes, leading to further entrenchment in crime. Reintegrative shaming evokes community disapproval but is followed by efforts "to reintegrate the offender back into the community of law-abiding or respectable citizens through words or gestures of forgiveness or ceremonies to decertify the offender as deviant."[12] Braithwaite's work points to the importance of different types of societal response and how those types are shaped by underlying social conditions and commitments. He points toward the United States, defined by urbanization, heterogeneity, residential mobility, and individualism, as a site where social control has a distinct disintegrative orientation. Here, lawbreakers carry permanent stigmatized identities as ex-offenders deserving of few resources, especially when attempting to reenter society.

A powerful counterargument to such stigmatizing practices is found under the umbrella of restorative justice, an emergent paradigm in international criminal justice that rejects the conventional role of the state in defining crime.[13] Rather, restorative justice advocates argue that the guiding principle of social reaction should be to decrease harm (as opposed to crime) by restoring (not severing) the relationships damaged in the harmful act. This approach includes a new and privileged place for the victim, clear processes of accountability for the offender, and his or her reintegration within the community. As opposed to a conventional trial, restorative justice sessions rely upon mediation and the active participation of the community to help both the victim and the offender move forward with their lives. Restorative justice attempts to reverse the stigmatizing effects of state-imposed labels.

Finally, a special realm of studies, built in part upon labeling perspectives, is committed to examinations of *moral panics*. Groundbreaking work by Stanley Cohen in *Folk Devils and Moral Panics* (1972) illustrates many of the classic features of a moral panic. He writes that "societies appear to be subject, every now and then, to periods of moral panic. A condition, episode, person or group of persons emerges to become defined as a threat to societal values and interests,"[14] just as the harmless British youth gangs, the Mods and Rockers, were depicted in 1960s Britain. In *Policing the Crisis*, another classic study of this kind, Stuart Hall and colleagues add:

When the official reaction to a person, groups of persons or series of events is out of all proportion to the actual threat offered, when "experts," in the form of police chiefs, the judiciary, politicians and editors perceive the threat in all but identical terms, and appear to talk "with one voice" of rates, diagnoses, prognoses and solutions, when the media representations universally stress "sudden and dramatic" increases (in numbers involved or events) and "novelty" above and beyond that which a sober, realistic appraisal could sustain, then we believe it is appropriate to speak of . . . a moral panic.[15]

The media have played an unprecedented role in such labeling processes, communicating specific kinds of selected knowledge and upholding particular interpretations of events in their production of moral panics. From a contemporary perspective, these media events have become quite complex. As Jeff Ferrell and Clinton Sanders argue in their influential formulation of cultural criminology:

It is no longer possible to retain the quaint, linear view of a world in which criminal acts and other objective happenings occur, are then observed and reported by the news media, and are finally transformed into quasi-factual stories or offered as fictionalized representations for the entertainment of the public audience. Instead, the most viable model is one in which media presentations, real-life events, personal perceptions, public policies, and individual actions spiral about each other in a complex, mutually affecting and ever-changing structure of inner-relationships.[16]

Capturing the Friedmans is a documentary that reflects the power of this shifting media environment, where differing accounts and perspectives run up against one another, leaving its viewers in the uncomfortable space of spiraling meanings with no clear resolution. The film also ties in with one of the most startling moral panics in recent history, the 1980s furor over child sexual abuse in day care centers and similar educational sites.

Capturing the Friedmans

Capturing the Friedmans is the true story of a typical middle-class Jewish American family living in Great Neck, Long Island, where Arnold and Elaine, both in their fifties, have raised three sons: David, Seth, and Jesse. An award-winning high school science teacher, Arnold conducts after-school computer classes for kids in his home basement and is helped by his young-est son Jesse, age eighteen. In November 1987, on the eve of Thanksgiving, Arnold and Jesse are arrested on charges of repeated sexual abuse of boys who attended their classes. The police raid marks a dramatic turning point in the Friedman's lives, giving rise to denigrating rumors and suspicions, a media frenzy, neighborhood outrage, and—within the Friedman home—family arguments over the best strategy to keep Arnold and Jesse out of jail. In the end, the family collapses around conflicting emotions of guilt, doubt, suspicion, and loyalty. David, the oldest son, chooses the side of his father and brother and bitterly resents his mother. Elaine has difficulty supporting her husband as she is never convinced of Arnold's innocence, given that he has lied to her about his sexual past. Her efforts to save Jesse, by urging both father and son to plead guilty, inadvertently backfire. In separate hearings, Arnold and later Jesse enter guilty pleas and are sentenced to substantial jail time. Arnold commits suicide in 1995 while imprisoned, and Jesse is released in 2001 after having served thirteen years of his sentence.

An exemplary film from which to consider labeling perspectives, *Capturing the Friedmans* presents multiple and often conflicting accounts, rendering the truth elusive even as Arnold and Jesse are constructed by the community, media, and criminal justice system as deviants and criminals. The viewer is left to piece together his or her own version of events, with the reality of the Friedman lives a puzzle without closure. This narrative openness reflects shifting conventions in contemporary documentary where films rely upon the use of memory and testimony, with rare consensus, to construct social reality. In the case of the Friedmans, this approach culminates in a paradox where we gain access to many individual states of mind but no solid evidence. Reality is never clear in its entirety even as we come to believe some things to be true and not others. Such an approach highlights labeling processes and the social construction of reality where meanings are shaped through social interactions and the disparate, often conflicting efforts of individuals and groups to make sense of and impose meaning upon reality. The film's opening juxtaposition of image and audio presents us with such a moment: As we screen idyllic home movies of father and sons, Jesse is recorded saying, "I still feel like I knew my father very well. I don't think that just because there were things in his life that were private and secret and shameful that that means that the father who I knew and the things I knew about him were in any way not real." Already, image and word are counterposed, building an ambiguous, subjective reality.

Given its constructionist approach, the film is best analyzed with attention to its recording and editing structure, all of which reflects the new and expansive role of film and video in everyday life. Made up of footage from more than fifty hours of Friedman home movies, twenty-five hours shot by Arnold Friedman during his sons' childhood and another twenty-five shot by David after Arnold's and Jesse's arrests, the documentary relies heavily on juxtaposition. The early movies are of happy times: trips to the beach, David playing the piano, holiday dinners and birthday parties. Later footage, shot by David, is volatile and filled with emotional outbursts among family members. Director Andrew Jarecki recorded key interviews with the Friedman family, Arnold's former students, law enforcement officials, and psychologists, and he also incorporated footage from the trials (the judge allowed cameras in the courtroom during both Friedman trials).

Jarecki's directing skills are most evident in the exhaustive editing and mixing of the cumulative footage. He chops up interviews and plays with chronology in the film, choosing images from various points in time. Individual statements are placed in contradictory combinations: former students with radically different experiences of the basement computer class are cross-edited; interviews with experts are positioned against police accounts. Jarecki reveals information at key moments, actively shaping viewer questions and assumptions. The effect is both provocative and sensational, with disparate chunks of found footage, often seemingly innocent and happy, poised against the harsh realities of the Friedman trial. The film runs up against the challenge of how to trigger discussion about the multiple meanings that circulate in any crime account without reveling in the spectacle of human suffering. How the documentary fares in its efforts is, like the case it chronicles, an open question.

A closer examination of the film's depiction of the ways in which Arnold and Jesse are accused and convicted demonstrates many of labeling's propositions. Events in the Friedman family are triggered when a postal inspector suspects that Arnold is exchanging pornography by mail. During a raid of the family's home, authorities find a stack of magazines featuring nude adolescent males. When local police learn of Arnold Friedman's afternoon computer classes, they begin questioning students enrolled in the courses. Police tell the parents of these students that they suspect their children may have been molested by Arnold and his son Jesse. In the course of police interviews with the children, a horrific and massive list of offenses, including physical violence (slapping, hair pulling, etc.), threats, rape, sodomy, and other sexual acts, materializes. One student describes being taken into a separate room in

Figure 8.1. In *Capturing the Friedmans* (2003), director Andrew Jarecki relies upon a wide array of archival footage to depict the processes by which Arnold and Jesse Friedman are labeled as sexual predators. In this shot, a news media photograph, father and son handcuffed together while escorted by law enforcement. Jesse's supportive embrace of his father captures the complexity of their situation. Photo used by permission of Photofest.

the basement and raped repeatedly. He also tells of a bizarre game of nude leapfrog that occurred during class. Another student portrays the accusations as "grotesque fantasy," remembering his class as being ordinary and boring. A detective describes the class setting as a sexual "free-for-all." Such contradictions in testimonies prove critical. As Debbie Nathan, an expert on child sex abuse who figures prominently in the film, argues, in such cases, there is generally blood, semen, soiled clothes, and disturbed, upset children. However, even though victims testify that the crimes occurred routinely and for months at a time, there is no physical evidence in the case to support the accusations. Following the time line provided by one victim, thirty-one incidents of molestation occurred across a ten-week course. The student then reenrolled, citing forty-one additional offenses. The absence of physical evidence and contradictions in accounts do not check the seemingly fantastic accusations that continue to mount throughout the community. Great

Neck, characterized as an insular community of wealthy professionals, competitive, affluent, and powerful, is polarized. Families who do not claim to have been victimized are told by other community members that they are in denial. Death threats are left on the Friedmans' answering machine. Jesse is attacked by outraged family members at the courthouse the morning of his sentencing.

Experts in the film remind us that the 1980s and 1990s were defined by a wave of moral panics surrounding the sexual abuse of children. Characterized by widespread fear of child abuse and molestation, satanic ritual abuse, and sex rings, the social climate was indisputably ripe for the prosecution and persecution of sex offenders. In *Capturing the Friedmans*, experts discuss how the use of hypnosis and highly leading questions by police during the interviews with children may have created a situation that casts doubt on the accuracy of police findings. We see evidence of this in the film. Retired sex crimes detective Frances Galasso describes "pornography in foot-high stacks" around the Friedman household, but photos reveal this to be false. Detective Anthony Sgeugloi openly describes his efforts to describe to the families and students what happened before questioning, raising the possibility that testimony was intentionally or inadvertently coerced by authorities asking leading questions with no physical evidence. In this way, both police officers and the local community play powerful, questionable roles in the labeling of Arnold and Jesse Friedman as sexual deviants and offenders.

Capturing the Friedmans would be fairly straightforward if possible police misconduct and community hysteria were its main messages; however, the film is far more complex. Jarecki relies upon editorial and narrative techniques to build tension and ambiguity in the film that commentators have both praised and criticized. For instance, the film incorporates odd pieces of information. We learn that David is New York City's most popular professional clown, specializing in children's entertainment. Debates about the sexual incompatibility of Arnold and Elaine are foregrounded and openly discussed by their children and extended relatives. The one student in the film who claims to have been abused is shot in a darkened room, where, dressed in a T-shirt and shorts, he lounges casually on a sofa as he offhandedly recounts being raped, a directing and editorial choice that seems designed to question the legitimacy of his claims. Even the homosexuality of Arnold's brother, Howard, is strangely implicated in Jarecki's documentation of the Friedman family woes. Clearly, none of this information is relevant to the legal issues the Friedmans face; however, the footage heightens the titillation factor in a film that feels voyeuristic from start to finish.

Jarecki also builds suspense and confusion across the film by timing the revelation of information, first establishing, then undermining, the credibility of witnesses and accounts. For instance, after building a case against the police and community, we learn that Arnold's history and sexual orientation are quite complex. Arnold's brother, Howard, recounts a childhood where, after the death of their sister, he and his brother shared their mother's bedroom and witnessed her having sex with multiple partners. Arnold claimed that, out of this early trauma, he had experimented in adolescence with his brother, then boys his own age, resulting in a lifelong attraction to boys; however, his brother Howard denies this. In written correspondence with Debbie Nathan, Arnold voices fears of molesting his own children and admits to pedophilic acts with two boys in the past while on family vacations. Complicating the case further, Jesse's attorney, Peter Panaro, claims that Jesse admitted to being abused by his father, a confession that is difficult to interpret as Jesse argues the admission was constructed solely in order to gain leniency in his case.

While Arnold and Jesse are home under house arrest, the home movies continue, but this time as a record of the family's complex interpretations of events and a memorial to the family's collapse. David relentlessly records family arguments and the debates over the proper course of action in the pending criminal cases. He and his brothers quickly turn against their mother, making harsh claims that she is cold, distant, and "sexually ignorant." Sad attempts to foster a normal family life do not cover an accumulating rage. The sons scream angrily at their mother, Elaine, in defense of their father. She becomes increasingly antagonistic and alienated in the process, lashing back: "I don't believe your father because your father has never been honest with me." Gradually, their fights assume the tenor of cross-examination, and preexisting cracks in deep family structures gape open under the pressure of accusation. Everyone's worth and identity are redefined in the process as the Friedmans are forced to organize their lives around the stigma of sexual deviance. Against his sons' insistence that the police are railroading him, Arnold decides to "take the blame" and pleads guilty to the charges against him. We learn from Arnold's brother, Howard, that in prison Arnold fears for his life as he is pushed down stairs, his eyeglasses are crushed, and urine is thrown at him. Studies of imprisonment have noted that child molesters carry the highest level of stigma in prison and are often the targets of other prisoners. Even while incarcerated, Arnold continues to be labeled and stigmatized. He ultimately commits suicide while incarcerated in what the family describes as an effort to provide Jesse with some financial compensation upon his release from prison.

Facing gross overcharging and looking at a lengthy prison sentence, Jesse becomes the subject of much of the film's conclusion. With positive character statements, the possibility that he is a victim of abuse himself, and no previous record, Jesse appears more vulnerable than his father in many ways. The family and Jesse's attorney agonize over the best possible legal strategy in his case even as the odds turn against him. His father's plea of guilt troubles Jesse's efforts to clear his name. In the end, he is advised by his mother and his attorney to plead guilty in the hopes of receiving a shorter sentence, regardless of his guilt or innocence. Even here, the facts are confusing. Jesse is shown in court giving a seemingly heartfelt, tear-filled confession where he admits guilt and apologizes for all the pain he has caused. Yet on the morning of his sentencing, he calmly asserts his innocence in a car ride with his brothers to court. A brief time later, just before being sent to prison, he engages in a loud, boisterous portrayal of a comedy skit on the steps of the courthouse, drawing the attention and criticism of observers who view his behavior as grossly inappropriate. In a harsher ruling than anyone expects, Jesse is sentenced to six to eighteen years in prison, with the judge recommending full sentence. He is shown at the conclusion of the film a middle-aged man who has lost his youth to prison. At this point, now a registered sex offender, he anticipates a difficult transition into the free world.

Capturing the Friedmans leaves us with far more questions than it resolves. How is the viewer left to feel about the imprisonment and ultimate suicide of Arnold Friedman, a convicted pedophile and dearly loved father? What is to be made of the imprisonment of his son Jesse—is this justice or its miscarriage? Why had Arnold's pedophilia not surfaced previously? Suppressed memories of abuse? Willed amnesia? And what do his confessions of sexual abuse and arousal mean exactly? Did the community of Great Neck, Long Island, engage in a form of moral panic, making the Friedmans victims of a modern-day witch hunt? Why had the families' and children's accusations not emerged earlier across the weeks, months, and years in which Arnold conducted a class that students happily attended? What is to be done with all the contradictions in memories and facts surrounding the case? What are the costs of the justice system's reliance upon eyewitness testimony alone? What are the effects upon the Friedmans when Arnold and Jesse waive their due process rights and rely upon plea bargaining, the most powerful mechanism of case processing in the criminal justice system? Fascinatingly, a wealth of visual materials, collected meticulously, obsessively across time and during the course of the trial, provides us with no clear answers.

One of the true feats of *Capturing the Friedmans* is its ability to leave us not simply with questions but, consistent with labeling theory, also a complicated and nuanced form of compassion for those caught up in the criminal justice system. The film tackles sexuality, one of the classic domains of deviance studies and a difficult arena in which to create understanding. In that pursuit, it seems fair to assume, based upon his own statements, that Arnold Friedman engaged in questionable sex acts with children in his lifetime, possibly even with his own children; however, this reality does not necessarily mean he also committed multiple and lurid acts of sex abuse in his basement. Nor does it preclude him from the complicated adoration of his sons. Whatever the reality, Arnold is, aside from a pedophile, also a beloved father, well-intentioned husband, and highly respected teacher. Similarly, Jesse's acts, whatever they may have been, do not restrict him from being a caring son and brother who is also still a teenager. In the film, we see the disintegration of these positive identities, all of which are supplanted by the label of sexual predator. As ties with social institutions weaken and the family is further stigmatized, we observe Arnold assume blame and responsibility for his acts while Jesse gives contradictory performances of guilt and innocence. From a labeling perspective, such inconsistencies might be read as attempts by Arnold and Jesse to make meaningful and strategic use of the labels they can no longer escape. We see the effects of labeling not in the escalation of criminal acts (which we cannot assess from the point of view of the film) but rather in the isolation of institutionalization, the demise of the family, Arnold's suicide, and Jesse's permanent status as sex offender.

The contemporary perspectives built upon labeling theory encourage us to ask other questions of *Capturing the Friedmans*. For instance, what if the community and authorities had pursued Braithwaite's reintegrative shaming as opposed to the dominant disintegrative model? What might a move away from stigmatization and exclusion look like? How might a restorative justice model have shifted the roles of victims, perpetrators, and the community? Given the emphasis by these perspectives upon both accountability and community reintegration, we might imagine a far more meaningful and positive outcome for everyone involved in the case, especially the Friedmans.

In documentaries such as *Aileen Wuornos: The Selling of a Serial Killer* (1992), *Aileen: The Life and Death of a Serial Killer* (2004), and *Paradise Lost: The Child Murders at Robin Hood Hills* (1996), we see similar processes at work in real-life cases. As with *Capturing the Friedmans*, these films depict radically different crime realities, constructed through opposing accounts. Even as the films expose the uncertainties and fallibility of justice, individuals are subjected to the worst labels and given the harshest, most irrevocable of punishments, death sentences. Nick Broomfield's two-part documentary series on Aileen Wuornos, the woman heralded as America's "first female serial killer," focuses on the nefarious, greedy motives of her adoptive mother, self-serving lawyer, and corrupt law enforcement who all profited from Aileen's tragic life and death. *Paradise Lost* chronicles a horrific triple child murder in Arkansas where three nonconformist teenagers were tried and convicted of the crimes with no physical evidence. Instead, the convictions were based primarily upon a possibly coerced confession by one of the teens, Jesse Misskelly, and the deviant reputation of another, Damien Echols, who was known for dressing in black, listening to heavy metal music, and reading books on Wicca.

Conclusion

Because labeling theories are ultimately concerned with the meanings of crime, open-ended documentaries in which the realities of crime are intensely debated make both excellent and cautionary cases. With the newest wave of independent documentaries marked by a relative freedom from corporate control over content, they are often strikingly partisan, moving away from conventional claims to neutrality and objectivity. Rather, they construct arguments, aim to inform, persuade and even incite. For many commentators, this development has raised new questions and debates about the legitimacy and dangers of contemporary documentary, including its ability to manipulate viewers. From a social constructionist and labeling perspective, the turn toward the subjective is welcome in its efforts to reveal the uncertainties and open-ended nature of justice. No series of images or assertions is able to display the raw and perfect real. Images beget more images. Meanings multiply and compete. In the process, public expectations of crime, criminals, and film are altered.

In the years since the DNA revolution, criminologists have been forced to confront the fact that the single greatest cause in wrongful conviction is faulty eyewitness testimony. In traumatic instances of high emotion, memory proves tricky and unstable, scientists have found. Films like *Capturing the Friedmans* encourage us to treat complications in memory, even errors, not as anomalies or nuisances to be explained away or minimized but as revelatory of the very real processes of interpretation at play in the world around us. Here, memory is alterable, disorganized, fragmented, and repetitive, especially in cases that involve uncomfortable accusations and taboo behaviors, like sexuality. Labeling theorists have encouraged us to consider a negotiated space for reconciling polarized and plural claims and their role in the construction of crime and deviance. Against the compulsion to collect, record, and authenticate actuality, we are encouraged to think of reality as a generative space where all sorts of meanings circulate. The question of how certain meanings become dominant and the impact of those "truths" or labels upon the lives of others remains a critical problem for criminology. No longer are we in a simple world of binary true/false, either/or accounts, if ever we were.

FURTHER VIEWING

Accused, The (1988)
American History X (1998)
Chicago (2002)
Let Him Have It (1991)
One Flew Over the Cuckoo's Nest (1975)
Lives of Others, The (2006)
Titicut Follies (1967)
12 Angry Men (1957)
Woodsman, The (2004)
X-Men series (2000, 2003, 2006, 2009)

9

Fight the Power

Conflict Theories and Do the Right Thing

Violence is immoral because it thrives on hatred rather than love. It destroys community and makes brotherhood impossible. It leaves society in monologue rather than dialogue. Violence ends up defeating itself. It creates bitterness in the survivors and brutality in the destroyers.

—Martin Luther King

I am not against using violence in self-defense. I don't even call it violence when it's self-defense, I call it intelligence.

—Malcolm X

Criminologists have long confronted the fact that those who get caught up in the criminal justice system are disproportionately drawn from the lower social classes. Some have examined biological, psychological, and social factors that may help explain this disparity, while others—conflict theorists—go further, questioning the very processes through which crime and criminality are constructed in a class-based society, one where elites define crimes in the first place. Conflict theorists look to social imbalances in power to explain the disproportionate representation of poor and marginal people in the criminal justice system. Conflict theory is rooted in Marxism, but the nineteenth-century political philosopher Karl Marx himself actually said little about crime and criminality. Thus conflict theorists have extracted principles from Marxism and applied them to crime.

To illuminate these principles, we turn to a film that at first glance may not seem to be about crime at all: director Spike Lee's *Do the Right Thing* (1989). This was one of the first films to deal with the complex tensions that informed race politics in the late twentieth century. Lee's depiction of characters who are neither good nor evil but complicated and flawed was groundbreaking, and today the film is considered a cultural touchstone, a movie against which to compare more recent efforts (such as the 2004 movie *Crash*) that deal with the politics of race. Lee frankly addressed the dilemmas of a multiethnic and multirace community trapped by both capitalism and its own failures, posing the solutions in terms of nonviolence or its alternative, revolution. So what can *Do the Right Thing* tell us about the causes of crime and about conflict theory?

Do the Right Thing

> 1989 the number another summer. . . .
> We got to fight the powers that be
> Lemme hear you say
> Fight the power.
>> —The hip-hop group Public Enemy on the
>> soundtrack of *Do the Right Thing*

Do the Right Thing begins with a dancer (Rosie Perez), now in a bodysuit, now in boxing clothes, thrusting and punching against a backdrop of Brooklyn brownstone stoops, her motions choreographed to Public Enemy's rap anthem "Fight the Power." The song, one of the film's central motifs, continuously reminds viewers of *Do the Right Thing*'s political engagement. As the film opens, we hear an alarm clock while a local radio DJ, Mister Señor Love Daddy (Samuel Jackson), tells his morning listeners to "Wake up!" He begins his daily report by describing how hot it is, with temperatures expected to reach above 100 degrees. In fact, it is going to be the hottest day of the year. And the color of the day, Love Daddy says, is black. Through these few quick reference points, Lee sets the stage symbolically for a revolutionary day, one in which neighborhood tensions will grow heated, escalate, and end violently.

Next, we are introduced to Smiley (Roger Guenveur Smith), a character who is mentally and physically disabled. Smiley roams the neighborhood, stuttering in his attempts to sell copies of an image of Martin Luther King and Malcolm X, together and smiling. The photo captures a moment of good-natured exchange between men known for their ideological opposition. Smiley informs us that although both are dead, they still call out to us to fight against hatred. Here the film introduces its key question: whether violent or nonviolent means are best in the struggle against oppression and for political empowerment. Next we meet the main character, Mookie (Spike

Lee), who is sitting on a bed counting his weekly pay—an introduction to another key theme, that of capitalism and the poverty of black people. Playful and charming, Mookie teases his sister, Jade (Joie Lee), who is trying to sleep and, annoyed, tells him to "go to work." Mookie replies with "gotta get paid" and heads to his delivery job at Sal's Famous Pizzeria, the neighborhood's main food establishment.

At the pizzeria, we see Sal (Danny Aiello), the owner, and his two sons, Pino (John Turturro) and Vito (Richard Edson), arrive at work. Because the storefront sidewalk is littered with garbage, Sal instructs Pino to sweep it up; Pino then delegates the work to his younger brother, Vito. Bickering ensues. Pino, who dislikes blacks, tells his father, "I hate this place." Sal, immediately defensive, asks, "Do you think you can do better? . . . Have some respect." Watching his sons argue, he predicts, "I'm gonna kill somebody today." Mookie arrives and immediately Pino comments on his lateness. When asked to do the sweeping, Mookie replies, "I deliver pizzas." Pino responds, "You get paid to do what we say." Another of the film's many tensions is introduced as Pino attempts to exploit Mookie's employee status while Mookie resists Pino's attempts to downgrade his labor. Another character, the neighborhood drunk, known as Da Mayor (Ossie Davis), arrives, disheveled and in search of money for beer. Ultimately, Sal hires him to do the sweeping, thereby demonstrating a compassionate understanding for Da Mayor's predicament while Pino disgustedly compares his father's generosity to "welfare." Next we meet Radio Raheem (Bill Nunn), who is larger than life and literally "walks in stereo," carrying a massive boom box through the neighborhood, blasting Public Enemy's "Fight the Power." A quiet giant of a man, his commanding presence elicits respect, awe, and fear from the community. Camera work includes sweeping shots of Raheem's body and extreme closeups of his boom box.

Buggin' Out (Giancarlo Esposito), the local activist-intellectual, arrives at Sal's to purchase a slice of pizza, a bit of food that quickly becomes a site of contest. Buggin demands more cheese; Sal insists he pay for it. Buggin' accuses Sal of skimping and being cheap. Grudgingly sitting down with his slice and looking around, he becomes furious with the pictures on Sal's Wall of Fame, all of which depict Italian American celebrities. He asks Sal why there are "no brothers on the wall?" Sal responds with, "Get your own place. This is my pizzeria." Buggin' replies, "But you own this and Italian Americans don't eat here"—nearly all of Sal's customers are black. Sal looks to Mookie, his black employee, to usher Buggin' out of the establishment, while Buggin' yells, "Boycott Sal's!" Later, when Mookie tells Sal that "people are free

Figure 9.1. It's the hottest day of the year, and race relations escalate across the Bedford-Stuyvesant neighborhood of Brooklyn. As members of the community go about their day, the structural roots of violence become clear, including the relationship between criminal justice and the inequality of the underlying economic order. In this early scene from *Do the Right Thing* (1989), the stark division between black neighborhood residents and white police officers foreshadows the violence to come. Photo used by permission of Photofest.

to do whatever the hell" they want, Sal answers with "Free? There's no free here. I'm the boss." Thus early in the film, the workplace becomes a location for struggle over ownership, control, and identity. Mookie, caught in contradictions, leaves to make another delivery. Along the way, he encounters Da Mayor, sitting on a stoop. Da Mayor calls him over and instructs him mysteriously, "Always do the right thing."

Tensions escalate as the day grows hotter. The playful use by neighborhood residents of a fire hydrant to cool off ends with the police arriving. A group of Puerto Rican men engage in a standoff with Radio Raheem as he passes their stoop. Buggin' Out angrily derides a white man in a Celtics jersey who accidentally runs into him, scuffing his new Air Jordan sneakers: "Why you want to live in a black neighborhood? Fuck gentrification." A group of older, unemployed black men sit on the corner discussing the neighborhood; passing white police officers call them "waste." The older men direct their frustration at the local Korean grocers, commenting that they probably had not "been off the boat for one year" before opening a business in the neighborhood. "Either those Koreans are geniuses or you black assess are dumb," one of these street corner philosophers comments. "I will be one happy fool when we open up a business in our neighborhood." Again, issues of labor, employment, ownership, and identity rise to the surface. Intergenerational conflict, too, breaks out as local youths accost Da Mayor. When he invokes his past, telling them that they have no idea what it is like to have "five hungry children crying for bread and you can't do a damn thing about it," one of the youths responds callously, "I don't want to know your pain. You did it yourself." Thus the community turns inward on itself, internalizing responsibility for the social constraints in which it is caught. We also see how neighborhood tensions affect family life, including Mookie's relationship with his son's mother, Tina (Rosie Perez), who is frustrated by Mookie's casual attitude toward work, child support, and their relationship.

Midway through the film, racial tensions overflow in a wave of racial slurs and vitriolic stereotyping. Pino urges African Americans to "Take your fucking pizza and go back to Africa." An Italian police officer sneers at Puerto Rican Americans: "Fifty in a car goya bean eatin'." The Korean grocer stereotypes Jewish Americans: "Bagel eating cream deluxe." African Americans stereotype Italians, and on and on. Love Daddy calls a "time-out" across the airwaves, and Radio Raheem tells us the story of the struggle of "love" and "hate," words emblazoned on a gold band across his knuckles. We next see Radio at Sal's buying two slices of pizza, his boom box blasting. Sal yells, " No service 'til you turn it off. You are disturbing me. You are disturbing my customers. No music." Radio grudgingly acquiesces and, like Buggin', demands more cheese while Sal again asserts that extra cheese costs more. The struggle for autonomy, expression, and rights continues.

As the unbearably hot day turns into an overheated evening, Pino and Sal engage in another lengthy discussion in which Pino, alienated and angry, argues that they should move the pizzeria out of the neighborhood. Sal responds that there are already too many pizzerias in Italian neighborhoods and discloses a real fondness for his local customers: "I've had no trouble with these people. They grew up on my food and I'm proud of that. Sal's Pizzeria is here to stay." When Smiley shows up at the window with his Martin and Malcolm placards, a simmering Pino moves out onto the street, shoving Smiley away.

Tensions and ironies continue to mount. Sal and Jade flirt with one another, to the dismay of Mookie and Pino. Radio Raheem has a stressful encounter with the Korean grocers. A young boy is nearly hit by a speeding car but rescued by Da Mayor. As the day concludes and the pizzeria is closing, Sal makes a big announcement: It has been a great day. (His sons and Mookie look on in cynical disbelief.) He is changing the name of the pizzeria to Sal and Sons. There will always be a place for Mookie as well, for he is like a son. When several local youths show up at the door, Sal good-naturedly agrees to let them in, even though it is past closing time. They are followed by Radio Raheem, Smiley, and Buggin' Out, who continues his call for a boy-cott. The situation rapidly escalates, and Sal, grabbing a baseball bat, destroys Raheem's boom box. Enraged, Raheem pulls Sal across the counter, and they begin fighting, drawing the attention of the entire neighborhood and, even-tually, the police. Attempting to restrain Raheem, one police officer places him in a chokehold with his baton, lifting him off the ground and eventually strangling him to death as the community looks on, horrified. The police leave quickly with Raheem's body. Smiley breaks down, crying. In disbelief, people say, "They killed him." One of the old heads mutters, "They didn't have to kill the boy," but Sal responds, "You do what you have to do."

At this point the neighborhood turns its anger toward Sal and his sons. Da Mayor pleads with everyone to go home, pointing out that Sal had noth-ing to do with the police brutality. Someone cries out, "He died because he had a fucking radio." In the climactic and most enigmatic moment of the film, Mookie walks over to a stoop, takes a garbage can, carries it to the front of Sal's establishment, and throws it through the window, initiating the total destruction of Sal's property. Da Mayor yells "No," as does Mother Sis-ter (Ruby Dee), the community matriarch. Sal beseeches them: "That's my place—that's my fucking place." Pino mutters, "Fucking niggers." And the scene erupts. Smiley sets fire to the pizzeria, engulfing the Wall of Fame in flames. The fire department and police arrive, with the neighborhood on one side and authorities on the other. As a police officer yells through a mega-phone, "Please disperse—one more warning: Please go home," Mookie yells back, "This *is* our home!" The imagery—fire hoses turned on the protesters, blacks being arrested—echoes the civil rights imagery of the 1960s. (In fact, one man yells "fucking Birmingham," invoking one of the most famous of all civil rights clashes.)

As the violence subsides and night settles in, Mookie and Jade sit emo-tionless on the curb. "Fight the Power" plays on the soundtrack. For better or worse, the community (or parts of it) have "fought the power." Smiley places the picture of Martin and Malcolm on Sal's charred Wall of Fame.

In the final scene, morning arrives. The street is covered with stray shoes, pizza boxes, and pizzeria cups. Love Daddy calls out again for everyone to wake up, asking, "Are we going to live together or are we going to live?"

Mookie leaves Tina and his son at home to demand his pay from Sal, who responds, "I don't believe this shit." "Believe it," Mookie says, and Sal pays him. When Sal asks Mookie what he is going to do now, he replies, "Go make that money. Get paid." They seem to have a faint but mutual respect for one another. In the background, life returns to the neighborhood, and we hear over the radio that a blue-ribbon panel has been established to investigate the disturbance: "The city of New York will not let property be destroyed." This is followed by a call to "register to vote." The film ends with the two quotations, one from King and the other from Malcolm X, that head this chapter.

After two decades of film and political commentary,[1] audiences still wonder: Did Mookie do the right thing? What were his motives? Did he throw the trash can through the window to deflect violence onto property and away from Sal and his sons? Did he do it out of a sense of futility and because he lacked a meaningful alternative? Or was he a revolutionary, protesting inequalities in race and class? Debates about Mookie's behavior center on the Martin-Malcolm polarity: Is violence immoral, or is it intelligent action? Some commentators ask whether it is possible to make the right choice or even figure out what the right thing might be in late modernity; in their view, Lee has created a classic hard case, one with no clear answers and inevitably tragic outcomes. The film poses other issues as well. What is to be made of its cautious—perhaps improbable—reconciliation between Mookie and Sal after the fiery climax? Why does Mookie demand to be paid? Why does Sal pay him? Conflict criminology frames the answers to such questions in terms of the way capitalist society values white property over a black life.

Do the Right Thing was not the first film to take a black perspective on social issues. It was preceded in the 1970s by a series of "blaxploitation" films, including *Sweet Sweetback's Baadasssss Song* (1971), *Shaft* (1971), and *Superfly* (1972), and like them, *Do the Right Thing* is grounded in the grittiness of black daily experience with shades of resistance. However, unlike its predecessors, Lee's film depicts real issues and more conflicts than it can resolve. He chooses messy realism over moral tidiness or plot resolution. Property and its unequal distribution lie at the heart of *Do the Right Thing*. Sal and Radio Raheem both live for what they own, although what they own is radically different. And in the film's final moments, Mookie clearly associates pay for a fair day's work with masculine self-worth. Still, we are left with the sense that he neither denies nor fully embraces either of the ideological extremes of nonviolence or revolutionary violence, rather choosing to work on the edges, in the "double truth, Ruth." The film's conclusion only tentatively reaffirms capitalism, and it does so, as it were, over Raheem's dead body.

The Principles of Conflict Theory

For conflict theorists, the criminal justice system reflects at a fundamental level the capitalist system of ownership and production. The foundations of this system are rarely challenged because they appear to be natural and rational—the only "right" way in which to govern ourselves and the economy. The criminal law seems to be fair. (As the French communist and author Anatole France famously observed, "The law, in its majestic equality, forbids the rich as well as the poor to sleep under bridges, to beg in the streets, and to steal bread.")[2] However, conflict theorists insist that such a system allows only a small number of individuals to control property and resources, out of which two classes emerge: the proletariat (or working class) and the bourgeoisie (or ruling class). (*Do the Right Thing* suggests that although Sal is an owner, he and Mookie actually have a great deal in common in their disempowerment; the real solution would be for them to form an alliance against the system that keeps them marginal and at odds.) Such a system is fundamentally biased toward those in power.

The power of capitalism, ideologically, as conflict theorist Jeffrey Reiman writes in his well-known book *The Rich Get Richer and the Poor Get Prison*, is its ability to appear "as a system of free exchanges between people with equal rights (over unequal amounts of property)."[3] For Karl Marx, the ideological dimensions of revolution were bound up with the ability of people to become conscious of the exploitation underpinning capitalism and, in his words, "fight it out."[4] With his colleague Friedrich Engels, Marx put forth a series of propositions: (1) conflicts of interest will be increased by inequality in the distribution of resources; (2) this inequality will eventually be recognized by those receiving less, who will then challenge the legitimacy of existing relationships; (3) these groups will start to organize and bring conflict into the open, where it will culminate in revolutionary violence that will lead to a more equitable redistribution of resources.

Marx wrote in response to the massive changes brought on by the Industrial Revolution, including its violent restructuring of the social relations of production and the ways in which the positioning of individuals in the economic sphere, as owners and workers, shaped social interactions and life possibilities. Under capitalism, he argued, society would polarize into two groups, one growing smaller while getting richer, the other growing larger while getting poorer. Marx labeled this polarization the "contradiction" of capitalism. At a point of extreme polarization, Marx argued, a revolutionary restructuring of society would become inevitable. Although Marx paid little attention to crime, he did address crime-related issues such as the concepts of demoralization and alienation. According to Marx, everyone wants to be productive through work, but industrialized capitalist societies always generate unemployment, and underemployed people, in their discontent, become susceptible to crime and vice. In *Do the Right Thing*, we see community members struggling with demoralization through unemployment or underemployment, although this type of demoralization does not affect the owners, Sal and the Korean grocers.

For conflict theorists, law reflects the values and interests of the groups in power.[5] Consequently, in a capitalist society law will undergird capitalism, both functionally and ideologically. The material reality of the law manifests itself in police, courts, and prisons as well as guns, legislation, and other types of state force, all of which are intended for the protection of property. But these institutions and practices, like capitalism itself, are perceived not as coercive but rather as natural and justified. Social inequality seems to be due simply to differences in what individuals own. The power of elites recedes from view, becoming invisible as everyone assumes the right of the individual to own property and do as they will with it—a philosophy that Sal enunciates about his ownership of the pizzeria throughout the film. The problem with this perspective is that while some people own corporations, others own small pizzerias or radios or nothing at all, resulting in fundamentally mismatched exchanges. Thus capitalism is an exploitive system based on the unjust distribution of wealth, specifically the exclusive ownership by a few of the means of production. Ultimately, capitalism pits class against class and worker against worker, just as we see in *Do the Right Thing*. Crime, criminality, and violence flow from these antagonisms, but ultimately crime is produced by the capitalist system itself. Ironically, the criminal justice system, which is supposed to treat everyone equally and to protect the interests of all, contributes to alienation, degradation, and inequality. It kills Raheem.

Whether social transformation is possible through revolution is a question that haunts *Do the Right Thing*, where at the end it seems that nothing has actually changed. The film's conclusion may reflect Spike Lee's own ambivalence—his own inability to choose between Martin and Malcolm. Or it may reflect a more sophisticated view that revolution—true improvement in the conditions of African Americans—can occur only when they, like Mookie, recognize ways in which their interests coincide with barely less marginalized owners such as Sal.

The Evolution of Conflict Theory

Before we investigate the evolution of conflict theory, a word on language and theory subfields. Criminologists often use *conflict theory* interchangeably with other terms, including *Marxist criminology* and *critical criminology*. In this chapter, we deal with conflict theory as a derivative of Marxist theory, treating it as a broader perspective centered upon the work and principles of Marx. Critical criminology is an umbrella term that includes both conflict and Marxist criminology, as well as other perspectives, including radical, left realist, and feminist accounts of crime. This progression is evident in the evolution of conflict theory, which began early on as a Marxist perspective. Dutch scholar Willem Bonger, in *Criminality and Economic Conditions* (1916), developed one of the first Marxist accounts of crime; it continues to serve as a foundation for conflict theorists. Bonger argued that a capitalist system encourages individuals to value material accumulation and individual success. Capitalist societies breed greed and selfishness, encouraging people to pursue their own interests without regard for others. Pitting people against each other, capitalist societies produce the economic struggles, egoism, and self-interest that encourage crime.

This hyperindividualism is, of course, a real problem in *Do the Right Thing*, where few characters other than Da Mayor and Mother Sister value the community above their own needs. When Da Mayor instructs Mookie to "do the right thing," there is a clear implication that doing right is doing good for the community—which Mookie may be doing when he tosses the garbage can through Sal's window. In Bonger's view, both the decline of social solidarity and the rise of a dangerous individualism derive from capitalism itself. He argued that only a truly socialist society would eliminate crime, for it would promote concern for the welfare of others and eradicate biases in favor of the rich and propertied.

After Bonger, from the 1920s to the 1970s, criminologists paid little attention to Marxist explanations. It was not until the social upheavals of the 1960s, with their rebellions against the status quo and inequality, that Marxist-inspired theory moved to the very center of criminological analysis. The perspectives developed by conflict theorists reflected a new attention to the sociology of law and power as well as to social context.[6]

In 1969, criminologist Austin Turk developed a general conflict theory of crime built upon a series of key questions and propositions.[7] Turk asked, under what conditions are differences between authorities and citizens transformed into legal conflicts, and under what conditions are those who violate laws or norms criminalized? His response to these questions led him to enunciate several key principles. First, Turk argued that cultural and behavioral differences between authorities and subjects would lead to conflict (such as the Italian American/African American divide in *Do the Right Thing*). In fact, the law is more likely to be enforced at key sites of difference. The more powerless the resisters and norm violators, the higher the probability that they will become targets of enforcement. Nowhere is this more evident than in Radio Raheem's death. Turk pictures crime and deviance in a modern, complex, and heterogeneous society as an ongoing struggle. Equality is difficult, if not impossible, to achieve, as *Do the Right Thing* suggests. The behavior of any group and, perhaps most important, the cultural meaning and significance attached to that behavior are destined to provoke a negative reaction from another group. In particular, authority groups will continuously strive to maintain and expand their control over social resources by defining the activity of "subject groups" as threatening (deviant and/or criminal) to the existing order. (Implicit here is the idea that the existing order is *the* order, the only legitimate order.) Historically these subject groups were called the "dangerous classes"; in Turk's day, they were called the "permanent underclass." For Turk, criminality is not a label but a "status" assigned by those in power.

Sociologist William Chambliss pursued a similar line of thought simultaneously. His volume *Crime and the Legal Process* (1969), published the same year as Turk's *Criminality and Legal Order*, was followed in 1971 by *Law, Order, and Power*;[8] in both books, Chambliss argued that the more complex the society, the more law and the interests of the powerful become prevalent as a sanctioning mechanism. Chambliss and his coauthor legal scholar Robert Seidman laid out five propositions: (1) the conditions of one's life affect one's values and norms; (2) complex societies are composed of groups living under widely different life conditions; (3) complex societies, therefore, are characterized by highly disparate and conflicting sets of norms; (4) the probability that a given group will have its particular normative system embodied in law is not equal but rather closely related to the group's political and economic position; and (5) the higher a group's political or economic position, the greater the probability that its views will be reflected in law. This they termed a *theory of law in action*. Instead of contributing to social solidarity, law in action tends to fragment communities by negatively labeling and excluding its more powerless members. The law in practice creates a vicious circle, reinforcing the social conflicts out of which law grows in the first place. Chambliss subsequently refined his position, pointing out that crime diverts the lower class's attention from exploitation, directing it instead toward members of its own group rather than the political economy—a phenomenon depicted in *Do the Right Thing*.

In the early 1970s, the best-known conflict criminologist was Richard Quinney, who published influential books such as *The Problem of Crime* and *The Social Reality of Crime*. According to Quinney,

> The actions of the criminally defined are not so much the result of inadequate socialization and personality problems as they are conscientious actions taken against something . . . , the only appropriate means for expressing certain thoughts and feelings—and the only possibilities for bringing about social changes.[9]

The violence that spins out of control in *Do the Right Thing* illustrates Quinney's point; it seems to be the community's only way to express its frustration. Over time, Quinney's thought became more radical. He critiqued mainstream and critical crime theories for accepting the existing economic and social order; he pointed out ways in which a capitalist system generates a surplus population of unemployed laborers, some of whom adapt to their situation through crime; and he noted the sense of alienation, including a loss of feeling and hope about the future, that pervades contemporary capitalist contexts.

However, unlike other Marxist thinkers who called for revolution, Quinney moved toward "peacemaking criminology." He and his collaborator, Hal Pepinsky of Indiana University, argued that conflict can be resolved best by building social bonds, trust, and a sense of community. Implicit in the peacemaking perspective is the idea that marginalized or oppressed peoples cannot better their condition simply by overpowering their oppressors. In its effort to reduce harm by forging better relationships among victims, offenders, and communities, peacemaking criminology echoes the nonviolent stance advocated by Martin Luther King. In recent years it has been reinforced by the restorative justice movement, which seeks to heal the wounds of crime through meetings of offenders with their victims and to reintegrate offenders, through moral restoration, with their communities.[10]

After the 1980s conflict theory broke up into several different perspectives. So-called radical criminologists retained the earlier focus on the political economy of crime even as they expanded conflict theory to study variations in the causes and effects of crime by race, gender, culture, and historical period.[11] Marxist feminists argued that, in accordance with patriarchy (the domination of women by men), men control the division of labor in capitalist societies. Female criminality, in their view, is often defined in terms of acts that threaten both the capitalist and the patriarchal underpinnings of society. That over time women have been punished predominantly for extramarital sexual activity relates to the fact that these acts threaten men's control over women's bodies as property. Left realism, a third variation on conflict criminology, criticized conflict theory's traditional inattention to the harmful effects of street crime on the disempowered. The more vulnerable people are economically and socially, left realists argued, the more likely they are to be caught up in crime as victims or perpetrators. Strong concern for victims led left realists to stress the problem of violence against women and the experience of victimization in daily life.[12] Their work nonetheless continues to draw on Marxist theory, especially the idea that social and economic conditions such as high unemployment affect definitions of criminality.

By now, we can begin to anticipate some of the criticisms that conflict theorists might face.[13] First, many mainstream criminologists who subscribe to the idea of rational choice theories clearly do not foreground social and economic conditions but instead emphasize human nature itself. They argue that Marxist criminology does not take into account the possibility of free will and individual autonomy. A classic critique is one that argues the theory overestimates the explanatory power of economic factors in the direct causation of crime and punishment, although recent work has carefully disputed this claim.[14] Others point to conflict criminology's privileging of class over gender and race—although most critical criminologists would concede that conflict must be analyzed in terms of other factors in addition to class, particularly race. As we see in *Do the Right Thing*, conflict falls along many axis points. In this case, race is the most critical. Some insist that conflict theory is too deterministic— a totalizing narrative that omits subjective and "real" experiences of crime and capitalism and romanticizes criminals as an oppressed or revolutionary class. Finally, some scholars are critical of conflict theory's definition of crime as primarily a matter of power—whatever the state and criminal justice system define as criminal. *Do the Right Thing* supports conflict theorists in this definition, however: the film's conflict and violence hardly appear as criminal but rather as actions borne out of social structure and interpersonal disputes. Yet, the film ends with a person's death by criminal justice and state intervention. In such contexts, Marxist perspectives should not be confused with the idea that deprivation itself (an inability to buy things, for instance) leads to crime; rather, they hold that when poverty is experienced as unjust or unfair, it leads to discontent. Without recognition of this discontent and consequent efforts to change the status quo, crime and violence emerge.

Conclusion

Conflict theory, by asking us to consider crime in relation to the way societies organize their economic and political institutions, raises a different set of questions than those posed by mainstream criminology. It reminds us that everyday experience and face-to-face interactions are shaped by larger social structures. Because social structures constrain the behaviors of individuals, there are limits to the kind of change that is possible to induce in individuals without altering social structure itself. In terms of crime, this means that individuals have only limited responsibility for their actions and cannot be "rehabilitated" if the social structures in which they live are not rehabilitated at the same time. *Do the Right Thing* depicts the complex interactions of individuals and social structures during a single day in a single neighborhood.

Conflict criminology was conceived of as a criminology of resistance in which actors would challenge the status quo, pursue structural transformation in ways that empowered the less powerful, and become actively involved in movements representing oppressed social groups (workers, the poor, prisoners, African Americans, women, gays and lesbians, etc.). At the heart of this theoretical perspective, then, was a notion of action, a form of praxis—engaged action in which actors seek to transform social structure. Conflict criminologists gave up the idea of criminology as a value-free enterprise, openly acknowledging their own political positions and alliance with the disadvantaged. They protested police brutality, excessive bail, prison conditions, and the death penalty. Many advocated more informal dispute settlement processes outside of the criminal justice system and state control.

At a time when accusations of socialism from the conservative Right are pervasive in American public discourse, conflict theory reminds us of a marked historical moment in criminology when theorists embraced unabashedly utopian commitments, believing one could improve the human condition through social change. The deepening economic crises of the twenty-first century demand greater attention to inequality and poverty, making Marxist accounts in crime theory ever more relevant. As globalization rewrites the class structure of the planet and the very meanings of citizenship, inequality, violence, and resistance will intensify, and conflict criminologists will continue to interrogate how we do the right thing.

Battle in Seattle (2007)
Bicycle Thief, The (1948)
Capitalism: A Love Story (2009)
Civil Action, A (1998)
Erin Brockovich (2000)
Matewan (1987)
Michael Clayton (2007)
Modern Times (1936)
Monsieur Verdoux (1947)
Sympathy for Mr. Vengeance (2002)
Trainspotting (1996)
25th Hour (2002)

10

"Let Her Go"

Feminist Criminology and Thelma & Louise

The open road. Blue skies. The great American West. Traditionally these have been settings for cowboy movies about men's adventures, masculinity, and male bonding. So how do two women wind up in this landscape, on the lam with state and federal law enforcement in close pursuit, speeding through conventionally masculine terrain in an attempt to reach Mexico? In a word, violence. Specifically, violence against women. *Thelma & Louise* (1991) stands out as one of film history's first, most celebrated, and most controversial visions of women on a crime spree. In some respects their story parallels the way in which feminist criminologists forged ahead into mainstream criminology, a criminology, they will tell you, created largely by and for men.

Feminist Criminology

For feminist criminologists, there are no grand theories to explain crime; rather, there are multiple forms of experiences with crime that derive from the ordinary lives of women. Feminist perspectives in criminology are consequently very much concerned with ways of knowing and respectful of the multiplicity of perspectives that gendered experience offers. The way criminological questions are framed and research results interpreted are issues to which feminists give careful attention, for criminological knowledge itself has a masculine bent that to most seems simply universal or natural.

Feminist criminology focuses on ways in which crime and its social contexts are structured by sex (meaning biological characteristics) and gender (meaning the characteristics attributed to men and women). Feminist criminologists analyze both female and male criminality, since gender affects both. Similarly, feminist criminologists study the impact of gender on the treatment of women and men within the criminal justice system, whether they be offenders or workers. It has become clear that gender even shapes the nature of criminal justice institutions.[1]

Another aspect of the feminist agenda is to analyze ways in which gender and crime intersect with race. Black females, white females, black males, and white males, because they are all differently located in social structure, have radically different experiences with crime and criminal justice. Ethnicity, age, social class, and even geographical region affect the crime and punishment of men and women. Yet another central concern of feminist criminology is violence against women—rape, sex crimes, and intimate partner abuse—and it also studies traditional theories of crime, not only to uncover the male-centered biases that have shaped them but to understand the gendered nature of criminological knowledge more generally.

Kathleen Daly, an important theorist in feminist criminology, speaks of four major areas of inquiry within contemporary feminist scholarship.[2] First comes the nature of gender in relationship to crime, including the factors that can explain male-female differences in rates of lawbreaking and arrests (the famous "gender gap," in which over time and in all countries, females have had much lower rates of offending). Second, Daly mentions differences in the pathways that lead girls and women on the one hand, boys and men on the other, to lawbreaking. A third major focal point of feminist research has been gender differences in the social organization of offenses—how different kinds of illegal acts are defined and ranked in seriousness in relation to gender. A fourth major area concerns the role of gender in broader areas of life, including the effects of criminality on ways in which men and women take care of themselves and find food and shelter.

Daly's work does not stop here. She and another well-known feminist theorist, Meda Chesney-Lind, have written about ways in which their field differs from conventional criminological inquiry.[3] Their points are widely cited and particularly useful in that they define the key concept of gender upon which feminist criminology is built. They define gender not as a natural fact but as a complex social construction that plays a key role in the ordering of all aspects of social life and social institutions. In a patriarchal society, gender relations and constructs of masculinity and femininity are not balanced but biased in favor of men, who maintain social, economic, and political dominance. Consequently, systems of knowledge, including criminology, reflect men's views, meaning that the production of knowledge is always gendered. Finally, they insist that women should be at the center of criminological inquiry, not peripheral, invisible, or "add-ons" to theories about male offending.

Feminist criminology began with a critique of conventional criminology. It argued, first, that criminology had traditionally overlooked or marginalized women. The result was an overgeneralized approach to explaining crime that, while it spoke about why "people" commit crime, actually studied only why *men* commit crime. Not only did traditional criminology allow theories about men to speak for the experiences of women; it also ignored ways in which gender structures male crime. In short, it produced biased and limited explanations of criminal behavior.

Another facet of the feminist critique objected to offensive stereotypes of female offenders that traditional criminology produced when it did pay attention to them. Historically, criminology pictured them as passive, weak, overly emotional, and, by nature, asexual. Early writers on women and crime explained their lawbreaking in terms of individual pathology and emotional or sexual disorders, even while attributing men's crimes to external, social forces.[4] Female criminals were pathological individuals; male criminals were victims of social conditions.

The first book on female offending—Cesare Lombroso and Guglielmo Ferrero's *Criminal Woman* (1893), contrasts "the" criminal woman with "the" normal woman, arguing that both are inferior to men and inherently deviant. This study, which remained the standard source on female crime for nearly a century, explained that criminal women were merely more pathological than their "normal" counterparts—more sexual, more prone to lying, more infantile, but much more bloodthirsty than serious male offenders. The mid-1950s saw the arrival of a "chivalry" thesis, according to which women are treated more leniently than men by criminal justice officials, regardless of the seriousness and frequency of their offenses.[5] These and other early accounts, nearly all composed by men, explained female crime purely in relation to sexuality, biology, and pathology.[6] A central contribution of feminist criminology has been to expose the biases at the foundations of criminology.

Evolution of Feminist Criminology

The first feminist responses to these biased explanations of female crime appeared in the late 1960s, emerging out of the liberation movements of the era. "Second-wave" feminists (so-called to distinguish them from the original feminists of the nineteenth century) fought for equal pay for equal work, child care, abortion rights, and the rights of women who were victimized by domestic violence and rape. For them, as a phrase popular at the time put it,

"The personal is the political"; private problems became social issues. "In the United States," as Nicole Rafter and Frances Heidensohn explained,

> and to a lesser extent other countries, the [women's] movement carried women on to campuses, where they demanded more opportunities for female scholars and students, together with courses in women's studies. Female students increased in number; in some North American departments, women scholars became regular faculty members, eligible (at last) for tenure and promotion; and the colleges and universities began to approve subjects such as women's history. But the victories were costly, and they remain contested to this day.[7]

Marie-Andree Bertrand, Frances Heidensohn, and Dorie Klein—writing without knowledge of one another's work, in Canada, England, and the United States, respectively—were the first three feminists to challenge mainstream criminology's patriarchal assumptions.[8] They were followed by two theorists—Freda Adler in *Sisters in Crime* (1975) and Rita Simon in *Women and Crime* (1975)—who put forth the first feminist (or protofeminist) explanations of female offending. Adler and Simon formulated versions of a "liberation/emancipation" thesis according to which the women's rights movement led to increases in female crime. Both implied that as women's social roles grew more equal to men's roles, so too would their criminal behavior. While the liberation explanation of female offending focused attention on female crime and attracted a great deal of attention, feminists who had thought more deeply about the issues realized that the implications of liberation theory were negative: to control women's crime, deny women's rights.

As feminist criminology developed, theorists became more careful in framing their inquiries. Some pointed out that simply to ask what factors cause the gender gap in offending may assume a male norm from which women are merely deviations. Feminist criminologists began to question whether a better way to approach the issue would be to study the nature of women's (and men's) participation in crime. This pursuit would pose criminological questions differently from the past, asking: What is it about being male or female that accounts for patterns in offending?[9] How do men and women "do gender"—or act in gendered ways? With the problem framed this way, we are better able to see the role in crime causation of social and cultural norms that dictate what it means to be a man or woman, boy or girl, straight or gay. Crime becomes one pathway through which these social roles are enacted. This kind of questioning has led to a better understanding of why men are more likely to participate in some crimes (robbery or rape, for instance) and women in others (like street-level sex work). Robbery and rape permit men to construct a particular type of masculinity, built upon money, power, and male dominance. Similarly, prostitution and other forms of sex work fit with role definitions dictating that women serve as sexual objects for male pleasure.

In his classic study of hegemonic or dominant masculinity, criminologist James Messerschmidt analyzes ways in which actors "do gender." *Masculinities and Crime* argues that men must constantly "accomplish" or demonstrate their masculinity in relationship to a dominant cultural script. This script endorses the performance of traditional masculine values such as labor, subordination of women, and hypersexuality. If their routes to such performance are blocked, then boys and men must find other ways to demonstrate their masculinity—and crime may serve as a key resource. Violence can be a way of defining oneself as a "real man." Such performances, across time, reproduce patriarchal social structures. Here, gender—and in particular features of masculinity—is critical in understanding crime's causation.[10]

Focusing on the ways in which African American girls and women engage in gender performance, criminologist Jody Miller has explored what it means for female gang members to "do gender."[11] She holds that by studying the "doing" of gender, we can see both the role of individual choices (or agency) in behavior and the social (or structural) constraints that limit those choices in the production of crime. Crime may be a powerful resource for expression, one that liberates women from constricting cultural stereotypes, even while it has ultimately destructive effects on young women's lives. Gang members' crimes, being embedded in the conditions of their lives, often reflect a personal and seemingly liberating personal behavior with their limited structural opportunities. In analyzing such "gendered pathways" to lawbreaking, feminist criminologists such as Daly, Messerschmidt, and Miller study social contexts across a lifetime, the ways in which those contexts are shaped by gender, and the turning points that lead toward or away from crime. They have provided a bridge between the classic poles of structure and agency that tended to divide (and limit) criminological and sociological study.

Another key contribution in the development of feminist criminology centers on the way in which victims and perpetrators tend to "bleed together" or overlap. A wealth of empirical studies of crime and victimization points to the reality that most female offenders were abused before they committed a crime. The textbook case for this kind of blurring is the battered woman who ultimately kills her abusive partner. In their efforts to understand the effects of victimization, researchers have turned to victims themselves, asking about their histories of abuse and crime. Kathleen Daly and criminologist Lisa Maher assert that a key part of the feminist agenda is to "connect studies of 'real women' with 'women of discourse,'" the latter being experts' constructions of women that are actually disconnected from the tragic realities of female offenders' everyday lives.[12]

Many women who are arrested have spent lives marginalized by their gender, ethnicity or race, and poverty. Most come from unstable homes where they were exposed to drugs and relatives who had been in prison. Emotional, sexual, and physical abuse has led to patterns of dependence, including reliance on alcohol, drugs, and bad relationships. In some cases, women take to the streets and the world of drugs to avoid the violence in their home life. Undereducated and underemployed, these girls and women exist in what some criminologists call a "spiraling marginality": chronic abuse leads to crime, crime to substance abuse, substance abuse to more crime or perhaps another abusive relationship, and so on.[13]

Women constitute the most rapidly growing group in terms of criminal justice supervision and incarceration. Over half of this penal population are African American women. Over half have not finished high school. Over half have experienced some form of sexual abuse prior to incarceration. A quarter have a history of mental illness. Ninety percent are single mothers. Ninety-five percent entered prison with annual incomes below $10,000. And 40 percent used drugs daily in the month before their arrest.[14]

Nearly all feminist criminologists are committed to the transgression or fundamental critique of mainstream, male-dominated criminology that will make it impossible for the traditionalists to continue their refusal to acknowledge their masculinist perspective on female victims and offenders.[15] Feminists' critique grows out of their analysis of gender and power. For them, rape, for example, is a crime not of sex but of male power, control, and domination—a tool by which men seek to render women submissive. Feminists situate the violence of rape along a continuum of violation that includes (for some) pornography, sexual harassment, incest, and battering.[16] Calling for a transformation of traditional attitudes toward female victimization, feminists argue for woman-centered definitions of violence that will take into account experiences from intimidation through coercion and physical violence to death.

Feminist criminology, like other theoretical perspectives, is criticized less for what it does than for what it does not do. Critics argue that in emphasizing gender, feminists overlook other factors related to criminality. Some simply see it as an appendage of mainstream criminology, a peripheral specialty focused upon women. Finally, to critics who value conventional scientific research models, feminist criminology is overly personal and subjective.

Thelma & Louise

"The law is some tricky shit, isn't it?"
—Thelma

Thelma & Louise opens with a credit sequence set against the expansive, cinematic American West. The film immediately evokes other American road movies—*Easy Rider, Bonnie and Clyde, Badlands*—but in this case, the heroes are women. The film begins with them planning a weekend getaway to a friend's cabin. Louise (Susan Sarandon) is a waitress at a diner, working the busy breakfast shift. Thelma (Geena Davis) is a housewife, preparing breakfast for her self-important husband, Darryl (Christopher McDonald), a Corvette-driving regional district manager for a carpet company who is dissatisfied with every move Thelma makes. When she asks what he would like for dinner, he announces that he doesn't "give a shit" and she should not expect him home that evening.

Louise, neat and meticulous, leaves her home in perfect order. She is in a relationship with a musician (Michael Madsen) but has grown dissatisfied with his inability to settle down. She smokes, is clear about her likes and dislikes, and is not afraid to speak her mind. Thelma is more passive and accommodating. Angry at Darryl but also afraid of him, she leaves without telling him of her plans. More disorganized than Louise and unable to decide what she needs for the weekend, she overpacks. When Louise arrives in the car, she teases Thelma about all her gear. Thelma playfully shows that she has even brought a gun. "Why in the hell did you bring that?" Louise asks, instructing Thelma to pass it over. Louise tucks it in her own purse. Then the women set off in Louise's blue Thunderbird convertible.

Excited by her newfound freedom and eager to have some fun, Thelma persuades Louise to stop at a honky-tonk roadhouse, the Silver Bullet. Louise observes that she hasn't "seen a place like this since I left Texas," hinting at something mysterious in her past. Thelma and a hesitant Louise order shots of alcohol. A man arrives at their table, flirting with both women. While serving the women drinks, the waitress asks the man, whose name we learn is Harlan (Timothy Carhart), "You bothering these poor girls?" He replies,

"Just being friendly." Louise is put off by Harlan, but Thelma engages him in a good-natured conversation, promising to dance with him. While Louise is in the restroom, Thelma starts dancing but gets sick, and Harlan takes her outside for some "fresh air." When Harlan has her outside and safely isolated from the bar, he becomes sexually aggressive. Thelma refuses him, and he hits her in the face, forcing her down onto the hood of a car and preparing to rape her. Suddenly, from outside of the frame, we hear the voice of Louise and see a gun pointed at Harlan's neck.

LOUISE: Let her go.
HARLAN: Get the fuck out of here. (Louise presses the gun to Harlan's head.)
LOUISE: You let her go, you fucking asshole, or I'm going to splatter your ugly face all over this nice car. (Harlan releases Thelma.)
HARLAN: Now calm down. We were just having a little fun.
LOUISE: Looks like you've got a fucked-up idea of fun. In the future, when a woman's crying like that, she isn't having any fun. (Both women turn to walk away.)
HARLAN: Bitch. I should have gone ahead and fucked her.
LOUISE: What did you say?
HARLAN: I said suck my cock.

Louise takes two steps back and shoots Harlan in the head.

The most critical moment in the film, the rape scene merits careful analysis. Typical Hollywood rape scenes reach completion, but this rape is interrupted—and by a woman. Louise clearly communicates that "no" means no, and having made her point, she and Thelma prepare to leave. However, Harlan continues to be verbally abusive and humiliating. When Louise fires, it is not because either of them is under imminent threat but because of something else—perhaps Harlan's lack of remorse and unrelenting effort to control and degrade them. Louise's actions, although perhaps not ultimately justifiable, have a quality of self-defense to them.

Thelma thinks they should go to the police, but Louise does not believe the police will buy the fact that Harlan was trying to rape Thelma; even though she is scratched and bruised, she was seen drinking and dancing with him. Louise understands (and Thelma later comes to agree with her) that society holds women responsible for their own victimization. From this point forward, the women are driven by their mistrust of the criminal justice system. Thelma admits in the film's concluding moments that Louise was right to shoot Harlan and that the law would not have afforded them any recourse:

Nobody would believe us. We'd still get in trouble. We'd still have our lives ruined. And you know what else? . . . That guy was hurting me. And if you hadn't come out when you did, he'd a hurt me a lot worse. And probably nothing would have happened to him. 'Cause everybody did see me dancing with him all night. They would have made out like I asked for it. My life would have been ruined a whole lot worse than it is now.

As they evade the law, every male they encounter either betrays them or is powerless to assist them.

During their flight, the women grow more assertive, competent at crime and the use of the gun. When Louise decides that she is going to Mexico to escape arrest, she tells Thelma she has to decide what to do for herself. Thelma hesitates, and eventually Louise calls her out, stating that at times of big decisions, Thelma always goes "blank" or "pleads insanity or some such shit." Louise tells her "everything has changed" and that such reactions won't fly anymore. It is a compelling moment that challenges Thelma's conventional behavior as weak, submissive, even ditzy, woman. Thelma decides to continue on to Mexico with Louise and eventually grows more self-assured. When she phones Darryl for the first time, he tells her, "You get your butt back here now." After listening to him patiently, Thelma concludes the conversation with "Darryl, go fuck yourself."

Another way in which the film speaks back to patriarchy is in its assertion of female desire. When the women encounter a good-looking young hitch-hiker, J.D. (a breakout role for Brad Pitt), he initiates a sexual awakening for Thelma but not without stealing all the money that Louise's boyfriend, Jimmy, had loaned them to make it to Mexico. When she realizes what has occurred, Louise breaks down in their motel room. Reversing roles, Thelma takes it upon herself to make things right. Since J.D. has taught her the ropes, she will rob a store. In one of the film's most comical moments, Thelma is shown by security camera, flawlessly and charismatically committing the robbery. As the camera pans out, we realize that the tape is being watched by her husband and police officers, all of whom express utter disbelief. The women grow increasingly aware of the sexism around them, commenting with disgust as they pass an oil-rig truck that has silhouettes of nude women on its mud flaps and a driver who gestures lewdly as they pass.

As they journey farther into the desert, the women are gradually transformed. A traumatized and disheveled Louise, while waiting for Thelma at a convenience store, realizes she is being watched by two older women in a diner. She begins to apply lipstick in response but, after carefully examining herself in the rearview mirror, quits. Exhausted and disillusioned, Louise gives up on any effort to meet the gendered expectations of others that she should look presentable and appropriately "feminine" by way of cosmetics. Later, at an abandoned outpost where an old man is sitting, Louise wordlessly exchanges her jewelry for his old, battered cowboy hat. On a night drive into vast rock formations and desert beauty, Louise watches the sunrise, and we sense that both women are experiencing a spiritual reawakening. Thelma, celebrating her newfound freedom, states, "I always wanted to travel—just never got the opportunity." In a critical scene, Thelma carefully prods Louise for details about what happened to her in Texas, saying "It [rape] happened to you, didn't it?" Louise responds emphatically with "I'm not talking about it." Regardless of their freedom and new sense of agency, both women have experienced patriarchal violence so deeply that it can never achieve articulation, even though this violence structures narrative events.

When Louise is pulled over by a muscle-bound state trooper in sunglasses (the "Nazi," Louise calls him), another reversal of gender power occurs. Thelma pulls a gun on the police officer and using polite but forceful language locks him in the trunk of his squad car. On the phone with the only empathetic male in the film, Detective Hal Slocum (Harvey Keitel), who is camped out with other officers at Thelma's home, Louise confesses that there is a "snowball effect" going on that makes their journey look like a crime spree. He asks her to come in for questioning, but she says that certain words keep running through her mind—"incarceration," "cavity search," "death by electrocution," "life imprisonment"— and that she will have to think about it. Louise suspects that Thelma is contemplating turning herself in, but Thelma says, "Something's . . . crossed over in me and I can't go back. I just couldn't live." As they near their fate, Thelma observes that she feels awake—more awake than she ever has been.

In the final moments, they once again encounter the vulgar oil-rig driver; this time they gesture to him to follow them to a turnout. When the expectant driver pulls off the road, the women surprise him with reprimands, demanding that he apologize for his sexist behavior. The truck driver, far from demonstrating remorse, initiates a flow of even more abusive language. Louise shoots out his tires and then together, Thelma and Louise blow up the truck. After this comedic and cathartic moment, the women screech away, with Thelma appropriating the driver's beat-up old hat.

Having pinpointed the women's last location, the police begin a high-speed chase that leads to the edge of the Grand Canyon. In the final scene, the law is visualized as a massive squad car formation pursuing the women

Figure 10.1. With the forces of a patriarchal state lined up behind them and the Grand Canyon ahead, Thelma (Geena Davis) and Louise (Susan Sarandon) must make an impossible decision. As *Thelma & Louise* (1991) and feminist theories demonstrate, the crimes of women are often linked to a lack of choices and the danger of striking out on one's own. Photo used by permission of Photofest.

to the canyon's edge. As the women (and film audience) look out over the canyon, a police helicopter suddenly rises from the below the cliffs, hovering directly in front of them. Louise disbelievingly says, "All this for us?" Faced by the overwhelming force of a patriarchal system, Thelma and Louise agree to "keep going," driving off the cliff into the canyon. But in a classic Hollywood twist, the frame is frozen, leaving the Thunderbird suspended in midair, then dissolving into happier moments in their friendship. This ending, which resists resolution and closure, has been a point of critical controversy in the film's reception. Should Thelma and Louise have given up, thereby returning to a justice system that could never acknowledge, much less understand, the nature of the violence they faced? Do self-assertion and self-awakening for women lead to death in a patriarchal system? Are you free if death is your only meaningful choice?

The film was released to immediate success and massive controversy, for its appearance coincided with a conservative backlash against feminism. *Thelma & Louise* was labeled everything from "fascist," "toxic," "a betrayal of feminism," "degrading to men," and filled with "inchoate rage and deranged violence"[17] to "a buttkicking feminist manifesto" and "the downright truth."[18] Susan Sarandon responded that the controversy demonstrated "what a straight, white male world movies traditionally occupy. This kind of scrutiny does not happen to *Raiders of the Lost Ark* or that Schwarzenegger thing (*Total Recall*) where he shoots a woman in the head and says 'Consider that a divorce!'"[19] The film continues to be nagged by feminist questions. Are revenge and violence compatible with the feminist principles of equality, sensitivity, responsibility, and peacemaking? When women take up the gun, are they appropriating, assimilating, or subverting the phallic tools of patriarchy? As a text subject to a feminist reading, the film has clearly offered women unique and complex spectatorship possibilities. Some feminists argue that the women's friendship and their expressions of passion and desire challenge patriarchy. Others admire the film for showing the heroines as ordinary women driven to extraordinary ends by male violence. Some viewers, admirers and critics, have detected a lesbian subtext within the film. Yet others criticize *Thelma & Louise* for what they consider to be dangerous caricatures of women engaging in masculine violence in order to be taken seriously. Like any mythic text, *Thelma & Louise* allows for multiple readings. The failure of public debate to achieve any kind of consensus about the movie shows that feminism is not a rigidly fixed or easily identifiable doctrine but rather contradictory and contested terrain. As popular culture scholar Elayne Rapping writes:

> It's not the movie itself—as text—that most interests me. I believe the most important things about Thelma & Louise are to be found in the media hullabaloo that followed its release—the fascinating, passionate public discourse it engendered—rather than in the merits or meanings of the film itself.[20]

Beyond controversy, *Thelma & Louise* vividly depicts how crime becomes a resource for expression, one that is sufficiently liberating that the women choose to go forward rather than back into their caged, domestic existences. This freedom grows into a kind of serenity late in the film, where two ordinary women achieve an extraordinary transcendence. Without makeup and jewelry, shorn of all their belongings, hot, sweaty, and dirty, the women grow more beautiful. The landscape itself becomes ever more stunning, right up to the Grand Canyon, invoking the cultural landscape of Hollywood Westerns. (In fact, *Thelma & Louise* is often read as a new version of two of Hollywood's seminal male Westerns, John Ford's *Searchers* and George Roy Hill's *Butch Cassidy and the Sundance Kid*.) This masculine iconography is further developed by the inclusion of vertically thrusting oil pumps, big-rig trucks honking on the highway, old, dusty filling stations with loitering men, and cowboys on horses. The women's westward passage is itself a defiant rite of passage into masculine territory, openness, and freedom, away from the claustrophobic clutter of conventionally female spaces: the kitchen and the diner.

Not surprisingly, many of the same issues raised by *Thelma & Louise* are also generated by other crime films centered on women. *The Silence of the Lambs* (1991) shows what life is like for a woman in the man's world of a criminal justice agency. Like *Thelma & Louise*, *Silence of the Lambs* stimulated public debate over its depictions of gender and sexuality. The film focuses on the experiences of an FBI agent-in-training, Clarice Starling (Jodie Foster). Petite, orphaned, and socially isolated, her identity struggle lies at the heart of the narrative. The plot pairs her with a series of men, some father figures, others potential lovers or sexual threats, some both. These include FBI director Jack Crawford, serial killer Jame ("Buffalo Bill") Gumb, and the incarcerated, cannibalistic psychiatrist Hannibal Lecter. Clarice is constantly presented as the object of the male gaze, and she often squirms uncomfortably under it as she maneuvers in the deeply masculine terrain of crime and criminal justice. Lecter serves as the primary vehicle for this visually gendered relationship: "We begin by coveting what we see every day. Don't you feel eyes moving over your body, Clarice? I hardly see how you couldn't." The film's complex viewpoints allow for a reading of Clarice as both vulnerable and empowered, both victim and victor.

Conclusion

Feminist criminologists, in part because they do not rely on or privilege any one theory, open up the criminological project to multiple ways of knowing and understanding the lives of women and men. Their efforts have revealed crime, punishment, victimization, and even professional life in the justice system to be profoundly shaped by masculine and feminine values. Even more pertinent, they have pointed to the process behind the formation of these values, how gender is a performance and crime a resource, when other, more acceptable avenues are blocked. These points of emphasis have in many ways brought criminology down to earth, closer to the lived experiences of its subjects. Merging the personal and the political, offender and victim, feminist criminology provides unique ways for us to think of the relationship between crime and punishment. In its effort to move women to the center of criminological inquiry, it encourages us to rethink how crime and criminology depend in their formation on what is thinkable in the larger cultural imagination, including how we understand ourselves as men and women.

FURTHER VIEWING

The Accused (1988)
Blue Steel (1990)
Bound (1996)
The Brave One (2007)
Chicago (2002)
Dolores Claiborne (1994)
Fargo (1996)
Heavenly Creatures (1994)
Lady Vengeance (2005)
La Femme Nikita (1990)
Maria Full of Grace (2004)
Monster (2003)
Ms. 45 (1981)
Precious (2009)
Set It Off (1996)
Silence of the Lambs, The (1991)
Vera Drake (2004)

11

A Matter of Time

Life-Course Theories and City of God

What would happen if criminologists took time more seriously? How might the field change if, instead of simply studying incidents of criminal behavior and types of crime, researchers examined offenders' personal histories from birth through old age, studying the impacts of crime on their entire lives? Would we have to modify our understandings of criminal behavior if we focused on why and how offenders exit from crime as well as why and how they get into it? And if we could figure out how to study the effects of historical contexts on offending, could we develop better theories of crime? These are the sorts of questions asked by life-course and developmental theories, the most recent reorientation in the study of criminal behavior.

This chapter has four main sections. The first covers life-course criminology, concentrating on work by John Laub and Robert Sampson and interspersing this discussion with examples from the movies *The Godfather* (1972) and *Falling Down* (1993). The second deals with Terrie Moffitt's developmental criminology, illustrating it with the films *Badlands* (1973) and *Angels with Dirty Faces* (1938). The third section covers desistance, the process of exiting from criminal behavior, a topic of central importance to Laub and Sampson, and to Moffitt as well, but here discussed primarily in terms of Shadd Maruna's book *Making Good*. This section is illustrated with the film *Malcolm X* (1992). The final section of the chapter discusses *City of God* (2002), the extraordinary Brazilian film that shows drugs ravaging a community. That community, which actually exists, almost forms a real-life experiment, for it is an entirely new town, built on the outskirts of Rio de Janeiro, opened in 1966, and allowed to operate with minimal interference from the city government or police. *City of God*, based on a true story, illustrates the life-course concept through the story of a youth named Rocket; with other characters it also illustrates late-onset criminality and desistance, concepts integral to life-course and developmental criminology. Our conclusion ties together the interest in time that lies near the heart of both theories discussed here and the film *City of God*. We suggest that in both cases, the interest in time is related to a third phenomenon, postmodernism, a movement in the arts and to a lesser extent the social sciences that calls for a rethinking of basic pre-conceptions, including assumptions about the nature of time.

Life-Course Criminology

Although there are several types of life-course criminology,[1] we will focus on the two books, *Crime in the Making* (1993) and *Shared Beginnings, Divergent Lives* (2003), that put the life-course perspective on the criminological map.[2] Written by John Laub of the University of Maryland and Robert Sampson of Harvard University, these books shifted the contours of the discipline.

As Laub and Sampson tell the story, in the mid-1980s they "stumbled across . . . dusty cartons of data in the basement of the Harvard Law School Library. Originally assembled by Sheldon and Eleanor Glueck of Harvard University, these cartons contained the original case files from their classic study, *Unraveling Juvenile Delinquency* (1950)."[3] Merely organizing the files was a daunting project—there were more than fifty boxes of data on delinquent subjects alone, along with files on a control group and the Gluecks' personal papers.

The Gluecks, who were prolific researchers, produced thirteen books, many of them focused on the causes of delinquency. Their studies were well known and innovative but not always admired, due partly to methodological problems and partly to the Gluecks' interest in trying to *predict* which youths would eventually become criminals, an aim that raised political and even constitutional questions. For reasons that Laub and Sampson identify, the Gluecks' delinquency research was not welcomed enthusiastically by criminologists: it was atheoretical, burdened by more than 2,500 variables, and not closely allied to their discipline, for the Gluecks examined psychological, psychiatric, and biological as well as social factors. Moreover, Edwin Sutherland, the most powerful criminologist of the day, attacked the Gluecks' research as insufficiently sociological.[4] In short, their work was unfashionable in mainstream criminology, which in the mid-twentieth century was almost exclusively sociological in focus. Thus the Gluecks' studies were neglected until Laub and Samson, stumbling over those dusty boxes, realized that they could use the data for new purposes.

The data consisted, first, of records on 500 delinquent boys, all white and aged ten to seventeen, who had been committed to Massachusetts reformatories for persistent, fairly serious offending. Second, the Gluecks' data included records on 500 nondelinquent Boston schoolboys, also white and aged ten to seventeen, who had *not* been involved in persistent delinquency. Case by case, they had matched the second group with the first in terms of age, ethnicity, neighborhood of residence, and measured intelligence. The Gluecks had also collected an enormous amount of information on each of the 1,000 boys and his family, including reports on their behavioral problems and delinquencies from parents, teachers, and the boys themselves. Third, the data included information that the Gluecks collected in follow-up studies when the boys were twenty-five and again thirty-two years old. Thus Laub and Sampson found an extremely rich, longitudinal data set that enabled them to study the lives of delinquents and a matched control group over time. Although the data pertained to men born in the 1920s, they might be reanalyzed, Laub and Sampson reasoned, to build a theory relevant to offending at other points in time. To supplement the Gluecks' data, in the 1990s they updated files on the original 500 delinquents, creating a record of their criminal activity (or desistance from it) until the age of seventy, and conducted in-depth interviews with 52 of the original delinquents about their criminal careers. Thus Laub and Sampson completed a data set on a relatively large group of serious offenders from age seven to seventy—apparently the most complete longitudinal data set on crime ever assembled.

Research led Laub and Sampson to realize that their subjects' lives had been heterogeneous—that the men had taken different pathways toward and away from crime. Then the problem became explaining how and why those routes differed, which led the researchers to describe the life course in terms of trajectories and turning points. They define a *trajectory* as a long-term pattern of behavior, a pathway or line of development through life in areas such as work, marriage, and criminal behavior. For an example we can turn to the movie *The Godfather* (1972), in which Michael Corleone (played by Al Pacino), although a son of an organized crime boss, is originally set on a noncriminal trajectory. College-educated and a decorated war hero, Michael explains to his girlfriend, Kay (Diane Keaton), that while he loves his family, he intends to stay out of its business. Moreover, unlike his brothers, who regard women essentially as chattel, Michael treats Kay as a companion of equal standing; this implies a second trajectory, parallel to the first, of a stable modern marriage.

A *turning point*, as defined by Laub and Sampson, is an event or realization that leads eventually to a shift in a trajectory. A moment when change begins in a life-course pattern, it can be marked by the onset of criminal behavior, its escalation, or a decision to desist or exit from crime. Or a turning point can be marked by marriage, a residential change, commitment to a reform school, or start of a new job that becomes a permanent part of one's life. In Michael Corleone's case, a key turning point comes when a rival mob tries to kill his father, leading Michael to realize that if the family is to survive, he has to assume his father's mantle. The realization is unwanted but, he feels, unavoidable. Eventually, it totally changes his trajectories in terms of work, marriage, and family relationships. (In fact, he later orders the death of close family members.)

Laub and Sampson speak of life-course transitions as *age-graded*, meaning appropriate to typical life sequences. For example, having a child as a young adult is an age-graded turning point that can alter one's criminal trajectory in a positive way, perhaps leading out of crime. On the other hand, having a child as a teenager, an "off-time" departure from the usual age-graded sequence, may negatively affect one's developmental trajectory, perhaps leading in the direction of crime. A jarring example of being off-time appears in *City of God* (2002), the film discussed in detail later in this chapter. In the 1960s, when the movie begins, virtually all males who live in the violent Brazilian slum known as City of God are criminals from the time they become adolescents—that is typical, age-graded behavior. However, by the 1980s we see armed four- and five-year-olds committing robberies—and being shot by rival gangsters. To be a baby gangster is not age-graded behavior, at least not in the experience of most viewers (critics unanimously referred to this as the film's most horrific scene), and not even in the City of God itself in earlier times.

When Laub and Sampson reanalyzed the Glueck data, two of their many findings seemed particularly significant. First, about 20 percent of the original *non*delinquent control group initiated criminal behavior as adults ("late-onset offending"), which suggested that other theories' almost exclusive emphasis on adolescent delinquency was misplaced and misleading. Second, while most adult criminal behavior was indeed preceded by childhood antisocial behavior, as many theories held, paradoxically, most antisocial children did not grow up to be adult offenders. That is, when the researchers introduced the time dimension, they discovered that there is a great deal of heterogeneity in criminal behavior over time. As Sampson puts it, "Variability is nearly ubiquitous."[5] Earlier studies, beginning with known delinquents or criminals and looking *back* to discover antecedents, usually concluded that antisocial behavior is stable from childhood onward. However, the Glueck data enabled Laub and Sampson to look *ahead* in time and discover successes as well as failures. These findings encouraged them to formulate a theory built around the concepts of trajectories and turning points.

Calling their explanation of criminal behavior an "age-graded theory of informal social control," Laub and Sampson define informal social control in terms of a person's bonds or ties to family, work, and community. (In contrast, formal social control consists of institutions such as the police and courts that are publicly mandated to maintain law and order.) According to the idea of informal social control, crime is more likely to occur when the individual's bonds to family, friends, work, and so on are weak or broken. Laub and Sampson stress the quality or strength of social ties rather than the mere occurrence of events. For example, they found that marriage alone did not prevent the offenders in the Glueck sample from committing crime but that good marriages with close emotional ties did, for the latter created strong bonds, strengthened informal social control, and gave the men reasons to keep out of trouble. Similarly, it was not employment per se that built up social bonds and thus informal social controls but rather *stable* employment to which the subject was committed. Those who desisted from crime were helped by good marriages, job stability, and other factors that helped them establish strong social bonds.

A cinematic example of the way in which the weakening of informal social controls can lead to crime appears in the film *Falling Down*, previously discussed in chapter 6. In *Falling Down*, a middle-aged man (D-FENS, played by Michael Douglas)—ordinary, politically conservative, and thoroughly obedient to the rules—becomes unhinged when his social bonds start to fray. His wife leaves him, his boss fires him, and immigrants and adolescent gangsters who corrode his image of American purity weaken his ties to his community. Finally, in a spectacular case of late-onset offending, he starts a slaughter-trek across L.A.[6]

The most innovative—and from our point of view, most welcome—aspect of Laub and Sampson's theoretical work is that they recognize offenders as people who make decisions and control their own lives. In a field long dominated by a condescending determinism and characterized by a search for factors that somehow force "them" to become delinquents and criminals, Laub and Sampson speak of human agency—offenders' freedom to make good and bad choices in life. They do not argue for free will, for "social actors are always embedded in space and time; they respond to specific *situations* (opportunities as well as constraints)."[7] But they do speak of "situated choice,"[8] combining the idea of turning points with that of choice and borrowing a line from sociologist Andrew Abbott that clearly expresses their view: "'A major turning point has the potential to open a system the way a key has the potential to open a lock . . . action is necessary to complete the turning.'"[9]

In addition to trajectories, turning points, and age-grading, *Shared Beginnings, Divergent Lives* draws on another time-related phenomenon by integrating information on the Glueck men's lives with the historical contexts in which they lived. It discusses the meanings of work to men's identities in a period in which men were typically a family's only breadwinner, and it points out that military service in the World War II period had special benefits, especially for young men with criminal records, in that it not only separated them from delinquent peers but also offered training that could set "in motion a chain of events (or experiences) in individuals' lives that progressively shape[d] future outcomes."[10] History, Laub and Sampson point out, also affected the type of substances that these men abused (many were alcoholics, but street drugs were not yet widely available), and it led to the intense ethnicity of the immigrant neighborhoods in which the men grew up.

Two Kinds of Delinquents?

Another well-known and influential time-based theory is developmental criminology, an explanation associated most strongly with name of Terrie E. Moffitt, now a professor at Duke University. Her 1993 article "Adolescence-Limited and Life-Course-Persistent Antisocial Behavior" is already a criminological classic—quite an achievement for an article-length work, especially one published in a journal (*Psychological Review*) that criminologists do not routinely read.[11]

Moffitt proposes an offender taxonomy with two categories, adolescence-limited offenders and life-course-persistent offenders. The distinction is not merely descriptive, for it "includes implications for etiology, course, prognosis, [and] treatment."[12] The *adolescence-limited* group, by far the larger of the two, includes the majority of all delinquents. Their involvement in crime peaks about the age of seventeen and falls off radically in their twenties; by the time they are adults, most have desisted from crime. Their participation in delinquency, a normal aspect of teen life, involves offenses such as theft, vandalism, and substance abuse. Motivation comes from the gap between their biological maturity and social maturity: in the modern world, adolescence is prolonged, leaving teenagers in a "5-to-10 year role vacuum" in which they are "biologically capable and compelled to be sexual beings, yet they are asked to delay most of the positive aspects of adult life."[13] During this period, they learn delinquent behaviors from antisocial peers—especially the life-course-persistents, who are already more practiced in crime and whom they therefore imitate.

Life-course-persistent offenders, in contrast, demonstrate conduct disorders as toddlers. Their antisocial behavior increases dramatically between the ages of seven and seventeen, and instead of tapering off, it remains stable over time. Moffitt's life-course-persistents are a smaller group, but they are responsible for a majority of serious crimes. Not only are they more aggressive and violent than adolescence-limiteds; they continue with antisocial behavior throughout the life course. They can be identified through the antisocial behavior that begins when they are very young children.

Dozens of crime movies can be used to illustrate Moffitt's taxonomy because scripts often include an ordinary bad guy to contrast with the *very* bad guy and thus make the latter seem even worse. For example, in *Badlands* (1973), Terrence Malick's film about teenage misfits on a killing spree, it is Kit, the male partner, who does the shooting. Holly, his girlfriend, is complicit, but she is more passive, and eventually, like Moffitt's adolescence-limiteds, she outgrows life on the lam. A more extreme contrast can be found in Michael Curtiz's *Angels with Dirty Faces*, about two young hoodlums who steal together—but only coal, to keep warm. When Rocky (played by James Cagney) wants to move on to bigger game, his pal Jerry (Pat O'Brien) holds back. Eventually Rocky becomes a killer and Jerry (definitely an adolescence-limited offender) a priest. Rocky is ready to go to the electric chair with his usual defiant élan, but at Jerry's pleading, at the last minute he pretends to be "yellow" and afraid to die so that his young followers will cease considering him a hero. Left to his own devices, however, Rocky would have maintained his life-course-persistent ways until the very end.

Moffitt argues that the antisocial behavior of the life-course-persistents "has its origins in an interaction between children's neuropsychological vulnerabilities and criminogenic environments."[14] Some of their neurological problems may be hereditary or linked to maternal drug use, poor maternal nutrition, or brain injuries during birth. Others may be caused by postnatal nutritional deprivation, lack of stimulation, or abuse. These problems may be self-perpetuating because vulnerable infants are disproportionately found in disadvantaged or deviant homes and adverse neighborhoods. Their neuropsychological disabilities—conduct disorders, impulsivity, inattentiveness—show up early and in many cases are exacerbated by their environments. These disabilities persist through the entire life course.

Moffitt's argument takes into account the history of adolescence. In pre-industrial societies, when youths began working on the family farm or in the family store as soon as they could help with the chores, there was no such thing as adolescence as we know it today. "Biological maturity came at a later age," Moffitt writes; "social adult status arrived at an earlier age, and rites of passage more clearly delineated the point at which youths assumed new roles and responsibilities."[15] But today, there can be a gap of a decade or more between biological maturity and entry into the labor force; adolescents are "trapped in a *maturity gap*"[16] during which they want to but cannot become adults. It is during this period that they engage in delinquent behaviors that signify adult status, imitating life-course-persistent peers who seem more grown up.

Moffitt's theory, like that of Laub and Sampson, derives from a longitudinal study, in this case a cohort investigation of more than 1,000 children born in Dunedin, New Zealand, in 1972 and 1973. She finds support for her theory not only in the Dunedin data but also in other studies showing, first, that nearly all adults with antisocial personality disorder had conduct disorders as children and, second, that more than half of all crimes are committed by a small proportion (5 to 6 percent) of high-rate offenders.[17] But Laub and Sampson dismiss Moffitt's theory, arguing that there is too much variability among offenders to create simple taxonomies and that even serious offenders eventually desist from crime.[18]

Desistance

Desistance from crime—a phenomenon that attracted little attention just a few years ago—has become a hot topic due in part to the greater sensitivity to time issues introduced by life-course and developmental criminology. Why do offenders desist? Why do some cease their involvement in crime earlier than others? What is the typical age of desistance, and are there really some offenders who commit crimes into old age? Having already indicated how Laub and Sampson and Moffitt would respond to these questions, we now turn to a book focused entirely on desistance: *Making Good: How Ex-Convicts Reform and Rebuild Their Lives* (2001) by Shadd Maruna, a specialist in human development.[19]

As Maruna points out, *desistance* is a difficult phenomenon to pin down. Should we define it in terms of total cessation of criminal activity for a period of years, and if so, how many years should be the criterion? How can we avoid confusing *intermittent* criminal behavior (say, one crime every five years) with desistance, and does that even matter if our main interest lies in the desistance of *frequent* offenders? How can we tell if desistance has occurred—are official records more reliable than what offenders themselves may tell us?

Maruna's approach was to interview offenders and ex-offenders, asking them about desistance. However, as he explains,

> Like every researcher who enters the field in search of these persisters or desisters, I soon reached the conclusion that such classification is purely a convenience for statistical classification and "hides a tremendous amount of variation." To be blunt, most of the persisters one finds do not seem to really persist, most desisters do not seem to really desist, and, honestly, it is getting harder than ever to find any "innocents." Individuals in the real world do not tend to fall into the neat dichotomies of desisters—persisters, innocents—offenders, victims—victimizers, or prosocial-antisocial consistently constructed in political and criminological discourse.[20]

To find his interviewees, Maruna got leads through probation officers and social workers; through ethnographic fieldwork (he actually went to Liverpool, England, and lived for a month in a seedy hotel where he thought, rightly, ex-offenders were also likely to live); and through references from ex-offenders (the "snowball sampling" technique). In all, he interviewed fifty-five men and ten women. These he divided into a desisting group (thirty subjects), a matched persisting group (twenty subjects), and a third group of fifteen subjects who did not match his criteria for either of the first two groups and so were dropped from the analysis. All of the persisters and desisters were (or had been) high-rate offenders (defined in terms of at least a crime a week for a period of at least two years), although most committed property and drug crimes, with few having been involved in violent offending. Those included in the "desisting" group (a useful, process-oriented term that allows for the possibility of change) reported more than a year of crime-free behavior and the intention to remain crime-free in the future.

Methodologically, Maruna's approach was to analyze his subjects' "self-narratives"—their own accounts of their lives—with an eye to what the narratives would reveal about how these desisters made sense of their lives.

> To desist from crime, ex-offenders need to develop a coherent, prosocial identity for themselves. As such, they need to account for and understand their criminal pasts . . . , and they also need to understand why they are

now "not like that anymore." Ex-offenders need a coherent and credible self-story to explain (to themselves and others) how their checkered pasts could have led to their new, reformed identities.[21]

This is not to say that Maruna listened without skepticism. Key to his analysis was the recognition that his interviewees consistently distorted their past—not lying about it but cognitively reinterpreting it with "an exaggerated sense of control over the future and an inflated, almost missionary sense of purpose in life." They "recast their criminal pasts. . . . I describe this process of willful, cognitive distortion as 'making good.'"[22]

Like Malcolm X in director Spike Lee's *Malcolm X*, Maruna's desisters developed "redemption scripts" according to which the offender was essentially good from the start but got involved with crime and drugs due to adverse circumstances. Finally, with the help of some outside force—someone who believes in his or her essential goodness—the narrator exits from crime to accomplish, as Maruna puts it, "what he or she was 'always meant to do.'"[23] Former offenders revise their self-narrative to make themselves good. In the case of Malcolm X, the redeemer is another prisoner named Baines who gets him off drugs, teaches him the value of study and self-discipline, and converts him to Islam, freeing Malcolm to denounce his former identity and become a leader of his people.

Many ex-offenders, Maruna suggests, borrow their narrative lines from crime movies, which often relate the story of the bad guy who secretly has a heart of gold and eventually reforms. Moreover, desisters are not really very different from the rest of us. "The peculiar combination of making excuses for past failures and yet taking responsibility for present and future accomplishments," Maruna wryly observes, "is a well-established characteristic of another group of interest to social psychologists—healthy adults."[24] But his desisters had a need for some kind of redemption ritual in the form, for instance, of letters from criminal justice officials recognizing that they had gone straight. Thus, Maruna concludes, if we want to encourage desistance, we should introduce such rituals into the criminal justice process. We should also eliminate laws that stigmatize ex-offenders by making it impossible for them to vote, hold certain jobs, and otherwise reintegrate themselves into lawful society.

Even an initial integration into lawful society can be difficult, as shown by *City of God*, the story of the youth named Rocket who lives in a government-created favela, or shantytown, saturated by crime. Drug selling and violence are the chief occupation of young men who reside in the City of God, but

Rocket discovers a way to escape into lawful society.[25] His story comes from an autobiographical novel by Paulo Lins; however, whereas Lins became a writer, Rocket (played by Alexandre Rodrigues) grows up to be a photographer. Narrated by Rocket, *City of God* takes us from his childhood to his exit out of, not so much crime, in which he participates only halfheartedly, but the favela, into a new life where crime is not necessary.

City of God (Cidade de Deus)

City of God was awarded literally dozens of honors for its direction, cinematography, and editing—testimony to its bravura visual style. Its cinematographer filmed with a handheld camera, using extremely rapid changes in point of view, zooms, split screens, overhead shots, close-ups, visual fragmentation (some images include only people's feet), speed (some scenes last just one second), and rapid changes in rhythm (other scenes linger) to create an impressionistic, elliptical approach to narration. Moreover, Rocket's story unfolds nonlinearly, with loops and flashbacks. The overall effect is one of frenetic yet exuberant violence and chaos, a cinematic counterpart to the lives of the city's hoodlums.

Behind the opening credits we see, first, a close-up of an enormous knife being sharpened on a stone, next the face of a youth behind a grill, then a barbeque with chickens in various stages of dismemberment and bits and pieces of people who seem to be partying, as well as a live chicken tied loosely by one leg to a post. With casual brutality the partygoers prepare to kill the chicken, but it escapes, tearing down favela streets and chased by a gang of kids with drawn guns. Suddenly, a freeze frame halts this commotion and we see the boy whom we later learn is Rocket trapped in the middle of the street with the chicken. At one end of the street is a solid wall of young men and children with guns; at the other end stand cops with *their* guns drawn. Not until the end of the film do we fully understand what is happening in this opening parable; however, Rocket's voice-over does explain, "In the City of God, if you run away, they get you, and if you stay, they get you too. It's been that way ever since I was a kid." At this point, the camera spins 360 degrees to show Rocket years earlier, as a kid of about eight playing soccer on a dusty field, his stance initially identical to the pose he held as a young man in the chicken scene. In a flashback, a transition cannot get much slicker than that.

Although the film includes a few professional actors, Meirelles and Lund mainly hired nonprofessionals from the City of God and other favelas, training them in workshops while at the same time learning from their improvisations and incorporating their dialogues into the script. The film gained its sense of authenticity and spontaneity from this process; it almost seems like a documentary, with Rocket's voice-over a kind of oral history. The setting, too, feels authentic, for instead of constructing sets, Meirelles and Lund filmed in favelas. (Few, if any, scenes were filmed in the City of God itself, however, for the location was deemed too dangerous.)[26]

As Rocket narrates segments of his story, moving from the 1960s through the early 1980s, we see how he and the City of God changed during that period. When the town opened in 1966, it was intended for poor people left homeless by flooding and arson in other parts of the metropolis. Its name may have been an homage to Saint Augustine's *City of God*, a fourth-century defense of Christianity; or it may have been an ironic appellation, given the town's tightly packed rows of tiny, identical, stucco houses, more hellish than heavenly. The first scenes show unpaved streets, electricity poles going up, more horses than cars. Dusty and treeless, this landscape gives off a warm yellow glow. Marijuana is ubiquitous, but kids play soccer together; they are supervised by their parents; and crime is an older boys' activity.

In later segments, the drugs become stronger, violence increases, weaponry grows warlike (bombs, machine guns), and very small children participate in the drug trade and its conflicts. The government lets the town deteriorate; whereas in the first segment the cops entered the City of God to chase criminals, later they approach only to collect payoffs, otherwise allowing the town to flourish as a subculture of violence. To exemplify the changes, Rocket tells "The Story of the Apartment," a place where he used to buy pot. Originally the apartment belonged to Doña Zelia, an aging woman who sold marijuana to support her daughters and pay young boys for sex. Hers was an entirely amateur operation, but one of her lovers seized control of her business and teamed up to sell cocaine with Carrot, who by the film's end heads one of two major gangs. Eventually the apartment ended up in the hands of Li'l Dice, a sadistic psychopath who changes his name to Li'l Ze and becomes head of the other major gang. The apartment decays into a filthy drug den where several young men meet their deaths. Like it, the entire favela becomes what one reviewer describes as "a cross between an orphanage and an abattoir."[27]

Rocket's story plays out in counterpoint with that of L'il Dice (L'il Ze), who is as good at crime as Rocket is inept at it. A bully from childhood, L'il Dice becomes a mass murderer about the age of eight. Older boys have taken him along as a lookout when they rob clients at a brothel. Miffed that the older boys will not let him accompany them into the brothel, L'il Dice stays behind

Figure 11.1. In *City of God* (2002), we follow Rocket (Alexandre Rodrigues) over a crucial segment of his life course, from childhood to early manhood, as his interest in photography saves him from violent death in the slum where he was born. This image is an emblem of his life-course trajectory. Photo used by permission of Photofest.

to shoot all the prostitutes and their clients, thus satisfying what Rocket calls "his lust to kill." (He is what Moffitt would term a life-course-persistent offender, although in this film, in which by the end the age for entry into crime is about four and nearly all participants are dead by the age of twenty-five, there is no such thing as Moffitt's adolescence-limited offenders.) Later, in a flashback, we watch L'il Ze kill Rocket's brother. But his violence is often tamped down by Benny, his best friend from childhood. Moreover, the film is not unsympathetic to L'il Ze, who, we learn, is self-conscious about his ugliness and humiliated by his inability to attract girls. He is simply a kid who learns more quickly than his friends that violence is power.

Rocket, an Afro-Brazilian, first tells "The Story of the Tender Trio," hoods who include his older brother Goose. Set in the 1970s, this story shows that in that period, informal social bonds still tied family members to one another. When Goose steals, he gives some of the money to Rocket to pass on to their father, "but don't tell him it's from me." The father, a fishmonger, bosses his sons around, telling them how to behave and forcing them to push his peddler's wheelbarrow through the streets. Rocket loves marijuana but avoids joining a gang because he is afraid of being shot, and he attends school because it saves him from physical work. When Shaggy, one of the Trio, is shot by cops and a newsman arrives to photograph the body, Rocket is entranced by the camera and its flashbulb. He buys a cheap camera with which he photographs friends at the beach. Later Benny gives him a good camera, with which he starts photographing street warfare. A roll of his film finds its way to a newspaper, which publishes one of Rocket's photos on its front page.

Rocket is sure L'il Ze will kill him over the photograph, but it turns out that L'il Ze is thrilled by the publicity and wants Rocket to take shots of him and his gang posing with assault rifles. That is in fact what they are doing in the chicken-chase scene that starts the movie; Rocket is focusing his camera in the middle of the street when the chicken runs between his legs. He goes on snapping pictures, and the newspaper, which does not dare send regular reporters into the favela, starts paying Rocket for his work. One of the reporters seduces him so he finally loses his virginity; another teaches him about lenses and light meters. He has found his ticket out of the City of God.

But that happens at the end of the film. It is preceded by a long climax starting with Benny's going-away party. He and his girlfriend have decided to get out of the drug trade, buy a farm, raise pot, and listen to rock music all day. Darkness takes over in this film that has been getting shadier since the sunny early scenes of boys playing soccer. Only by strobe lights can we see the hundreds of people dancing at Benny's party. However, desistance is impossible. Someone shoots Benny by mistake, and warfare breaks out, the hostilities intensified by the entry of a character named Knockout Ned. Here we get a case of late-onset offending: a law-abiding fare collector on a tram line, Knockout Ned is so handsome that out of spite, the ugly L'il Ze rapes Ned's girlfriend and shoots members of his family. Ned loathes violence, ignores drugs, and enjoys helping neighborhood kids. However, now he wants revenge, and because he was trained as a marksman in the army, he is able to get it. Ned joins Carrot's gang at the start of the "all-out war." "The slum had been purgatory," Rocket observes; "now it became hell. . . . That is how I became a reporter." With bodies lying everywhere, like "Vietnam," Rocket starts filming. Ned is killed. The cops capture L'il Ze, but because he has kept up his payoffs, they surreptitiously release him. (From behind a grill, Rocket photographs them taking L'il Ze's money.) But then the Runts—gangsters under the age of ten—find L'il Ze and in a spectacular scene group-shoot him in revenge for his earlier killing of a Runt.

The final scene shows the Runts walking away from the camera down the street, revolvers dangling from their small hands, compiling a blacklist of those they plan to kill. One tiny boy runs behind, trying to catch up. While *City of God* is not moralistic, it is deeply concerned about the way drugs can ruin a community, destroying the fabric of life and social ties. As one commentator notes, in it acts of violence "allow boys and young men to . . . attain a status as men that is independent of their chronological age." The result is a "juvenocracy," rule by violent young men.[28] Moffitt speaks of a maturity gap between biological and social maturity as a cause of adolescence-limited crime. In *City of God*, for most characters there is no gap whatsoever between traditional age-graded stages in the life course because all the stages, adolescence included, vanish. Boys come of age to violence before they are old enough to start school. Kids reach for power even when they are toddlers; childhood collapses, going out of existence along with the family, and youth is lost. As one little boy in the film explains, "I smoke, I snort, I've killed and robbed. I'm a man." That has become the typical life course. Rocket escapes because, despite his best efforts, he cannot avoid adolescence. He tries robbery but cannot force himself to steal from pleasant people; he tries seduction but has to wait for sex until, well into his teens, he is seduced. He could not join the Runts if he tried.

In this film, there are two types of time. The first is Rocket-time, the narrative of his development from childhood to early manhood, measured in years and the usual stages. The second is the edited film's time: fragmented, jumbled, hyper, chaotic, like the other boys' lives and the city's decline. In both cases, we get a crime film that incorporates time, telling the story of a boy and a place over several decades.

Conclusion

Over the past several decades, criminology and film have both questioned conventional assumptions about time: its linearity, its significance, ways in which it is experienced, its effects. In criminology, the increased thoughtfulness about time shows up in Laub and Sampson's interest in the life course, the effects of time on offenders' lives, and historical context. It shows up more faintly in Moffitt's work, but it does appear in her taxonomy based on the idea that groups of offenders behave differently over time and in her historical account of the development of adolescence. With Maruna, sensitivity to time shows up both in his interest in desistance and in his narrative approach to understanding offenders' lives over time. Related to this new willingness to fold the dimension of time into criminology is a growing questioning of traditional assumptions about homogeneity, fixity, and finality. Moreover, life-course and developmental criminologists make increasing efforts to think about crime in dynamic, not static, terms and to find methods that will capture changes in people's lives over time.

These new approaches to time reflect the influence of postmodernism, a phenomenon that is difficult to define but whose characteristics include a repudiation of determinism in favor of ideas about agency, fluidity, and chance; a rejection of traditional linear notions of time in favor of scrambling story parts to disclose new meanings; and replacement of trust in generalizations with a confidence that we can learn more from diversity, the concrete, and the unique.[29] No one would call Laub and Sampson, or Moffitt, or even Maruna postmodernists, and yet, as the cultural theorist Pauline Marie Rosenau observes, "Threads of post-modern arguments weave in and out of those [arguments that are] advanced by more conventional critics of modern social sciences."[30] While criminology is perhaps the most conventional of all the social sciences, even it has been brushed by the wing of postmodernism. We see this in a new willingness to consider the role of chance and choice in human development; in a search for meaning in the quotidian—the concrete, daily lives of offenders and ex-offenders; and in decisions to recognize diversity rather than to make blanket generalizations. Above all, we see it in efforts to develop criminologies that take account of time.[31]

Cinema has embraced postmodernism more enthusiastically than has criminology. The epitome of the postmodernist crime film is perhaps *Run Lola Run* (1998), which tells the same story with three different outcomes; but *City of God*, too, is alive to the importance of individuals' decisions and the randomness of events. Like *Run Lola Run*, *City of God* scrambles time to produce meanings that a linear plot cannot generate. Both films are open-ended, offering not traditional beginnings, middles, and endings but bits of stories and narrative fragments. Through its radical filming and editing, and its chopping up of the narrative line into segments of barely connected story lines, *City of God* forces viewers to participate in construction of the meaning of both characters and place through time. It forces us to participate—but does not dictate our interpretations. Some Brazilians have objected that the film exaggerates favela violence and stereotypes poor blacks. Whereas the City of God has more than 120,000 inhabitants, they argue, fewer than 1 percent of them are involved in the drug trade.[32] For postmodernists, however, the key question is not the accuracy of the films' representations but rather the filmmakers' willingness to let meanings proliferate and even contradict one another. Whereas a traditional Hollywood film like *Double Indemnity* (1944) straightjackets interpretation, leaving the viewer to passively accept the movie's meanings, postmodernist films like *City of God* encourage viewers' active engagement in the construction of multiple interpretations, irrespective of the issue of accuracy.

Boyz n the Hood (1991)
Catch Me If You Can (2002)
Clockers (1995)
Godfather, The, parts I, II, and III (1972, 1974, 1990)
Let Him Have It (1991)
Little Caesar (1931)
Of Mice and Men (1939)
Scarface (1983)
They Made Me a Criminal (1939)

Three films in combination about the serial killer Aileen Wuornos: *Aileen Wuornos: The Selling of a Serial Killer* (1992); *Aileen: Life and Death of a Serial Killer* (2003); and *Monster* (2003)

12

Conclusion

The Big Picture

What happens, then, when criminology goes to the movies? It has fun, of course, and sees itself in a new mirror, but there are a number of more important results.

When criminology goes to the movies, we discover, first, that domains that often seem to belong to different universes—academic discourses on crime, on the one hand, and popular culture, on the other—actually overlap. These overlaps are the topic of popular (or cultural) criminology, a relatively new discourse in the criminological world that takes its place alongside discussions of subcultural formations, rational choice models, strain theories, and other strands of academic criminology. Popular criminology shows how deeply academic criminology and popular culture are actually intertwined. Big-name criminologists such as Cesare Lombroso, Edwin Sutherland, and Robert Agnew do not float in a hot air balloon, exchanging ideas high above ordinary heads; rather, their ideas are part of an ongoing dialogue between formal criminology and popular culture.

Analyzing the area of overlap between academic criminology and popular culture, as we have done in this book, clears away underbrush that has prevented academic criminologists from finding a route into popular culture. It opens up a path along which, we hope, increasing numbers of criminologists will travel to discover connections with popular culture. Moreover, this path enables travel in both directions; it should also give specialists in popular culture a route into criminology, one that will enable them to see, for instance, how formal explanations of crime constitute important subtexts in the best crime films, shaping narratives and characters.

Second, when criminology goes to the movies, its boundaries open up. No harm is done to the specialized theories and methods currently contained by those boundaries, but criminology becomes interdisciplinary. More accurately: criminology becomes *more* interdisciplinary, for it has always been an eclectic, magpie sort of field, picking up useful ideas where it finds them.

Popular criminology adds new dimensions to what the field can study (images and representations) and new tools (standpoint theory; analysis of images and representations) to add to its other methods of studying of crime. Drawing criminological theory closer to the image, popular criminology makes the field conscious of ways in which representations carry meaning. With such consciousness, criminology can become more sensitive to how representations construct what we see and think. An example can be found in the documentary *Capturing the Friedmans* (2003), in which a cop states with certainty that she saw stacks of magazines of child pornography all over Arnold Friedman's house. In fact, there was only one such magazine, and it was hidden behind the piano. What made the officer think that she had seen heaps of child pornography? Stereotyped representations of child molesters, or so we can assume.

Third, when criminology goes to the movies, it rediscovers aspects of crime that are left out of academic criminology. These include the emotive aspects of crime that scientific study washes out—the pain of crime, victims' feeling of having lost control, the anger, the sense of loss, the fear. Whereas academic criminology offers rather flat images of crime (when it offers images at all), movies provide something closer to hologram, three-dimensional images on a two-dimensional surface that you feel you can walk around and examine from various angles. Movies present narratives, which most academic criminologists (with the exception of members of the 1930s Chicago school) do not—stories that enable us to follow crime incidents or criminals through time and space. And they offer a different kind of complexity than one finds in the usual criminological study. Think, for example, of Norman Bates, the central character of *Psycho* (1960), whose mazelike psychology would be difficult to capture in a scientific study. Similarly, *Psycho*'s overall sense of entrapment by the gaze of others would not provide much material for scientific discussion, although feelings of entrapment by the gaze of others are ubiquitous among crime victims—and perpetrators as well. Moreover, *Psycho*, like many good crime films, brings up ethical issues that are seldom raised in more formal criminology, questions about sadism, for instance, and the sources of good and evil. While academic criminology does many things better than popular criminology, the reverse is also true.

Fourth, when criminology goes to the movies, it learns new approaches to analyzing crime. It engages in close textual examination, analyzing images for what they contribute to the explanation of crime. It learns the value of "thick" description—portrayals that explain not only criminal behavior but also the context in which it occurs, since context holds the keys to interpretation.[1] At the movies, criminology also learns the value of standpoint theory, the notion that seeing events from a specific person's point of view is sometimes more valuable than striving for an elusive objectivity. *Thelma & Louise* (1991), for instance, forces us to give up "objective" views of criminology and instead to see crimes from the standpoint of the two women who are fleeing the law on an apparent crime spree. Other films, such as *Before the Devil Knows You're Dead* (2007), shift among different standpoints in their depictions of criminal events. Contrast this richness in perspectives on crime with that of a large numerical dataset. Statistical analysis is invaluable, but so are textual analysis, thick description, and standpoint theory.

Popular criminology helps us understand crime itself. This is a fifth effect of criminology's trip to the cinema. The point is not only that movies can give us fresh perspectives on crime; it is that representations organize our worlds. We cannot think without them. Representations construct our realities, shaping how we think, define crimes, organize our thinking about "crime problems," define who is criminal, who is a good law enforcement officer, and how we should "fight" crime. We were not born with opinions on these matters; rather, we build up (and change) our opinions over time in light of cultural encounters. Some of us may also derive our opinions from the lessons of formal criminology, but the great majority of people get their ideas about crime and punishment from popular culture.

Sixth and finally, when criminology goes to the movies, the theories that students love to hate become more accessible and, we hope, more meaningful to them and other consumers of academic criminology. Movies translate the theories into narratives, enabling us to visualize a theory in action. They make theory exciting and fluid; they stimulate vigorous arguments about theory; and sometimes they take a formal criminological theory and run with it, stretching it beyond its academic formulation.

At the start of this book, we set ourselves the goal of contributing to criminological theory. We have tried to show how one can conceptualize the vast amount of theorizing about crime that goes on in popular culture. We have suggested ways of incorporating this type of speculation into more formal academic discourse by identifying and defining a related type of discourse, popular criminology. We have also tried to build bridges between criminology and the study of popular culture, so that specialists in the latter field, who have sometimes been hesitant to tackle crime movies and other crime-related artifacts, will have a way to—well, take movies to criminology. Above all, we have attempted to uncover the vast amount of criminological material that can be found in movies. When criminology goes to the movies, it finds itself.

Appendix of Films

What follows is an alphabetical list of all films referenced in the text of *Criminology Goes to the Movies*. We do not include the films mentioned only in our "Further Viewing" lists.

Aileen: Life and Death of a Serial Killer (2003)
Aileen Wuornos: The Selling of a Serial Killer (1992)
American Gangster (2007)
American History X (1998)
American Me (1992)
Angels with Dirty Faces (1938)
Asphalt Jungle, The (1950)
Babel (2006)
Badlands (1973)
Bad Seed, The (1950)
Before the Devil Knows You're Dead (2007)
Bicycle Thief, The (1948)
Blackboard Jungle (1955)
Bonnie and Clyde (1967)
Boston Strangler, The (1968)
Bottle Rocket (1996)
Boyz n the Hood (1991)
Brave One, The (2007)
Brother's Keeper (1992)
Butch Cassidy and the Sundance Kid (1969)
Capturing the Friedmans (2003)
City of God (2002)
Civil Action, A (1998)
Clockers (1995)
Clockwork Orange, A (1971)
Coffy (1973)

Collateral (2004)

Crash (2004)

Death Wish (1974)

Departed, The (2006)

Dirty Harry (1971)

Do the Right Thing (1989)

Double Indemnity (1944)

Easy Rider (1969)

Enron: The Smartest Guys in the Room (2005)

Falling Down (1993)

Fargo (1996)

Fight Club (1999)

Frankenstein (1931)

Fury (1936)

Gattaca (1997)

Godfather, The (1972)

Godfather II, The (1974)

Goodfellas (1990)

Green Mile, The (1999)

Hand That Rocks the Cradle, The (1992)

I Am a Fugitive from a Chain Gang (1932)

Insider, The (1999)

I Want to Live (1958)

John Q (2002)

L.A. Confidential (1997)

Let Him Have It (1991)

M (1931)

Malcolm X (1992)

Menace II Society (1993)

Michael Clayton (2007)

Monster (2003)

Ms. 45 (1981)

Mystic River (2003)

New Jack City (1991)

No Country for Old Men (2007)

Oceans 11 (1960; 2001)

Of Mice and Men (1939)

One Flew Over the Cuckoo's Nest (1975)

Paradise Lost: The Child Murders at Robin Hood Hills (1996)

Psycho (1960)
Public Enemy (1931)
Rebel without a Cause (1955)
Reefer Madness (1936)
Requiem for a Dream (2000)
Reservoir Dogs (1992)
Roger & Me (1989)
Run Lola Run (1998)
Scarface (1932)
Searchers, The (1956)
Serpico (1973)
Shaft (1971)
Shawshank Redemption, The (1994)
Sicko (2007)
Silence of the Lambs, The (1991)
Sleepers (1996)
Sling Blade (1996)
Sudden Impact (1983)
Sunset Blvd. (1950)
Superfly (1972)
Super Size Me (2004)
Sweet Sweetback's Baadasssss Song (1971)
Sympathy for Lady Vengeance (2005)
Syriana (2005)
Taxi Driver (1976)
Thelma & Louise (1991)
There Will Be Blood (2007)
Titicut Follies (1967)
Traffic (2000)
Trainspotting (1996)
Yes Men, The (2003)
Woodsman, The (2004)

Notes

1. Rafter, "Crime, Film and Criminology," 406.

2. Garland and Sparks, "Introduction," 3.

3. Here, we borrow from Austin Sarat's terminology, "law in the image," as elaborated in his 1999 Law and Society Association presidential address. Sarat, following the line of argument that law is present everywhere in everyday life, insists that film is not simply a reflection of law but is a means through which to project alternative realities. For this reason, it is central to explorations of the legal imagination. See Sarat, "Presidential Address: Imagining the Law of the Father."

4. Recently, film has been given a more pivotal place in the study of crime and society by way of specialized journals (*Media, Culture, & Society; New Media & Society*) and key volumes. Studies with criminal justice institutional focal points include Bailey and Hale, *Popular Culture, Crime, and Justice*; King, *Heroes in Hard Times*; and Wilson and O'Sullivan, *Images of Incarceration*. Studies focused on film, crime, and popular culture include Tzanelli, O'Brien, and Yar, "'Con Me If You Can'"; O'Brien et al., "'The Spectacle of Fearsome Acts'" and "'Kill n' Tell, and All That Jazz'"; Brown, "Prison Iconography"; Simpson, *Psycho Paths*; Staiger, *Perverse Spectators*; Walkowitz, *City of Dreadful Delight*; Young, *Judging the Image*; Asimow and Mader, *Law and Popular Culture*; Chase, *Movies on Trial*; Freeman, *Law and Popular Culture*; Sherwin, *When Law Goes Pop*; and Greenfield and Osborne, *Readings in Law and Popular Culture*. More broadly, sociologist Norman Denzin's work with cinema often attempts to integrate film with theoretical perspectives (see *Images of Postmodern Society; The Cinematic Society; Reading Race*). Meanwhile, within the fields of film studies and popular culture, books such as Leitch, *Crime Films*; Lenz, *Changing Images of Law in Film and Television Crime Stories*; and Campbell, *Marked Women*, as well as a wealth of film studies volumes focused upon film noir, feminist film theory, horror, and violence, all converge with criminological concerns.

5. See Brown, "Beyond the Requisites"; Jewkes, *Media and Crime*; Hebdige, *Subculture*.

6. See groundbreaking work by Cohen, *Images of Deviance; Folk Devils and Moral Panics*; and *States of Denial*. See also Cohen and Young, *The Manufacture of News*; Hall et al., *Policing the Crisis*; and Fishman, "Crime Waves as Ideology." Building from moral panic perspectives are these key social constructionist texts: Surette, *Media, Crime, and Criminal Justice*; Jenkins, *Using Murder*; Sasson, *Crime Talk*; Scheingold, *Politics of Law and Order*; Potter and Kappeler, *Constructing Crime*; Barak, *Media, Process, and the Social Construction of Crime*; Best, *Random Violence*; Chermak, *Searching for a Demon: The Media Construction of the Militia Movement* and *Victims in the News*; Chermak, Bailey, and Brown, *Media*

Representations of September 11; Reinarman, "The Social Construction of Drug Scares"; Beckett, *Making Crime Pay*; Sarat, *When the State Kills*. For contemporary critiques, see McRobbie and Thornton, "Rethinking 'Moral Panic' for Multi-mediated Social Worlds"; Garland, "On the Concept of Moral Panic."

7. Criminological journals publish an increasing number of articles on crime films, and within the field of criminology a whole new specialty—cultural criminology—has sprung up, replete with its own journals (*Crime, Media, Culture*, for instance) and conferences. Cultural criminology is particularly well known for its analyses of texts, images, and discourse and for its detailed ethnographic reflections on criminality in everyday life. It encourages us to rethink media representations as not simply exaggerations or distortions of real-life crime but cultural forces in and of themselves, capable of creating and elaborating complex criminologies of their own. See Ferrell, "Cultural Criminology"; Ferrell et al., *Cultural Criminology: An Invitation*; Hayward, "Opening the Lens: Cultural Criminology and the Image"; Ferrell and Sanders, *Cultural Criminology*; Ferrell and Hamm, *Ethnography at the Edge*; Ferrell and Websdale, *Making Trouble: Cultural Constructions of Crime, Deviance, and Control*; Presdee, *Cultural Criminology and the Carnival of Crime*.

8. McRobbie and Thornton, "Rethinking 'Moral Panic' for Multi-mediated Social Worlds," 571.

9. See Glassner, *Culture of Fear*; Furedi, *Culture of Fear*; Best, *Random Violence*; Jenkins, *Using Murder*; Schmid, *Natural Born Celebrities*.

10. Katz, *Seductions of Crime*.

11. Rafter, *Shots in the Mirror*.

12. See Rafter, "Crime, Film and Criminology," 406.

13. Hayward, "Opening the Lens," 9.

14. Carrabine, *Crime, Culture and the Media*, 120.

15. Rafter, "Crime, Film and Criminology," 415.

16. Carrabine, *Crime, Culture and the Media*, 187.

17. Ibid.

18. Young, "The Scene of the Crime," 87 (emphasis in original).

19. Ibid., 87–88.

NOTES TO CHAPTER 2

1. It is worth noting that the definition of film noir is hotly debated, including its status as a genre, style, cycle, mood, or movement. See Borde and Chaumeton, "Toward a Definition of Film Noir"; Durgnat, "Paint It Black"; Naremore, *More Than Night*; Schrader, "Notes on Film Noir."

2. For instance, *Double Indemnity* is ranked by *Time* magazine and the American Film Institute as one of the top 100 films of all time. It is also ranked consistently in the top 50 of all films by Internet Movie Database users.

3. Beccaria, *On Crimes and Punishments*, 7.

4. Ibid., 113.

5. Ibid., 19.

6. For a more thorough explication of Beccaria's argument, see Radzinowicz, *Ideology and Crime*; Vold et al., *Theoretical Criminology*; Beirne, "Towards a Science of Homo Criminalis."

7. See Bottoms, "Environmental Criminology"; Cohen and Felson, "Social Change and Crime Rate Trends"; Felson, *Crime and Everyday Life*; Garland, "The Limits of the Sovereign State"; Hindelang, Gottfredson, and Garofalo, *Victims of Personal Crime*; Kelling and Coles, *Fixing Broken Windows*; Wilson, *Thinking about Crime*; Wright and Decker, *Armed Robbers in Action*.

8. See Wilson, *Thinking about Crime*; Martinson, "What Works?"; Bennett et al., *Body Count*; Kelling and Coles, *Fixing Broken Windows*.

9. Wilson, *Thinking about Crime*, 250.

10. Hall et al., *Policing the Crisis*; Beckett, *Making Crime Pay*; Garland, *Mass Imprisonment*.

11. See Cornish and Clarke, *The Reasoning Criminal*; Clarke and Cornish, "Modelling Offenders' Decisions"; Felson, *Crime and Everyday Life*; Clarke and Felson, *Routine Activity and Rational Choice*; Newman et al., *Rational Choice and Situational Crime Prevention*.

12. Felson, *Crime and Everyday Life*, 174.

13. Ibid., 50.

14. For instance, the plot of *Sunset Blvd.* (1950) is told from the flashback point of view of a protagonist (played by William Holden) who is found dead at the beginning of the film, floating face-down in the pool.

15. Beccaria, *On Crimes and Punishments*, 9.

16. Paris, "'Murder Can Sometimes Smell Like Honeysuckle,'" 14.

17. The production decision to omit the execution scene reflects the movie industry's then-current censorship guidelines, known as the Hays Production Code. Criminal behavior and, in particular, the methods of committing crime had to be carefully presented so as not to encourage such behavior by providing models for crime's enactment. Similarly, murder scenes could not be brutal in detail and, perhaps most important, the audience's sympathy, it was suggested, should never be on the side of crime or wrongdoing, necessitating Hollywood plots where the criminal is ultimately and always inevitably punished. However, the details of punishment in representation, in particular the death penalty, were to be either portrayed very carefully or avoided when possible due to underlying assumptions related to its possibility as spectacle and cruelty. Film noir challenged many of the code's guidelines in its portrayal of sympathetic criminals and punishment.

NOTES TO CHAPTER 3

1. Rafter, *The Criminal Brain*; Raine, *Psychopathology of Crime*; Wright, Tibbetts, and Daigle, *Criminals in the Making*.

2. Lombroso, *Criminal Man*, 222.

3. Ibid., 336.

4. Lombroso, *L'uomo bianco et uomo di colore*; Rafter, *The Criminal Brain*.

5. Lombroso, *Criminal Man*, 48.

6. Lombroso and Ferrero, *Criminal Woman*, 120.

7. Lombroso and Ferrero, *Criminal Woman*; Lombroso, *Palimpsestes des prisons*.

8. Regener, "Criminological Museums."

9. Rafter, *Creating Born Criminals*.

10. Bruinius, *Better for All the World*; Rafter, *Creating Born Criminals*.

11. Hooton, *The American Criminal*; Hooton, *Crime and the Man*.

12. Hooton, *The American Criminal*, 309.

13. Sheldon, *Varieties of Delinquent Youth*, 762.

14. Ibid., 752.

15. Ibid., 759.

16. Ibid., 826.

17. Wilson and Herrnstein, *Crime and Human Nature*.

18. Herrnstein and Murray, *The Bell Curve*.

19. Gould, "Curveball," 139.

20. Sutherland, *Principles of Criminology*. For the story of this boundary hardening, see Laub and Sampson, "The Sutherland-Glueck Debate."

21. Eysenck, *Crime and Personality*.

22. Ibid.

23. Ibid., 100, 172.

24. Moffitt, "'Adolescence-Limited' and 'Life-Course-Persistent' Antisocial Behavior."

25. Farrington, "Implications of Biological Findings"; Raine, *Psychopathology of Crime*.

26. Rafter, *The Criminal Brain*.

27. Shelley, "Author's Introduction" to the 1831 edition of Frankenstein, 9.

28. Shelley, *Frankenstein*, 147.

29. Lombroso and Ferrero, *Criminal Woman*.

NOTES TO CHAPTER 4

1. Ash, "Psychology," 251.

2. Gay, *Freud*, 491.

3. Beirne and Messerschmidt, *Criminology*.

4. Watson, *Behaviorism*, 82.

5. Raine, *Psychopathology of Crime*, 217.

6. Eysenck, *Crime and Personality*, chap. 5.

7. The scantiness of Freud's interest in criminal behavior is documented in Gay, *Freud*.

8. Freud, "Criminals from a Sense of Guilt," 333.

9. Aichhorn, *Wayward Youth*; Alexander and Healy, *Roots of Crime*; Redl and Wineman, *Children Who Hate* and *Controls from Within*. Healy (*The Individual Delinquent*) bridged abnormal psychology and psychoanalysis, as did White (*Crimes and Criminals*). For an overview, see Fitzpatrick, "Psychoanalysis and Crime."

10. Lunbeck, *The Psychiatric Persuasion*. In the early twentieth century, psychiatrists began attributing mental disease to factors such as maladjustment that assumed it to be independent of brain matter, but the older organicist tradition faded slowly.

11. Hare, *Without Conscience*. Hare, a psychologist, has wrested authority over the concept of psychopathy from psychiatrists. The best-selling book is one of the leading texts on psychopathy.

12. Rebello, *Alfred Hitchcock and the Making of* Psycho.

13. Wood, *Hitchcock's Films*, 143.

14. Evans, *Rituals of Retribution*, 530.

15. At Walpole, apparently just before he was about to retract his strangler confession and identify someone else as the actual killer, DeSalvo was stabbed to death. In 2001,

exhumations and DNA testing of DeSalvo and one victim proved that he was not the man who had sexually assaulted her; it followed that, in this case at least, he had not been the killer. Much about the Boston strangler case remains unresolved, with some speculating that there could have been as many as six or eight different assailants involved in the murders.

16. The film was released before DeSalvo was murdered.

17. As Maruna (*Making Good*, 3–4) explains, Burgess's original novel included a final chapter in which Alex grew up and became ashamed of his past behavior.

NOTES TO CHAPTER 5

1. As cited in Bulmer, *The Chicago School of Sociology*, 45.

2. As cited in ibid., 90.

3. See Hawley, "Ecology and Human Ecology" and *Human Ecology*.

4. McKenzie, "The Ecological Approach," 69.

5. Bulmer, *The Chicago School of Sociology*, 93.

6. Taxi dance halls are places where professional dancers (generally, women) were paid to dance with patrons (generally, men). These dance halls flourished in the 1920s and 1930s in U.S. cities as a site where strangers temporarily connected with each other. In his study of taxi dance halls, Paul Cressey found these establishments to be functional sites for human needs fueled by the dramatic transformations in urban life and the loneliness and isolation that accompanied such shifts.

7. See Thomas and Znaniecki, *The Polish Peasant in Europe and America*; Cressey, *The Taxi-Dance Hall*; Wirth, *The Ghetto*; Whyte, *Street Corner Society*; Anderson, *The Hobo*; Reckless, *Vice in Chicago*; Shaw, *The Jack-Roller*.

8. Burgess, "The Growth of the City," 57.

9. Ibid., 54.

10. Shaw and McKay, *Juvenile Delinquency in Urban Areas*.

11. Short, *The Social Fabric of the Metropolis*, 244.

12. Ibid., 250.

13. Sampson, "Whither the Sociological Study of Crime?" 713.

14. In these definitions, we rely upon the following works: Sampson, "Neighborhood and Community"; Sampson and Raudenbush, "Systematic Social Observation of Public Spaces"; Sampson et al., "Beyond Social Capital: Spatial Dynamics of Collective Efficacy for Children."; Sampson et al., "Neighborhoods and Violent Crime."

15. Sampson et al., "Neighborhoods and Violent Crime," 918.

16. Ibid.

17. Kelling and Coles, *Fixing Broken Windows*.

18. Sampson and Raudenbush, "Systematic Social Observation of Public Spaces." See also Beckett and Herbert, *Banished*.

19. Sampson, "Neighborhood and Community," 112.

20. Ibid., 112–13.

21. Burgess, "The Growth of the City," 56.

22. The so-called child savers were reformers whose work in some ways set a precedent for the Chicago school; however, the two groups approached social reform differently. See Platt, *The Child Savers*; Rothman, *Conscience and Convenience*.

1. On the Criterion Collection edition of *Traffic*, Soderbergh explains how he achieved the film's color effects. In addition, the Wikipedia entry on *Traffic* (http://en.wikipedia. org/wiki/Traffic_(movie)), includes information on how he achieved the different "look" for each plot.

2. In his director's commentary on the Criterion Collection edition of *Traffic*, Soderbergh tells how he and scriptwriter Stephen Gaghan over time simplified and in a sense purified Javier's character. Traces of Javier's earlier characterization seem to linger in the early scenes, adding to audience involvement, for we are forced to figure out what this enigmatic man is like. In contrast, most films simply tell us who is good and who is bad; they lack *Traffic*'s moral complexity.

3. See Boyd, *Hooked*, 83. Boyd argues that *Traffic* perpetuates this stereotype, thus perpetuating racism. However, this is a questionable interpretation.

4. See the sources cited in note 1.

5. Dargis, "*Traffic*."

6. Durkheim, *On Suicide*.

7. DuBois, *The Philadelphia Negro*, 282–84.

8. For the biographical details on Merton, see Lilly, Cullen, and Ball, *Criminological Theory*, 59; we have used the spelling of his original surname ("Schkolnick") that appears in the Wikipedia entry on Merton (http://en.wikipedia.org/wiki/Robert_k._Merton). Schkolnick never explained why he changed his name, but the switch was probably a good idea, professionally, in view of the period's anti-Semitism (see Laqueur, *The Changing Face of Anti-Semitism*, and, for examples pertaining particularly to criminology in the early to middle twentieth century, Laub, *Criminology in the Making*, 185, and Rafter, "Somatotyping," 823).

9. Merton, "Social Structure and Anomie," 676.

10. Ibid., 678.

11. Ibid., 674, 679.

12. Ibid., 676.

13. Ibid,. 677.

14. Another interpretation is also possible here. If we view the circumstances of poverty and crime in which Javier lives in terms of social disorganization theory (chapter 5), then Javier's effort to improve recreation for the youngsters can be compared to the efforts of the "child savers" (Platt, *The Child Savers*) who, in the early twentieth century, attempted to intervene in the lives of Chicago's delinquents in the hope of reforming them.

15. Some scholars maintain that Merton actually developed two related but conceptually separate theories of crime, a theory of anomie and a strain theory; see Murphy and Robinson, "The Maximizer." Strain theory, in this view, engendered the work of Cloward and Ohlin on differential opportunity structures, while anomie theory led to Messner and Rosenfeld's work (discussed below) on the American Dream. Furthermore, Murphy and Robinson ("The Maximizer," 502) propose adding a new adaptation to Merton's famous chart, that of the Maximizer, "someone who simultaneously uses and incorporates legitimate and illegitimate means of opportunity in the pursuit of profit and/or monetary gain."

16. Cloward and Ohlin, *Delinquency and Opportunity*.

17. See Laub, *Criminology in the Making*, 213–17.

18. Also see the film *John Q* (2002).

19. Agnew, *Why Do Criminals Offend?* Also see Agnew, "Foundation for a General Strain Theory," which ignores Durkheim and mentions Merton only in passing.

20. Agnew, *Why Do Criminals Offend?* 12 (emphasis in original).

21. Ibid., 26.

22. Agnew, "Foundation for a General Strain Theory," 64.

23. Agnew, *Why Do Criminals Offend?*

24. On biological theories, see chapter 3; on the so-called general theory of crime, see Gottfredson and Hirschi, *A General Theory of Crime.*

25. See, especially, Agnew, "Foundation for a General Strain Theory," 51, 74.

26. Agnew et al., "Strain, Personality Traits, and Delinquency," 43–44.

27. Tittle, *Control Balance*, 87.

28. Messner, Thome, and Rosenfeld, "Institutions, Anomie, and Violent Crime."

29. Rosenfeld and Messner, "The Origins, Nature, and Prospects of Institutional-Anomie Theory," 165 (emphasis in original).

30. Ibid., 165–66; also see Messner, Thome, and Rosenfeld, "Institutions, Anomie, and Violent Crime." 168.

31. Rosenfeld and Messner, "The Origins, Nature, and Prospects of Institutional-Anomie Theory," 169.

32. Ibid., 166.

33. Ibid., 170; also see Messner and Rosenfeld, *Crime and the American Dream*, 1994.

34. On the internationalization of GST, see Botchkovar, Tittle, and Antonaccio, "General Strain Theory"; on the internationalization of IAT, see Frerichs, Munch, and Sander, "Anomic Crime in Post-welfarist Societies"; Passas, "Global Anomie Theory"; and the entire issue (vol. 2, no. 2 [2008]) of the *International Journal of Conflict and Violence* devoted to institutional anomie theory.

35. Dargis, "*Traffic.*"

NOTES TO CHAPTER 7

1. Gaylord and Galliher, *The Criminology of Edwin Sutherland*, 162.

2. Sutherland, "Development of the Theory," 15–16.

3. Ibid., 16–17. The story of the selection of culture conflict as the topic for their Social Science Research Council report is told by Sellin in Laub, *Criminology in the Making*, 174. For the results of the collaboration, see Sellin, *Culture Conflict and Crime.*

4. Sutherland, "Development of the Theory," 17–19.

5. See, especially, Carrabine, *Crime, Culture and the Media*; also see Rafter, *Shots in the Mirror*, esp. pp. 8–11.

6. Sutherland, *Principles of Criminology*, 6. Italics in original.

7. By "priority" Sutherland meant that behavior (lawful or unlawful) that is learned in childhood may persist throughout life. He used "intensity" to refer to the prestige of the source and emotional reactions to the associations. Sutherland, *Principles of Criminology*, 7.

8. Ibid., 6–7.

9. The seemingly simple change in label washed out the social-structural implications inherent in the older "social disorganization" label, instead emphasizing culture conflict

among groups with varying norms. See Costello, "On the Logical Adequacy of Cultural Deviance Theories," 413–14, on the implications of this shift and p. 417 for its consequences. With "social disorganization," Costello argues, one can analytically separate social structure from individuals' values and thus empirically assess the theory, but with "differential social organization," testing is impossible.

10. Sutherland, *Principles of Criminology*, 8.

11. Also see the introduction to Laub, *Criminology in the Making*. Examples of Sutherland's reports and book reviews are collected in Cohen, Lindesmith, and Schuessler, *The Sutherland Papers*. For a particularly critical view of the way Sutherland dealt with those who strayed from the sociological true path, see Laub and Sampson, "The Sutherland-Glueck Debate."

12. Laub, *Criminology in the Making*, 9.

13. Donald R. Cressey, "Epidemiology and Individual Conduct: A Case from Criminology," *Pacific Sociological Review* 3 (1960): 47–58, p. 57, as cited and quoted in Laub, *Criminology in the Making*, 18.

14. Cohen interview in Laub, *Criminology in the Making*, 189–90.

15. Hirschi and Gottfredson, "Introduction: The Sutherland Tradition in Criminology," 8. Leading the pack of Sutherland attackers was Ruth Kornhauser, *Social Sources of Delinquency*, who sarcastically declared that Sutherland's "delinquents never violate norms, for they are all well-socialized members of well-knit subsocieties to whose cultural codes they invariably conform. . . . Delinquents are the neutral recipients of quantities of definitions emanating from subcultures. . . . [The delinquent] is a norm violator only in the eyes of those who are powerful enough to make and enforce law. In his own and his companions' eyes, he is simply conforming to group norms" (181). In other words, Kornhauser ridiculed Sutherland's assertion that members of subcultures have norms entirely at variance with the norms of the broader culture and that their norms and behaviors are determined by subcultural definitions.

16. Laub and Sampson, "The Sutherland-Glueck Debate."

17. A subculture is a group smaller than the larger group of which it is a part and different by virtue of its beliefs, values, interests, and activities. The term seems to have been used first by late nineteenth-century biologists who, when breeding microcosms, would separate some to reproduce in different colonies and thus become "subcultures."

18. Laub, *Criminology in the Making*, 19.

19. Cohen, *Delinquent Boys*, 14.

20. See, in addition to Cohen's *Delinquent Boys*, his interview in John Laub's *Criminology in the Making*.

21. Cohen, *Delinquent Boys*, 86.

22. Ibid., 68.

23. Ibid., 153 (emphasis in original).

24. See the interview with Ohlin in Laub, *Criminology in the Making*.

25. Cohen does mention middle-class delinquency and girl gangs in Delinquent Boys, but his research focused on lower-class male delinquency.

26. Ohlin as quoted in Laub, *Criminology in the Making*, 213.

27. On the "culture of poverty" (a concept subsequently much criticized for pathologizing the poor), see Lewis, *Five Families*, and Monihan, *The Negro Family*. Walter B. Miller, although not as influential as Cohen or Cloward and Ohlin, was another of the period's well-

known researchers of delinquent subcultures; see, for example, Miller, "Lower Class Culture as a Generating Milieu of Gang Delinquency." The classic study of police subcultures and corruption is Knapp Commission, *The Knapp Commission Report on Police Corruption*. For the classic study of inmate subcultures, see Sykes, *Society of Captives*, and for the ur-work in the subculture of violence literature, see Wolfgang and Ferracuti, *Subculture of Violence*.

28. Merton, "Social Structure and Anomie."

29. Clemmer's book *The Prison Community* did appear in an earlier, 1940 edition, published in Boston by Christopher Publishing House. However, it did not appear as a trade book until Rinehart released it in 1958.

30. Cohen as quoted in Laub, *Criminology in the Making*, 192.

31. Offenders, journalists, and other authors had been publishing criminal life histories for decades, as indicated by citations in Sutherland, *The Professional Thief*. However, before *The Jack-Roller*, criminal life histories had little criminological import; they were rather produced as exposés or parts of larger descriptions of the underworld.

32. *The Jack-Roller* was published over a decade before the first of the films that came to be labeled "noirs"—black-and-white movies with shadowy underworld settings and characters.

33. Also see Shaw, *Natural History of a Delinquent Career*, the autobiography of Sidney, a young gang member convicted of rape and robbery.

34. Also see The Jack-Roller et al., *The Jack-Roller at Seventy*.

35. Sutherland, *The Professional Thief*.

36. Ibid., 206.

37. Ibid.

38. Ibid., iv.

39. Also see Gaylord and Galliher, *The Criminology of Edwin Sutherland*, 110–11.

40. Snodgrass, "The Criminologist and His Criminal," as discussed in Gaylord and Galliher, *The Criminology of Edwin Sutherland*, 110–11.

41. Sutherland, *The Professional Thief*, iii.

42. For a later example, see Steffensmeier, *The Fence*. On the life-history approach more generally, see Bennett, *Oral History and Delinquency*, and Presser, "The Narratives of Offenders."

43. Scorsese grew up in the midst of a criminal subculture in New York City and has said that his early experiences shaped many of his movies.

44. Death does not necessarily limit a movie character's ability to narrate his or her life history, as demonstrated by *Sunset Blvd.* (1950), in which we first encounter the narrator floating face-down in a swimming pool.

45. Sutherland, *White Collar Crime*. Also see Sutherland, *White Collar Crime: The Uncut Version*.

46. Sutherland, "White-Collar Criminality," 59.

47. Sutherland, *White Collar Crime: The Uncut Version*, xi–xii, explains, "The term white-collar crime was incorporated into the language of scholarly work overseas as well as in the United States" and gives examples.

48. It is easier to portray in documentaries, as testified by the many documentaries that touch in one way or another on white-collar crime, for example, *Roger & Me* (1989), *The Yes Men* (2003), *Super Size Me* (2004), *Enron: The Smartest Guys in the Room* (2005), *Sicko* (2007), and *Capitalism: A Love Story* (2009).

49. See, for example, Hirschi and Gottfredson, "Introduction: The Sutherland Tradition in Criminology," and Costello, "On the Logical Adequacy of Cultural Deviance Theories."

50. See, especially, Hirschi, *Causes of Delinquency*.

51. Sutherland, *The Professional Thief*, 181.

52. Burgess and Akers, "A Differential Association-Reinforcement Theory."

53. See, especially, Matsueda, "'Cultural Deviance Theory.'"

54. See, for example, Lilly, Cullen, and Ball, *Criminological Theory*.

NOTES TO CHAPTER 8

1. Becker, *Outsiders*, 9.

2. For additional foundational labeling texts, see Becker, *The Other Side*; Erikson, "Notes on the Sociology of Deviance"; Garfinkel, "Conditions of Successful Degradation Ceremonies"; Kitsuse, "Societal Reaction to Deviant Behavior"; Lemert, "Beyond Mead"; Lemert, *Human Deviance, Social Problems and Social Control*; Lemert, *Social Pathology*; Tannenbaum, *Crime and the Community*.

3. Tannenbaum, *Crime and the Community*, 19–20.

4. Becker, *Outsiders*, 34.

5. See Western, *Punishment and Inequality in America*.

6. Scull, *Decarceration*; Miller, *Last One over the Wall*.

7. See Melossi, "Overcoming the Crisis in Critical Criminology"; Petrunik, "The Rise and Fall of 'Labelling Theory.'"

8. Best, *Deviance*, 35.

9. Liazos, "The Poverty of the Sociology of Deviance."

10. For some contemporary applications of labeling theory, see Beckett, *Making Crime Pay*; Ferrell, *Crimes of Style*; Sampson, "Effects of Socioeconomic Context on Official Reaction to Juvenile Delinquency"; Sasson, *Crime Talk*.

11. Sampson and Laub, "A Life-Course Theory of Cumulative Disadvantage," 150.

12. Braithwaite, *Crime, Shame, and Reintegration*, 100–101.

13. Zehr, *Changing Lenses*.

14. Cohen, *Folk Devils and Moral Panics*, 1.

15. Hall et al., *Policing the Crisis*, 16.

16. Ferrell and Sanders, *Cultural Criminology*, 308.

NOTES TO CHAPTER 9

1. See film commentaries: Baraka, "Spike Lee at the Movies"; Davis, "Black Independent or Hollywood Iconoclast?"; Gates, "Do the Right Thing: Issues and Images"; hooks, "Counter-hegemonic Art: Do the Right Thing"; McKelly, "The Double Truth, Ruth: Do the Right Thing and the Culture of Ambiguity"; Williams, "Why Spike Lee's New Film Ultimately Fails."

2. France, *The Red Lily*.

3. Reiman, *The Rich Get Richer and the Poor Get Prison*, 207.

4. Marx, *The Marx-Engels Reader*, 5. Also, see these works by Marx: *Capital, Volume One*; "Class Conflict and Law"; *The Eighteenth Brumaire of Louis Bonaparte*; and *The Communist Manifesto* (with Engels).

5. See Chambliss, "A Sociological Analysis of the Law of Vagrancy"; Chambliss and Mankoff, *Whose Law? What Order?*; Pashukanis, *The General Theory of Law and Marxism*; Quinney, *Critique of Legal Order*; Thompson, *Whigs and Hunters*; Hay, *Albion's Fatal Tree*.

6. See Greenberg, *Crime and Capitalism*; Spitzer, "Towards a Marxian Theory of Deviance"; Sykes, "The Rise of Critical Criminology"; Schwendinger and Schwendinger, *Adolescent Subcultures and Delinquency*; Rusche and Kirchheimer, *Punishment and Social Structure*; Platt, *The Child Savers*; Melossi and Pavarini, *The Prison and the Factory*; Rafter, *Partial Justice*; Taylor et al., *The New Criminology*; Triplett, "The Conflict Perspective, Symbolic Interactionism, and the Status Characteristics Hypothesis"; Irwin, *The Jail*.

7. See Turk, "Conflict and Criminality" and *Criminality and Legal Order*.

8. Also, see Chambliss, *On the Take*.

9. Quinney, *The Problem of Crime*, 180.

10. See Zehr, *Changing Lenses*; Sullivan and Tifft, *Handbook of Restorative Justice*.

11. See Lynch and Michalowski, *The New Primer in Radical Criminology*; Platt, "Prospects for a Radical Criminology in the United States."

12. See DeKeseredy, "The Left Realist Perspective on Race, Class, and Gender," and Schwartz and DeKeseredy, "Left Realist Criminology." Also, Young and Matthews, *Rethinking Criminology*, and Currie, *Confronting Crime*.

13. For a particularly cogent critique, see Sparks, "A Critique of Marxist Criminology."

14. Western and Beckett, "How Unregulated Is the U.S. Labor Market?"; Western, *Punishment and Inequality in America*.

NOTES TO CHAPTER 10

1. See Belknap, *The Invisible Woman*; Kruttschnitt, "Social Status and Sentences of Female Offenders"; Daly, *Gender, Crime, and Punishment*; Freedman, *Their Sisters' Keepers*; Rafter, *Partial Justice*; Carlen, *Women's Imprisonment*; Rafter, "Gender, Prisons, and Prison History."

2. Daly, "Gender, Crime, and Criminology."

3. Daly and Chesney-Lind, "Feminism and Criminology," 504.

4. See Rafter and Gibson, "Editors' Introduction."

5. Pollak, *The Criminality of Women*.

6. However, Eleanor Glueck as well as Sheldon Glueck wrote *Five Hundred Delinquent Women*, according to which female offenders are genetically defective, the trash of society, and should be locked up so long as they are capable of bearing children as their offspring will also be criminal. Another early account by a male criminologist that merges biological and psychological perspectives is Otto Pollak's *Criminality of Women*.

7. Rafter and Heidensohn, *International Feminist Perspectives in Criminology*, 3.

8. Bertrand, "The Myth of Sexual Equality before the Law"; Heidensohn, "The Deviance of Women"; Klein, "The Etiology of Female Crime."

9. Messerschmidt, *Masculinities and Crime*; Miller, *One of the Guys*.

10. Messerschmidt, *Masculinities and Crime*.

11. Miller, *One of the Guys*.

12. Daly and Maher, *Criminology at the Crossroads*, 13.

13. Owen, *In the Mix*.

14. See O'Brien, *Making It in the "Free World"*; Owen, *In the Mix*.

15. Cain, "Towards Transgression"; Maidment, "Transgressing Boundaries"; Naffine, *Female Crime*; Naffine, *Feminism and Criminology*; Simpson, "Feminist Theory, Crime, and Justice"; Young, *Imagining Crime*.

16. See Brownmiller, *Against Our Will*; Dobash and Dobash, *Violence against Women*; MacKinnon, *The Sexual Harassment of Working Women*; Schwartz and DeKeseredy, *Sexual Assault on the College Campus*; Schwendinger and Schwendinger, *Rape and Inequality*; Stanko, *Intimate Intrusions*.

17. Bowers, "'Thelma & Louise' Debuts," 74.

18. Grundman, "Hollywood Sets the Terms of the Debate," 35.

19. Ibid.

20. Rapping, "Feminism Gets the Hollywood Treatment," 30.

NOTES TO CHAPTER 11

1. For a strong contrast to Laub and Sampson's work, see Wright, Tibbetts, and Daigle, *Criminals in the Making*. For an overview of other life-course and developmental criminologies, see Farrington, "Developmental and Life-Course Criminology."

2. Sampson and Laub, *Crime in the Making*; Laub and Sampson, *Shared Beginnings, Divergent Lives*.

3. Sampson and Laub, *Crime in the Making*, 1.

4. Laub and Sampson, "The Sutherland-Glueck Debate."

5. Sampson, "Foreword," vi.

6. Earlier we used *Falling Down* as an example of strain theory, but the film also illustrates Laub and Sampson's age-graded theory of informal social control. Movies, because they are often open-ended in meaning, can illustrate more than one theory at a time; indeed, they sometimes suggest how separate theories might be integrated.

7. Laub and Sampson, *Shared Beginnings, Divergent Lives*, 54, quoting Mustafa Emirbayer, "Manifesto for a Relational Sociology," *American Journal of Sociology* 103 (1997): 307.

8. Ibid., 281.

9. Ibid., 282.

10. Ibid., 49.

11. Moffitt, "'Adolescence-Limited' and 'Life-Course-Persistent' Antisocial Behavior."

12. Ibid., 674.

13. Ibid., 686.

14. Ibid., 679.

15. Ibid., 686.

16. Ibid., 687 (emphasis in original).

17. The first of these other studies was Wolfgang, Figlio, and Sellin, *Delinquency in a Birth Cohort*; Moffitt claims this support in her 1993 article on p. 676.

18. Laub and Sampson, *Shared Beginnings, Divergent Lives*, esp. pp. 193–94.

19. Maruna, *Making Good*.

20. Ibid., 43 (textual citations omitted). The quotation is from D. Glazer, *Effectiveness of a Prison and Parole System* (Indianapolis, IN: Bobbs-Merrill, 1964).

21. Ibid., 7–8.

22. Ibid., 9.

23. Ibid., 87.

24. Ibid., 147.

25. Some commentators have complained that this gives false impression of favela life. See, for example, Oliveira, "An Ethic of the Aesthetic."

26. According to Elbow, "Three Recent Brazilian Films," 128–29, "Only the final scenes of the film showing the gang war were actually made in Cidade de Deus." Cf. Siwi, "City of God, City of Man," 235, and Holden, "Gangs of Rio de Janeiro," both of whom state that for security reasons none of the film was shot in the actual City of God.

27. Bradshaw, "Film of the Week: *City of God*," page 2 of 2.

28. McDonald, "Performing Masculinity," 20.

29. Rosenau, *Post-modernism and the Social Sciences*.

30. Ibid., 5.

31. Some criminologists have been less hesitant than those discussed here to incorporate postmodernism; see Arrigo, Milovanovic, and Schehr, *The French Connection*, and Milovanovic, *Postmodern Criminology*.

32. Oliveira, "An Ethic of the Aesthetic," 42, 45, 48.

NOTES TO CHAPTER 12

1. Again, the Chicago school of criminology did acknowledge and act upon the need for thick description.

Bibliography

Abbott, Jack Henry. *In the Belly of the Beast: Letters from Prison*. New York: Vintage Press, 1991.

Adler, Freda. *Sisters in Crime*. New York: McGraw-Hill, 1975.

Agnew, Robert. "Foundation for a General Strain Theory of Crime and Delinquency." *Criminology* 30 (1992): 47-87.

———. *Why Do Criminals Offend? A General Theory of Crime and Delinquency*. Los Angeles: Roxbury, 2005.

Agnew, Robert, Timothy Brezina, Joan Paul Wright, and Frances T. Cullen. "Strain, Personality Traits, and Delinquency: Extending General Strain Theory." *Criminology* 40 (2002): 43-70.

Aichhorn, August. *Wayward Youth*. New York: Viking Press, 1963.

Akers, Ronald L. *Social Learning and Social Structure*. New Brunswick, NJ: Transaction Publishers, 2009.

Anderson, Nels. *The Hobo: The Sociology of the Homeless Man*. Chicago: University of Chicago Press, 1923 (1967).

Arrigo, Bruce A., Dragan Milovanovic, and Robert Carl Schehr. 2005. *The French Connection in Criminology*. Albany: State University of New York Press.

Ash, Mitchell G. "Psychology." *The Modern Social Sciences*. Ed. Theodore M. Porter and Dorothy Ross. Cambridge: Cambridge University Press, 2003: 251-74.

Asimow, Michael, and Shannon Mader. *Law and Popular Culture*. New York: Lang, 2004.

Bailey, Frankie Y. and Donna Hale, eds. *Popular Culture, Crime, and Justice*. Belmont, CA: West/Wadsworth, 1998.

Barak, Gregg. *Media, Process, and the Social Construction of Crime: Studies in Newsmaking Criminology*. New York: Garland, 1994.

Baraka, Amiri. "Spike Lee at the Movies." *Black Cinema*. Ed. Martha Diawartha. New York: Routledge, 1993: 154-76.

Beccaria, Cesare. *On Crimes and Punishments and Other Writings*. New York: Cambridge University Press, 2003.

Becker, Howard S. "Becoming a Marihuana User." *American Journal of Sociology* 59 (1953): 235-42.

———, ed. *The Other Side: Perspectives on Deviance*. New York: Free Press, 1964.

———. *Outsiders: Studies in the Sociology of Deviance*. New York: Free Press, 1963.

Beckett, Katherine. *Making Crime Pay: Law and Order in Contemporary American Politics*. New York: Oxford University Press, 1997.

Beckett, Katherine, and Steve Herbert. *Banished: The New Social Control in Urban America*. New York: Oxford University Press, 2010

Beirne, Piers. "Towards a Science of Homo Criminalis: Cesare Beccaria's *Dei delitti e delle pene (1764)*." *Criminology* 29 (1993): 777–820.

Beirne, Piers, and James Messerschmidt. *Criminology*. 3d ed. Boulder, CO: Westview Press, 2000.

Belknap, Joanne. *The Invisible Woman: Gender, Crime, and Justice*. Belmont, CA: Wadsworth, 1996.

Bennett, James. *Oral History and Delinquency: The Rhetoric of Criminology*. Chicago: University of Chicago Press, 1981.

Bennett, William J., John J. DiIulio Jr., and John P. Walters. *Body Count: Moral Poverty—And How to Win America's War against Crime and Drugs*. New York: Simon and Schuster, 1996.

Bertrand, Marie-Andree. "The Myth of Sexual Equality before the Law." *Proceedings of the Fifth Research Conference on Delinquency and Criminality*. Montreal: Quebec Society of Criminology, 1967.

Best, Joel. *Deviance: Career of a Concept*. Belmont, CA: Wadsworth/Thomson, 2004.

——. *Random Violence: How We Talk about New Crimes and New Victims*. Berkeley: University of California Press, 1999.

Bonger, Willem. *Criminality and Economic Conditions*. Boston: Little, Brown, 1916.

Borde, Raymond, and Étienne Chaumeton. *Panorama du Film Noir Américain*. Paris: Flammarion, 1955.

——. "Toward a Definition of Film Noir." *Film Noir Reader*. Ed. Alain Silver and James Ursini. New York: Limelight Editions, 1996: 17-25.

Botchkovar, Ekatarina V., Charles R. Tittle, and Olena Antonaccio. "General Strain Theory: Additional Evidence Using Cross-Cultural Data." *Criminology* 47 (2009): 131–76.

Bottoms, Anthony E. "Environmental Criminology." *The Oxford Handbook of Criminology*. Ed. Mike Maguire, Rod Morgan, and Robert Reiner. Oxford: Oxford University Press, 1994: 585-656.

Bowers, Michelle. "'Thelma & Louise' Debuts." *Entertainment Weekly*, May 23, 1997, 74.

Boyd, Susan C. *Hooked: Drug War Films in Britain, Canada, and the United States*. New York: Routledge, 2008.

Bradshaw, Peter. Film of the Week: *City of God*. *The Guardian*, January 3, 2003. Accessed July 30, 2009. http://www.guardian.co.uk/culture/2003/jan/03/artsfeatures2.

Braithwaite, John. *Crime, Shame, and Reintegration*. Cambridge, MA: Cambridge University Press, 1989.

Brown, Michelle. "Beyond the Requisites: Alternative Starting Points in the Study of Media Effects and Youth Violence." *Journal of Criminal Justice and Popular Culture* 14 (2007): 1–20.

——. "Prison Iconography: Regarding the Pain of Others." *The Culture of Punishment: Prison, Society, and Spectacle*. New York: NYU Press, 2009: 50–83.

Brownmiller, Susan. *Against Our Will: Men, Women and Rape*. New York: Bantam, 1975.

Bruinius, Harry. *Better for All the World: The Secret History of Forced Sterilization and America's Quest for Racial Purity*. New York: Vintage, 2006.

Bulmer, Martin. *The Chicago School of Sociology: Institutionalization, Diversity, and the Rise of Sociological Research*. Chicago: University of Chicago Press, 1984.

Burgess, Ernest W. "The Growth of the City: An Introduction to a Research Project." *The City: Suggestions for Investigation of Human Behavior in the Urban Environment*. Ed. Robert E. Park, Ernest W. Burgess, and R. D. McKenzie. Chicago: University of Chicago Press, 1967: 47-62.

Burgess, Robert L., and Ronald L. Akers. "A Differential Association-Reinforcement Theory of Criminal Behavior." *Social Problems* 14 (1966): 128–47.

Bursik, Robert J. "Urban Dynamics and Ecological Studies of Delinquency." *Social Forces* 63 (1984): 393–413.

Cain, Maureen. "Towards Transgression: New Directions in Feminist Criminology." *International Journal of the Sociology of Law* 18 (1990): 1–18.

Campbell, Russell. *Marked Women: Prostitutes and Prostitution in the Cinema*. Madison: University of Wisconsin Press, 2006.

Carlen, Pat. *Women's Imprisonment: A Study in Social Control*. London: Routledge and Kegan Paul, 1983.

Carrabine, Eamonn. *Crime, Culture and the Media*. Malden, MA: Polity, 2008.

Chambliss, William J. *Crime and the Legal Process*. New York: McGraw-Hill, 1969.

———. *On the Take: From Petty Crooks to Presidents*. Bloomington: Indiana University Press, 1988.

———. "A Sociological Analysis of the Law of Vagrancy." *Social Problems* 12 (1964): 150–70.

Chambliss, William J., and Milton Mankoff, eds. *Whose Law? What Order? A Conflict Approach to Criminology*. New York: Wiley, 1976.

Chambliss, William J., and Robert Seidman. *Law, Order, and Power*. New York, Longman Higher Education, 1971.

Chase, Anthony. *Movies on Trial: The Legal System on the Silver Screen*. New York: New Press, 2002.

Chermak, Steven. *Searching for a Demon: The Media Construction of the Militia Movement*. Boston: Northeastern University Press, 2002.

———. *Victims in the News: Crime and the American News Media*. Boulder, CO: Westview, 1995.

Chermak, Steven, Frankie Bailey, and Michelle Brown, eds. *Media Representations of September 11*. New York: Praeger, 2003.

Chesney-Lind, Meda. "Women and Crime: The Female Offender." *Signs* 12 (1986): 78–96.

Clarke, Ronald V., and Derek B. Cornish. "Modelling Offenders' Decisions: A Framework for Research and Policy." *Crime and Justice* 6 (1985): 147–85.

Clarke, Ronald V., and Marcus Felson, eds. *Routine Activity and Rational Choice*. New Brunswick, NJ: Transaction Publishers, 2004.

Clemmer, Donald. *The Prison Community*. New York: Holt, Rinehart and Winston, 1958.

Cloward, Richard A., and Lloyd E. Ohlin. *Delinquency and Opportunity: A Theory of Delinquent Gangs*. New York: Free Press, 1960.

Cohen, Albert K. *Delinquent Boys: The Culture of the Gang*. New York: Free Press, 1955.

Cohen, Albert K., Alfred Lindesmith, and Karl Schuessler. *The Sutherland Papers*. Bloomington: Indiana University Press, 1956.

Cohen, Lawrence E., and Marcus Felson. "Social Change and Crime Rate Trends: A Routine Activity Approach." *American Sociological Review* 44 (1979): 588–608.

Cohen, Stanley. *Folk Devils and Moral Panics: The Creation of the Mods and Rockers*. London, MacGibbon, and Kee, 1972.

———. *Images of Deviance*. Harmondsworth: Penguin, 1971.

———. *States of Denial: Knowing about Atrocities and Suffering*. Malden, MA: Blackwell, 2001.

Cohen, Stanley, and Jock Young, eds. *The Manufacture of News: Deviance, Social Problems, and the Mass Media*. London: Constable, 1973.

Coleman, James S. "Social Capital in the Creation of Human Capital." *American Journal of Sociology* 94 (1988): S95–S120.

Conrad, Mark T., and Robert Porfirio, eds. *The Philosophy of Film Noir*. Lexington: University Press of Kentucky, 2007.

Cornish, Derek B., and Ronald V. Clarke. *The Reasoning Criminal: Rational Choice Perspectives on Offending*. New York: Springer-Verlag, 1986.

Costello, Barbara. "On the Logical Adequacy of Cultural Deviance Theories." *Theoretical Criminology* 1 (1997): 403–28.

Cressey, Paul G. *The Taxi-Dance Hall: A Sociological Study in Commercialized Recreation and City Life*. Chicago: University of Chicago Press, 1932.

Currie, Elliott. *Confronting Crime: An American Challenge*. New York: Pantheon, 1985

Daly, Kathleen. "Gender, Crime, and Criminology." *The Handbook of Crime and Criminology*. Ed. Michael Tonry. New York: Oxford University Press, 1989.

———. *Gender, Crime, and Punishment*. New Haven: Yale University Press, 1994.

Daly, Kathleen, and Meda Chesney-Lind. "Feminism and Criminology." *Justice Quarterly* 5 (1988): 498–538.

Daly, Kathleen, and Lisa Maher, eds. *Criminology at the Crossroads: Feminist Readings in Crime and Justice*. New York: Oxford University Press, 1998.

Dargis, Manohla. "*Traffic*." Criterion Collection–Online Cinematheque, May 28, 2002. Accessed June 11, 2009. http://www.criterion.com/current/posts/203.

Darwin, Charles. *On the Origin of Species*. Orig. 1859. New York: Cambridge University Press, 2009.

Davis, Zeinabu Irene. "Black Independent or Hollywood Iconoclast?" *Cineaste* 17 (1990): 37–39.

Deegan, Mary Jo. *Jane Addams and the Men of the Chicago School, 1892–1918*. New Brunswick, NJ: Transaction Publishers, 1988.

DeKeseredy, Walter S. "The Left Realist Perspective on Race, Class, and Gender." *Race, Gender, and Class in Criminology: The Intersections*. Ed. Martin D. Schwartz and Dragan Milanovic. New York: Garland, 1997.

Denzin, Norman. *The Cinematic Society: The Voyeur's Gaze*. Thousand Oaks, CA: Sage, 1995.

———. *Images of Postmodern Society: Social Theory and Contemporary Society*. Newbury Park, CA: Sage, 1991.

———. *Reading Race: Hollywood and the Cinema of Racial Violence*. Thousand Oaks, , CA: Sage, 2002.

Dobash, Russell P., and Rebecca E. Dobash. *Violence against Women: A Case against Patriarchy*. New York: Free Press, 1979.

DuBois, W. E. B. *The Philadelphia Negro: A Social Study*. Philadelphia: University of Pennsylvania Press, 1899.

Durgnat, Raymond. "Paint It Black: The Family Tree of the Film Noir." *Film Noir Reader*. Ed. Alain Silver and James Ursini. New York: Limelight Editions, 1996: 37–52.

Durkheim, Émile. *On Suicide*. New York: Penguin Classics, 2007.

Elbow, Gary S. "Three Recent Brazilian Films: A Review." *Journal of Latin American Geography* 4 (2005): 125–31.

Erikson, Kai T. "Notes on the Sociology of Deviance." *The Other Side: Perspectives on Deviance*. Ed. Howard S. Becker. New York: Free Press, 1964: 9–22.

———. *Wayward Puritans: A Study in the Sociology of Deviance*. New York: Macmillan, 1966.

Eysenck, H. J. *Crime and Personality*. St. Albans: Paladin, 1964.

Farrington, David P. "Developmental and Life-Course Criminology." *Criminology* 41 (2003): 221–25.

———. 1987. "Implications of Biological Findings for Criminological Research." *The Causes of Crime: New Biological Approaches*. Ed. S. A. Mednick, T. E. Moffitt, and S. A. Stack. New York: Cambridge University Press, 1987: 42–64.

Felson, Marcus. *Crime and Everyday Life: Insights and Implications for Society*. Thousand Oaks, CA: Pine Forge Press, 1994.

Ferrell, Jeff. *Crimes of Style: Urban Graffiti and the Politics of Criminality*. Boston: Northeastern University Press, 1996.

———. "Cultural Criminology." *Annual Review of Sociology* 25 (1999): 395–418.

Ferrell, Jeff, and Mark S. Hamm. *Ethnography at the Edge: Crime, Deviance and Field Research*. Boston: Northeastern University Press, 1998.

Ferrell, Jeff, Keith Hayward, and Jock Young. *Cultural Criminology: An Invitation*. London: Sage, 2008.

Ferrell, Jeff, and Clinton Sanders. *Cultural Criminology*. Boston: Northeastern University Press, 1995.

Ferrell, Jeff, and Neil Websdale. *Making Trouble: Cultural Constructions of Crime, Deviance, and Control*. New York: Aldine De Gruyter, 1999.

Fishman, Mark. "Crime Waves as Ideology." *Social Problems* 25 (1978): 531–43.

France, Anatole. *The Red Lily*. 1894. Accessed July 20, 2010. Project Gutenberg, http://www.gutenberg.org/etext/3922.

Freedman, Estelle. *Their Sisters' Keepers: Women's Prison Reform in America, 1830–1930*. Ann Arbor: University of Michigan Press, 1981.

Freeman, Michael, ed. *Law and Popular Culture*. New York: Oxford University Press, 2004.

Frerichs, Sabine, Richard Munch, and Monika Sander. "Anomic Crime in Post-welfarist Societies: Cult of the Individual, Integration Patterns and Delinquency." *International Journal of Conflict and Violence* 2 (2008): 194–214.

Freud, Sigmund. "Criminals from a Sense of Guilt." *The Standard Edition of the Complete Psychological Works of Sigmund Freud*. Vol. 14. London: Hogarth Press, 1916: 332–33.

Furedi, Frank. *Culture of Fear: Risk-taking and the Morality of Low Expectation*. New York: Continuum, 2002.

Garfinkel, Harold. "Conditions of Successful Degradation Ceremonies." *American Journal of Sociology* 61 (1956): 420–24.

Garland, David. "The Limits of the Sovereign State: Strategies of Crime Control in Contemporary Society." *British Journal of Criminology* 36 (1996): 445–71.

———, ed. *Mass Imprisonment: Social Causes and Consequences*. Thousand Oaks, CA: Sage, 2001.

———. "On the Concept of Moral Panic." *Crime Media Culture* 4 (2008): 9–30.

Garland, David, and Richard Sparks. "Introduction" to *Criminology and Social Theory*. Ed. David Garland and Richard Sparks. New York: Oxford, 2000: 1–22.

Gates, Henry Louis, Jr. "Do the Right Thing: Issues and Images." *New York Times*, July 9, 1989, sec. 2:1.

Gay, Peter. *Freud: A Life for Our Time*. New York: Norton, 1998.

Gaylord, Mark S., and John F. Galliher. *The Criminology of Edwin Sutherland*. New Brunswick, NJ: Transaction Books, 1988.

Giallombardo, Rose. *Society of Women: A Study of a Woman's Prison*. New York: Wiley, 1966.

Glassner, Barry. *The Culture of Fear: Why Americans Are Afraid of the Wrong Things*. New York: Basic Books, 2000.

Glueck, Sheldon, and Eleanor T. Glueck. *Five Hundred Delinquent Women*. New York: Knopf, 1934.

Goffman, Erving. *Asylums: Essays on the Social Situation of Mental Patients and Other Inmates*. New York: Anchor Books, 1961.

———. *Stigma: Notes on the Management of Spoiled Identity*. New York: Simon and Schuster, 1963.

Gottfredson, Michael R., and Travis Hirschi. *A General Theory of Crime*. Stanford, CA: Stanford University Press, 1990.

Gould, Stephen Jay. "Curveball." *New Yorker*, November 28, 1994, 139–49.

Greenberg, David. *Crime and Capitalism: Readings in Marxist Criminology*. Philadelphia: Temple University Press, 1993.

Greenfield, Steve, and Guy Osborn, eds. *Readings in Law and Popular Culture*. New York: Routledge, 2006.

Grundman, Roy. "Hollywood Sets the Terms of the Debate," *Cineaste* 4 (December 1991): 35–36.

Gusfield, Joseph R. Symbolic Crusade: Status Politics and the American Temperance Movement. Urbana: University of Illinois Press, 1963.

Hall, Stuart, Charles Critcher, Tony Jefferson, John Clarke, and Brian Robert. *Policing the Crisis: Mugging, the State and Law and Order*. London: Macmillan, 1978.

Hawley, Amos H. "Ecology and Human Ecology." *Social Forces* 22 (1943): 398–405.

———. *Human Ecology: A Theory of Community Structure*. New York: Ronald Press, 1950.

———. *Social Pathology*. New York: McGraw-Hill, 1951.

Hay, Douglas. *Albion's Fatal Tree: Crime and Society in Eighteenth-Century England*. New York: Penguin, 1975.

Hayward, Keith. "Opening the Lens: Cultural Criminology and the Image." *Framing Crime: Cultural Criminology and the Image*. Ed. Keith Hayward and Mike Presdee. New York: Routledge, 2010: 1–16.

Hebdige, Dick. *Hiding in the Light: On Images and Things*. New York: Routledge, 1988.

———. *Subculture: The Meaning of Style*. London: Methuen, 1979.

Heidensohn, Frances. "The Deviance of Women: A Critique and an Enquiry." *British Journal of Sociology* 19 (1968): 160–75.

Herrnstein, Richard J., and Charles Murray. *The Bell Curve: Intelligence and Class Structure in American Life*. New York: Free Press, 1994.

Hindelang, Michael J., Michael R. Gottfredson, and James Garofalo. *Victims of Personal Crime: An Empirical Foundation for a Theory of Personal Victimization*. Cambridge, MA: Ballinger, 1978.

Hirschi, Travis. *Causes of Delinquency*. Berkeley: University of California Press, 1969.

Hirschi, Travis, and Michael Gottfredson. 1980. "Introduction: The Sutherland Tradition in Criminology." *Understanding Crime: Current Theory and Research*. Ed. Travis Hirschi and Michael Gottfredson. Beverly Hills, CA: Sage, 1980: 7–19.

Holden, Stephen. "Gangs of Rio de Janeiro." *New York Times*, January 17, 2003. Accessed July 20, 2009. http://www.nytimes.com/2003/01/17/movies/17CITY.html?.

hooks, bell. "Counter-hegemonic Art: Do the Right Thing." *Yearning: Race, Gender, and Cultural Politics*. Toronto: Between the Lines, 1990: 173–84.

Hooton, Earnest A. *The American Criminal*. Cambridge: Harvard University Press, 1939.

———. *Crime and the Man*. Cambridge: Harvard University Press, 1939.

Irwin, John. *The Jail: Managing the Underclass in American Society*. Los Angeles: University of California Press, 1992.

Jack-Roller, The, and Jon Snodgrass with Gilbert Geis, James F. Short Jr., and Solomon Kobrin. *The Jack-Roller at Seventy: A Fifty-Year Follow-Up*. Lexington, MA: Lexington Books, 1982.

Jackson, George. *Soledad Brother: The Prison Letters of George Jackson*. New York: Coward-McCann, 1970.

Jenkins, Philip. *Using Murder: The Social Construction of Serial Homicide*. Hawthorne, NY: Aldine de Gruyter, 1994.

Jewkes, Yvonne. *Media and Crime*. London: Sage, 2004.

Katz, Jack. *Seductions of Crime: Moral and Sensual Attractions in Doing Evil*. New York: Basic Books, 1988.

Kelling, George L., and Catherine M. Coles. *Fixing Broken Windows: Restoring Order and Reducing Crime in Our Communities*. New York: Simon and Schuster, 1997.

King, Neal. *Heroes in Hard Times: Cop Action Movies in the U.S.* Philadelphia: Temple University Press, 1999.

Kitsuse, John I. "Societal Reaction to Deviant Behavior: Problems of Theory and Method." *The Other Side: Perspectives on Deviance*. Ed. Howard S. Becker. New York: Free Press, 1964.

Klein, Dorie. "The Etiology of Female Crime: A Review of the Literature." *Issues in Criminology* 8 (1973): 3–30.

Knapp Commission. *The Knapp Commission Report on Police Corruption*. New York: George Braziller, 1973.

Kornhauser, Ruth Rosner. *Social Sources of Delinquency: An Appraisal of Analytic Models*. Chicago: University of Chicago Press, 1978.

Kruttschnitt, Candace. "Social Status and Sentences of Female Offenders." *Law & Society Review* 15 (1980–81): 247–65.

Laqueur, Walter. *The Changing Face of Anti-Semitism*. New York: Oxford University Press, 2008.

Laub, John. *Criminology in the Making: An Oral History*. Boston: Northeastern University Press, 1983.

Laub, John, and Robert J. Sampson. *Shared Beginnings, Divergent Lives: Delinquent Boys to Age 70*. Cambridge: Harvard University Press, 2003.

———. "The Sutherland-Glueck Debate: On the Sociology of Criminological Knowledge." *American Journal of Sociology* 96 (1991): 1402–40.

Leitch, Thomas. *Crime Films*. New York: Cambridge University Press, 2002.

Lemert, Edwin M. "Beyond Mead: The Societal Reaction to Deviance." *Social Problems* 21 (1974): 457–68.

———. *Human Deviance, Social Problems and Social Control*. Englewood Cliffs, NJ: Prentice Hall, 1972.

————. *Social Pathology: A Systematic Approach to the Theory of Sociopathic Behavior.* New York: McGraw-Hill, 1951.

Lenz, Timothy O. *Changing Images of Law in Film and Television Crime Stories.* New York: Lang, 2003.

Lewis, Oscar. *Five Families: Mexican Case Studies in the Culture of Poverty.* New York: Basic Books, 1959.

Liazos, Alexander. "The Poverty of the Sociology of Deviance: Nuts, Sluts, and Preverts." *Social Problems* 20 (1972): 103–20.

Lilly, J. Robert, Francis T. Cullen, and Richard A. Ball. *Criminological Theory: Context and Consequences.* Thousand Oaks, CA: Sage, 2007.

Lombroso, Cesare. *Criminal Man.* A new translation with introduction and notes by Mary Gibson and Nicole Rafter. Durham, NC: Duke University Press, 2006.

————. *Palimpsestes des prisons.* Lyon: A. Storck, 1894.

————. *L'uomo bianco et uomo di colore.* Padua: Sacchetto, 1871.

Lombroso, Cesare, and Guglielmo Ferrero. *Criminal Woman, the Prostitute, and the Normal Woman.* Newly translated and edited by Nicole Hahn Rafter and Mary Gibson. Durham, NC: Duke University Press, 2004.

Lynch, Michael J., and Raymond J. Michalowski. *The New Primer in Radical Criminology: Critical Perspectives on Crime, Power and Identity.* New York: Criminal Justice Press, 2000.

MacKinnon, Catharine A. *The Sexual Harassment of Working Women.* New Haven: Yale University Press, 1979.

Maher, Lisa. *Sexed Work: Gender, Race and Resistance in a Brooklyn Drug Market.* New York: Oxford University Press, 2000.

Maidment, MaDonna. "Transgressing Boundaries: Feminist Perspectives in Criminology." *Advancing Critical Criminology: Theory and Application.* Ed. Walter DeKeseredy and Barb Perry. Lanham, MD: Lexington Books, 2006: 43–62.

Mann, Coramae Richey. *Female Crime and Delinquency.* Tuscaloosa: University of Alabama Press, 1984.

Martinson, Robert. "What Works? Questions and Answers about Prison Reform." *Public Interest* 35 (1974): 22–54.

Maruna, Shadd. *Making Good: How Ex-Convicts Reform and Rebuild Their Lives.* Washington, DC: American Psychological Association, 2001.

Marx, Karl. *Capital, Volume One. The Marx-Engels Reader.* Ed. Robert C. Tucker. New York: Norton, 1978.

————. "Class Conflict and Law." *Karl Marx: Selected Writings in Sociology and Social Philosophy.* Ed. T. B. Bottomore and Maximilien Rubel. London: McGraw-Hill, 1964: 200-230.

————. *The Eighteenth Brumaire of Louis Bonaparte.* Chicago: Charles H. Kerr, 1913.

Marx, Karl, and Friedrich Engels. *The Communist Manifesto.* Moscow: Progress Publishers, 1969.

Matsueda, Ross L. "'Cultural Deviance Theory': The Remarkable Persistence of a Flawed Term." *Theoretical Criminology* 1 (1997): 429–52.

McDonald, Sarah. "Performing Masculinity: From *City of God* to *City of Men.*" *Journal of Iberian and Latin American Studies* 12 (2006): 19–32.

McKelly, James C. "The Double Truth, Ruth: Do the Right Thing and the Culture of Ambiguity." *African American Review* 32 (1998): 215–27.

McKenzie, R. D. "The Ecological Approach to the Study of the Human Activity." *The City: Suggestions for Investigation of Human Behavior in the Urban Environment*. Ed. Robert E. Park, Ernest W. Burgess, and R. D. McKenzie. Chicago: University of Chicago Press, 1967: 63–79.

McRobbie, Angela, and Sarah L. Thornton. "Rethinking 'Moral Panic' for Multi-mediated Social Worlds." *British Journal of Sociology* 46 (1995): 559–74.

Melossi, Dario. "Overcoming the Crisis in Critical Criminology: Toward a Grounded Labeling Theory." *Criminology* 23 (1985): 193–208.

Melossi, Dario, and Massimo Pavarini. *The Prison and the Factory: Origins of the Penitentiary System*. London: Macmillan, 1981.

Merton, Robert K. "Social Structure and Anomie." *American Sociological Review* 3 (1938): 672–82.

Messerschmidt, James W. *Masculinities and Crime*. Boston: Rowman and Littlefield, 1993.

Messner, Steven F., and Richard Rosenfeld. *Crime and the American Dream*. Belmont, CA: Wadsworth, 1994.

Messner, Steven F., Helmut Thome, and Richard Rosenfeld. "Institutions, Anomie, and Violent Crime: Clarifying and Elaborating Institutional-Anomie Theory." *International Journal of Conflict and Violence* 2 (2008): 163–81.

Miller, Jerome. *Last One Over the Wall: The Massachusetts Experiment in Closing Reform Schools*. Columbus: Ohio State University Press. 1991.

Miller, Jody. *Getting Played: African American Girls, Urban Inequality, and Gendered Violence*. New York: NYU Press, 2008.

———. *One of the Guys: Girls, Gangs and Gender*. New York: Oxford University Press, 2001.

Miller, Walter B. "Lower Class Culture as a Generating Milieu of Gang Delinquency." *Journal of Social Issues* 14 (1958): 5–19.

Milovanovic, Dragan. *Postmodern Criminology*. New York: Garland, 1997.

Moffitt, Terrie E. "'Adolescence-Limited' and 'Life-Course-Persistent' Antisocial Behavior: A Developmental Taxonomy." *Psychological Review* 100 (1993): 674–701.

Monihan, Daniel Patrick. *The Negro Family*. Washington, DC: U.S. Department of Labor, 1965.

Murphy, Daniel S., and Mathew B. Robinson. "The Maximizer: Clarifying Merton's Theories of Anomie and Strain." *Theoretical Criminology* 12 (2008): 501–21.

Naffine, Ngaire. *Female Crime*. Sydney: Allen and Unwin, 1987.

———. *Feminism and Criminology*. Sydney: Allen and Unwin, 1997.

Naremore, James. *More Than Night: Film Noir in Its Contexts*. Berkeley: University of California Press, 1998.

Newman, Graeme, Ronald V. Clarke, and S. Giora Shoham, eds. *Rational Choice and Situational Crime Prevention: Theoretical Foundations*. Brookfield, VT: Ashgate, 1997.

O'Brien, Martin, Rodanthi Tzanelli, S. Penna, and Majid Yar. "'Kill n' Tell, and All That Jazz': The Seductions of Crime in Chicago." *Crime Media Culture* 1, no. 3 (2005): 243–61.

———. "'The Spectacle of Fearsome Acts': Crime in the Melting P(l)ot in Gangs of New York." *Critical Criminology* 13 (2005): 17–35.

O'Brien, Patricia. *Making It in the "Free World": Women in Transition from Prison*. Albany: State University of New York Press, 2001.

Oliveira, Emanuelle K. F. "An Ethic of the Aesthetic: Racial Representation in Brazilian Cinema Today." *Vanderbilt e-journal of Luso-Hispanic Studies* 4 (2008): 42–53.

Owen, Barbara. *In the Mix: Struggle and Survival in a Women's Prison*. Albany: State University of New York Press, 1998.

Paris, James A. "'Murder Can Sometimes Smell Like Honeysuckle': Billy Wilder's *Double Indemnity*." *Film Noir Reader 4: The Crucial Films and Themes*. Ed. Alain Silver and James Ursini. New York: Limelight Editions, 1944: 9–24.

Park, Robert E. "The City: Suggestions for the Investigation of Human Behavior in the Urban Environment." *The City: Suggestions for Investigation of Human Behavior in the Urban Environment*. Ed. Robert E. Park, Ernest W. Burgess, and R. D. McKenzie. Chicago: University of Chicago Press, 1967: 1–46.

———. "The Natural History of the Newspaper." *American Journal of Sociology* 29 (1923): 273–89.

Pashukanis, Evgeny. *The General Theory of Law and Marxism*. New York: Transaction Publications, 2001

Passas, Nikos. "Global Anomie Theory and Crime." *The Essential Criminology Reader*. Ed. Stuart Henry and Mark M. Lanier. Boulder, CO: Westview Press, 2006: 174–82.

Petrunik, Michael. 1980. "The Rise and Fall of 'Labelling Theory': The Construction and Destruction of a Sociological Strawman." *Canadian Journal of Sociology* 5 (1980): 213–33.

Platt, Anthony. *The Child Savers: The Invention of Delinquency*. Chicago: University of Chicago Press, 1977.

———. "Prospects for a Radical Criminology in the United States." *Crime and Social Justice* 1 (1974): 2–10.

———. "The Rise of the Child-Saving Movement: A Study in Social Policy and Correctional Reform." *Annals of the American Academy of Political and Social Science* 381 (1969): 21–38.

Pollak, Otto. *The Criminality of Women*. Philadelphia: University of Pennsylvania Press, 1950.

Potter, Gary W., and Victor E. Kappeler, eds. *Constructing Crime: Perspectives on Making News and Social Problems*. Prospect Heights, IL: Waveland, 1998.

Presdee, Mike. *Cultural Criminology and the Carnival of Crime*. New York: Routledge, 2000.

Presser, Lois. "The Narratives of Offenders." *Theoretical Criminology* 13 (2009): 177–200.

Quinney, Richard. *Class, State, and Crime*. London: Longman Group, 1977.

———. *Critique of Legal Order*. Boston: Little, Brown, 1974.

———. *The Problem of Crime*. New York: Dodd, Mead, 1970.

———. *The Social Reality of Crime*. Boston: Little, Brown, 1970.

Radzinowicz, Leon. *Ideology and Crime: A Study of Crime in Its Social and Historical Context*. New York: Columbia University Press, 1966.

Rafter, Nicole Hahn. *Creating Born Criminals*. Urbana: University of Illinois Press, 1997.

———. *The Criminal Brain: Understanding Biological Theories of Crime*. New York: NYU Press, 2008.

———. "Crime, Film and Criminology: Recent Sex-Crime Movies." *Theoretical Criminology* 11 (2007): 403–20.

———. "Gender, Prisons, and Prison History." *Social Science History* 9 (1985): 233–47.

———. *Partial Justice: Women, Prisons, and Social Control*. New Brunswick, NJ: Transaction Publishers, 1990.

——. *Shots in the Mirror: Crime Films and Society.* 2d ed. New York: Oxford University Press, 2006.

——. "Silence and Memory in Criminology—The American Society of Criminology 2009 Sutherland Address." *Criminology* 48 (2010): 339–56.

——. "Somatotyping, Antimodernism, and the Production of Criminological Knowledge." *Criminology* 45 (2007): 805–33.

Rafter, Nicole Hahn, and Mary Gibson. "Editors' Introduction" to Cesare Lombroso and Guglielmo Ferrero, *Criminal Woman, the Prostitute, and the Normal Woman.* Durham, NC: Duke University Press, 2004: 3–33.

Rafter, Nicole Hahn, and Frances Heidensohn, eds. *International Feminist Perspectives in Criminology: Engendering a Discipline.* Philadelphia: Open University Press, 1995.

Raine, Adrian. *The Psychopathology of Crime.* San Diego: Academic Press, 1993.

Rapping, Elayne. "Feminism Gets the Hollywood Treatment." *Cineaste* 18 (1991): 30–33.

Reckless, Walter C. *Criminal Behavior.* New York: McGraw-Hill, 1940.

——. *Vice in Chicago.* Chicago: University of Chicago Press, 1933.

Regener, Susanne. "Criminological Museums and the Visualization of Evil." *Crime, History, and Societies* 7 (2003): 43–56.

Reiman, Jeffrey H. *The Rich Get Richer and the Poor Get Prison: Ideology, Class, and Criminal Justice.* New York: Pearson, 2004.

Reinarman, Craig. "The Social Construction of Drug Scares." *Constructions of Deviance: Social Power, Context and Interaction.* Ed. Patricia A. Adler and Peter Adler. Belmont, CA: Wadsworth, 1994: 92–103.

Reiss, Albert J., and Michael Tonry, eds. *Communities and Crime.* Chicago: University of Chicago Press, 1986.

Rose, Dina R., and Todd R. Clear. "Incarceration, Reentry, and Social Capital: Social Networks in the Balance." *Prisoners Once Removed: The Impact of Incarceration and Reentry on Children, Families, and Communities.* Ed. Jeremy Travis and Michelle Waul. Washington, DC: Urban Institute Press, 2004: 313–41.

Rosenau, Pauline Marie. *Post-modernism and the Social Sciences.* Princeton: Princeton University Press, 1992.

Rosenfeld, Richard, and Steven F. Messner. "The Origins, Nature, and Prospects of Institutional-Anomie Theory." *The Essential Criminology Reader.* Ed. Stuart Henry and Mark M. Lanier. Boulder, CO: Westview Press, 2006: 164–73.

Rothman, David. *Conscience and Convenience: The Asylum and Its Alternatives in Progressive America.* Boston: Little, Brown, 1980.

Rusche, Georg, and Otto Kirchheimer. *Punishment and Social Structure.* New York: Columbia University Press, 1939.

Sampson, Robert. "Effects of Socioeconomic Context on Official Reaction to Juvenile Delinquency." *American Sociological Review* 51 (1986): 876–85.

——. "Foreword." *Life-Course Criminology: Contemporary and Classic Readings.* Ed. Alex Piquero and Paul Mazerolle. Belmont, CA: Wadsworth, 2001: v–vii.

——. "Neighborhood and Community: Collective Efficacy and Community Safety." *New Economy* 11 (2004): 106–13.

——. "Whither the Sociological Study of Crime?" *Annual Review of Sociology* 26 (2000): 711–14.

Sampson, Robert J., and John H. Laub. *Crime in the Making: Pathways and Turning Points through Life*. Cambridge: Harvard University Press, 1993.

———. "A Life-Course Theory of Cumulative Disadvantage and the Stability of Delinquency." *Life-Course Criminology: Contemporary and Classic Readings*. Ed. Alex Piquero and Paul Mazerolle. Belmont, CA: Wadsworth, 2001: 146–69.

Sampson, Robert J., Jeffrey D. Morenoff, and Felton Earls. "Beyond Social Capital: Spatial Dynamics of Collective Efficacy for Children." *American Sociological Review* 64 (1999): 633–60.

Sampson, Robert J., and Stephen W. Raudenbush. "Systematic Social Observation of Public Spaces: A New Look at Disorder in Urban Neighborhoods." *American Journal of Sociology* 105 (1999): 603–51.

Sampson, Robert J., Stephen W. Raudenbush, and Felton Earls. "Neighborhoods and Violent Crime: A Multilevel Study of Collective Efficacy." *Science* 277 (1997): 918–24.

Sarat, Austin. "Presidential Address: Imagining the Law of the Father: Loss, Dread, and Mourning in *The Sweet Hereafter*." *Law & Society Review* 34 (2000): 3–46.

———. *When the State Kills: Capital Punishment and the American Condition*. Princeton: Princeton University Press, 2001.

Sasson, Theodore. *Crime Talk: How Citizens Construct a Social Problem*. Hawthorne, NY: Aldine de Gruyter, 1995.

Scheingold, Stuart. *Politics of Law and Order: Street Crime and Public Policy*. New York: Longman, 1984.

Schmid, David. *Natural Born Celebrities: The Serial Killer in American Culture*. Chicago: University of Chicago Press, 2005.

Schrader, Paul. "Notes on Film Noir." *Film Noir Reader*. Ed. Alain Silver and James Ursini. New York: Limelight Editions, 1996: 53-64.

Schur, Edwin M. *Crimes without Victims: Deviant Behavior and Public Policy; Abortion, Homosexuality, Drug Addiction*. Englewood Cliffs, NJ: Prentice-Hall, 1965.

———. *Labeling Deviant Behavior: Its Sociological Implications*. New York: Harper and Row, 1971.

———. *The Politics of Deviance: Stigma Contests and the Uses of Power*. Englewood Cliffs, NJ: Prentice Hall, 1980.

Schwartz, Martin D., and Walter S. DeKeseredy. "Left Realist Criminology: Strengths, Weaknesses, and the Feminist Critique." *Crime, Law, and Social Change* 15 (1991): 51–72.

———. *Sexual Assault on the College Campus: The Role of Male Peer Support*. Thousand Oaks, CA: Sage, 1997.

Schwendinger, Herman, and Julia S. Schwendinger. *Adolescent Subcultures and Delinquency*. New York: Praeger, 1985.

Schwendinger, Julia R., and Herman Schwendinger. *Rape and Inequality*. Newbury Park, CA: Sage, 1983.

Scull, Andrew. *Decarceration: Community Treatment and the Deviant*. Englewood Cliffs, NJ: Prentice-Hall, 1977.

Sellin, Thorsten. *Culture Conflict and Crime*. New York: Social Science Research Council, 1938.

Shakur, Sanyika. *Monster: The Autobiography of an L.A. Gang Member*. New York: Penguin, 1998.

Shaw, Clifford R. *The Jack-Roller: A Delinquent Boy's Own Story*. Chicago: University of Chicago Press, 1930.

———. *The Natural History of a Delinquent Career*. Chicago: University of Chicago Press, 1931.

Shaw, Clifford R., and Henry D. McKay. *Juvenile Delinquency in Urban Areas*. Chicago: University of Chicago Press, 1942.

———. "Social Factors in Juvenile Delinquency." *Report on the Causes of Crime*. Vol. 2. National Commission on Law Observance and Enforcement. Washington, DC: Government Printing Office, 1931.

Shaw, Clifford R., Henry D. McKay, and James F. MacDonald. *Brothers in Crime*. Chicago: University of Chicago Press, 1938.

Shaw, Clifford R., Harvey Zorbaugh, Henry D. McKay, and Leonard S. Cottrell. *Delinquency Areas*. Chicago: University of Chicago Press, 1929.

Sheldon, William H. *Varieties of Delinquent Youth: An Introduction to Constitutional Psychiatry*. With the collaboration of Emil M. Hartl and Eugene McDermott. New York: Harper and Brothers, 1949.

Shelley, Mary. *Frankenstein or the Modern Prometheus*. Orig. 1831. London: Penguin Books, 2003.

Sherwin, Richard. *When Law Goes Pop: The Vanishing Line between Law and Popular Culture*. Chicago: University of Chicago Press, 2002.

Short, James. *The Social Fabric of the Metropolis: Contributions of the Chicago School of Urban Sociology*. Chicago: University of Chicago Press, 1971.

Simon, Rita James. *Women and Crime*. Lexington, MA: Lexington Books, 1975.

Simpson, Philip L. *Psycho Paths: Tracking the Serial Killer through Contemporary American Film and Fiction*. Carbondale: University of Southern Illinois Press, 2000.

Simpson, Sally S. "Feminist Theory, Crime, and Justice." *Criminology* 27 (1989): 605–31.

Siwi, Marcio. "City of God, City of Man." *SAIS Review* 23 (2003): 233–38.

Smart, Carol. *Law, Crime and Sexuality: Essays in Feminism*. London: Sage, 1995.

———. "The Woman of Legal Discourse." *Criminology at the Crossroads*. Ed. Kathleen Daly and Lisa Maher. New York: Oxford University Press, 1998: 21-36.

———. *Women, Crime and Criminology: A Feminist Critique*. Boston: Routledge and Kegan Paul, 1976.

Snodgrass, Jon. "The Criminologist and His Criminal: The Case of Edwin H. Sutherland and Broadway Jones." *Issues in Criminology* 8 (1973): 1–17.

Sparks, Richard. "A Critique of Marxist Criminology." *Crime and Justice: An Annual Review of Research* 2 (1980): 159–210.

———. *Television and the Drama of Crime: Moral Tales and the Place of Crime in Public Life*. Philadelphia: Open University Press, 1992.

Spitzer, Stephen. "Towards a Marxian Theory of Deviance." *Social Problems* 22 (1974): 638–51.

Staiger, Janet. *Perverse Spectators: The Practices of Film Reception*. New York: NYU Press, 2000.

Stanko, Elizabeth. *Intimate Intrusions: Women's Experience of Male Violence*. London: Routledge and Kegan Paul, 1985.

Steffensmeier, Darrell J. *The Fence*. Lanham, MD: Rowman and Littlefield, 1986.

Sullivan, Dennis, and Larry Tifft, eds. *Handbook of Restorative Justice: A Global Perspective.* New York: Routledge, 2008.

Surette, Ray. *Media, Crime, and Criminal Justice: Images and Realities.* Pacific Grove, CA: Brooks/Cole, 1992.

Sutherland, Edwin H. *Criminology.* Philadelphia: Lippincott, 1924.

———. "Development of the Theory." 1942 Address to the Ohio Valley Sociological Society, as printed in Karl Schuessler, ed., *Edwin H. Sutherland on Analyzing Crime.* Chicago: University of Chicago Press, 1956: 13–20.

———. *Principles of Criminology.* Chicago: Lippincott, 1947.

———. *The Professional Thief: By a Professional Thief.* Chicago: University of Chicago Press, 1937.

_____. *The Sutherland Papers.* Ed. Albert Cohen, Alfred Lindesmith, and Karl Schuessler. Bloomington: Indiana University Press, 1956.

———. *White Collar Crime.* New York: Dryden Press, 1949.

———. *White Collar Crime: The Uncut Version.* New Haven: Yale University Press, 1983.

———. "White-Collar Criminality." *American Sociological Review* 5 (1940): 1–12, as reprinted in Karl Schuessler, ed., *Edwin H. Sutherland on Analyzing Crime.* Chicago: University of Chicago Press, 1956.

Sykes, Gresham. "The Rise of Critical Criminology." *Journal of Criminal Law and Criminology* 65 (1974): 206–13.

———. 1958. *The Society of Captives: A Study of a Maximum Security Prison.* Princeton: Princeton University Press, 1958.

Tannenbaum, Frank. *Crime and the Community.* Boston: Ginn, 1938.

Taylor, Ian, Paul Walton, and Jock Young. *The New Criminology: For a Social Theory of Deviance.* New York: Harper and Row, 1973.

Thomas, William I., and Florian Znaniecki. *The Polish Peasant in Europe and America.* Boston: Gorham, 1920.

Thompson, E. P. *Whigs and Hunters: The Origins of the Black Act.* New York: Penguin Books, 1990.

Thrasher, Frederic M. *The Gang: A Study of 1,313 Gangs in Chicago.* Chicago: University of Chicago Press, 1927.

Tittle, Charles. *Control Balance: Toward a General Theory of Deviance.* Boulder, CO: Westview Press, 1995

Triplett, Ruth. "The Conflict Perspective, Symbolic Interactionism, and the Status Characteristics Hypothesis." *Justice Quarterly* 10 (1993): 541–56.

Turk, Austin. "Conflict and Criminality." *American Sociological Review* 31 (1966): 338–52.

———. *Criminality and Legal Order.* Chicago: Rand McNally, 1969.

Tzanelli, R., M. O'Brien, and M. Yar. "'Con Me If You Can': Exploring Crime in the American Cinematic Imagination." *Theoretical Criminology* 9 (2005): 97–117.

Vold, George B., Thomas J. Bernard, and Jeffrey B. Snipes. *Theoretical Criminology.* 5th ed. New York: Oxford University Press, 2001.

Walkowitz, Judith. *City of Dreadful Delight: Narratives of Sexual Danger in Late-Victorian London.* Chicago: University of Chicago Press, 1992.

Watson, John B. 1930 *Behaviorism.* Rev. ed. Chicago: University of Chicago Press.

Western, Bruce. *Punishment and Inequality in America.* New York: Russell Sage Foundation, 2006.

Western, Bruce, and Katherine Beckett. "How Unregulated Is the U.S. Labor Market? The Penal System as a Labor Market Institution." *American Journal of Sociology* 104 (1999): 1030–60.

Whyte, William F. *Street Corner Society: The Social Structure of an Italian Slum.* Chicago: University of Chicago Press, 1943.

Williams, Juan. "Why Spike Lee's New Film Ultimately Fails." *Washington Post*, June 25, 1989, G1+.

Wilson, David, and Sean O'Sullivan. *Images of Incarceration: Representations of Prison in Film and Television.* Winchester, UK: Waterside Press, 2004.

Wilson, James Q. *Thinking about Crime.* New York: Vintage Books, 1985.

Wilson, James Q., and Richard J. Herrnstein. *Crime and Human Nature.* New York: Simon and Schuster, 1985.

Wirth, Louis. *The Ghetto.* Chicago: University of Chicago Press, 1928.

Wolfgang, Marvin E., and Franco Ferracuti. *The Subculture of Violence.* London: Tavistock, 1967.

Wolfgang, Marvin E., Robert M. Figlio, and Thorsten Sellin. *Delinquency in a Birth Cohort.* Chicago: University of Chicago Press, 1972.

Wright, Joan Paul, Stephen G. Tibbetts, and Leah E. Daigle. *Criminals in the Making: Criminality across the Life Course.* Los Angeles: Sage, 2008.

Wright, Richard T., and Scott H. Decker. *Armed Robbers in Action: Stickups and Street Culture.* Boston: Northeastern University Press, 1997.

Young, Alison. *Imagining Crime.* London: Sage, 1996.

———. *Judging the Image.* London: Routledge, 2004.

———. "The Scene of the Crime." *Framing Crime: Cultural Criminology and the Image.* Ed. Keith Hayward and Mike Presdee. New York, Routledge, 2010: 83–97.

Young, Jock, and Roger Matthews. *Rethinking Criminology: The Realist Debate.* London: Sage, 1992.

Zehr, Howard. *Changing Lenses: A New Focus for Crime and Justice.* Scottdale, PA: Herald Press, 1990.

Zorbaugh, Harvey W. *The Gold Coast and the Slum: A Sociological Study of Chicago's Near North Side.* Chicago: University of Chicago Press, 1929.

Index

Soderbergh, Steven, 11, 83
somatotyping. *See also* Sheldon, William
strain theories, 9, 11, 83–100
subcultural theories, 11, 105–108, 112
Sudden Impact, 95
Superfly, 144
Sutherland, Edwin, 34, 101–105, 106,
    113–114, 115–118, 168, 184
Sweet Sweetback's Baadasssss Song, 144
Sykes, Gresham, 107
symbolic interactionism, 120
Sympathy for Lady Vengeance, 95
Syriana, 6

Tannenbaum, Frank, 120, 123
Taxi Driver, 6, 9 11, 60, 68, 75–80,
    81, 82; *See also* Chicago school of
    criminology; social disorganization
    theories
Thelma and Louise, 5, 153, 159–164, 186;
    and critical response, 163–164; *See also*
    feminist criminology

theory, criminological, 2–4, 184–186. *See
    also names of specific theories*
There Will Be Blood, 6, 97
Thomas, W. I., 67
Titicut Follies, 51
Traffic, 6, 9, 83–87, 89–91, 93, 95, 97, 100. *See
    also* classic strain theory; strain theories
Turk, Austin, 147–148

vigilante films, 81

Watson, John, 48
Whale, James, 8, 10, 36–41
white collar crime. *See* professional and
    white collar crime
Wilder, Billy, 10, 14
Wilson, James Q., 17, 34

X, Malcolm, 138, 139, 144. See also *Malcolm
    X*

Young, Alison, 9

.

About the Authors

NICOLE RAFTER is Professor and Senior Research Fellow in the School of Criminology and Criminal Justice at Northeastern University and the author of many books, including *The Criminal Brain: Understanding Biological Theories of Crime* (NYU Press, 2008) and *Origins of Criminology: Readings from the 19th-Century* (Routledge-Cavendish, 2009). In 2009, she won the American Society of Criminology's Sutherland Award.

MICHELLE BROWN is Assistant Professor of Sociology at the University of Tennessee and Fellow at the Indiana University Poynter Center for the Study of Ethics and American Institutions. She is the author of *The Culture of Punishment: Prison, Society, and Spectacle* (NYU Press, 2009) and coeditor of *Media Images of September 11th* (Praeger, 2003).